Versus Israel

King David Versus Israel

How a Hebrew Tyrant Hated by the Israelites Became a Biblical Hero

Gary Greenberg

PEREJET PREJJ

New York, NY

A Pereset Press Book
All inquiries should be addressed to:
Pereset Press
P. O. Box 25
New York, NY 10008
Info@peresetpress.com

Second Edition, first published in 2008 by Pereset Press.
The first edition was published in 2002 under the title *The Sins of King David: A New
History*. This second edition is re-edited and revised.

Cover and interior design by JoAnne Chernow

ISBN:978-0-9814966-1-0

*F*or my mother, Selma Greenberg

Contents

Usage Notes

Unless otherwise noted, all biblical citations are to the King James Version of the bible.

Citations to ABD refer to the Anchor Bible Dictionary (New York: Doubleday, 1992)

Time Line for the United Monarchy

The dates below are based on the chronology of king reigns in the biblical books of 1 and 2 Samuel and 1 and 2 Kings and counting backward from the Babylonian conquest of Jerusalem in 587 B.C.E. There are some problems with that chronology because of synchronization with datable events outside of the biblical text and contradictions within the biblical texts. Therefore, scholars tend to move the United Monarchy starting dates forward about fifty to sixty years. The sequence of events in the time line draws upon the arguments in the main text and there are some variations between the sequence of events below and those in the bible. In addition, some of the events set forth do not appear in the biblical account and appear on the basis of arguments in the main text. Some events are undated because the approximate year can't be determined

1076 Saul becomes the first king over Israel.
—Samuel denounces Saul and withdraws Shiloh support for the monarchy.
—Samuel forms an alliance with David.
—Samuel and David plot to overthrow Saul by force of arms.
—The revolt fails and David flees to Bethlehem.
—Samuel anoints David as king over Israel.
—David withdraws to Moab.
—David forms a rebel army and seeks control over Judah.
—Nabal dies and David marries Nabal's wife, Abigail, giving him control over Hebron, a chief city of Judah.

1061 David becomes king over Judah. Saul still rules over Israel.
—David becomes a Philistine vassal.
—Saul offers David the right of succession if David ends his rebellion and endorses Saul.

1056   Saul dies. Eshbaal becomes king over Israel. David rules over Judah and declares war on Israel.

—Abner, Israel's military leader, is assassinated by Joab.

1054   Eshbaal is assassinated.

—David marches to Mahanaim to accept Israel's surrender and place Saul's family under house arrest.

1054   David becomes king over Judah and Israel.

—Sheba leads a revolt aimed at putting Saul's son, Mephibaal, on the throne. The revolt collapses.

—David moves Israel's capitol to Jerusalem. He appoints Zadok and Abiathar as co-priests.

—Famine strikes Israel.

—David executes seven of Saul's sons.

—David orders a census of Israel. Benjaminites rebel.

—Three months later, the rebellion is put down.

—The Bathsheba affair occurs, probably before 1046.

—David defeats the Ammonites.

—Absalom chases David from Jerusalem, probably after 1036.

—David flees to the Philistines for help. The Philistines help David recapture the throne.

—Absalom is killed by Joab.

1021   Solomon becomes king over Israel and Judah.

—Solomon retrieves the Ark from Gibeon.

1017   Solomon begins construction of the Temple.

981   Solomon dies. The kingdom breaks in two. Jeroboam becomes king over Israel in the north. Rehoboam becomes king over Judah in the south.

977   An Egyptian pharaoh named Shishak invades Judah and takes the Temple treasures.

965   Rehoboam dies. Abijam rules over Judah.

963   Abijam dies. Asa reigns over Judah.

960   Jeroboam dies. His son Nadab becomes king over Israel.

959   Nadab is assassinated. Jeroboam's dynasty ends. Baasha rules over Israel. Asa continues to rule over Judah.

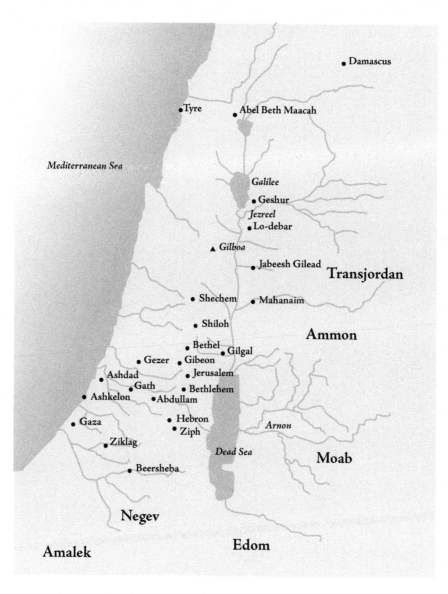

Important places in Israel and Judah in the time of David

Preface

This book was originally published under the title *The Sins of King David: A New History*. I was quite disappointed in that title (which the publisher selected without consulting me) as I thought it failed to even remotely connect to the controversial theme of this work, that David, rather than a heroic figure of his time much admired by the Israelites, was a widely despised monarch who imposed his will on Israel by military force. That previous title seemed to suggest little more than the traditional dull biographical roundup of David's handful of character flaws as depicted in the biblical account. This work penetrates much deeper into David's background than most biographies of David do. It also attempts to rescue the reputation of Saul who is usually dismissed as little more that a manic-depressive paranoid wrongly obsessed with the idea that David sought to usurp his throne. Saul, as I argue, was exactly right in his assessment of David.

In preparation for this new edition of the book I have re-edited the text to eliminate some typos and express some of my ideas in a clearer fashion. In response to some earlier criticism I have also inserted a great many more biblical citations for claims made in the book about what the bible says. In addition, I have added a few additional comments and observations to the text that did not appear in the earlier version. Lastly, I jettisoned three very minor arguments that I made in the previous edition.

First, in attempting to place Samuel's negative description of what a king of Israel would be like (1 Sam 8:10-18) into its proper historical chronological context, I suggested that the original speech, which appears prior to Saul's selection as king in the biblical chronology, probably originated as an attack by someone other than Samuel on King Solomon or that it may date to an even later time. In reviewing the evidence I have concluded that the attack was originally launched against Rehoboam, Solomon's son and successor and I have modified that portion of the text where the argument originally appeared to reflect my new understanding.

Second, in my discussion about whether David ever brought the Ark of the Covenant to Jerusalem, I challenged the biblical claim that he did so. I still hold to that position. However, in the course of the discussion I noted that there are two very different descriptions in the bible of what the Ark looked like and suggested the possibility that David may have created a second Ark in order to reinforce his claim to the leadership of Israel. I no longer believe that this "second Ark" theory is credible and I have removed it from the text. This in no way undermines my original claim that David never brought the Ark to Jerusalem and that it was Solomon who eventually seized control of the Ark and moved it to there.

Third, in analyzing the story of David's census sin I made a small error in reading the reported census data, mistakenly taking one reported number as a separate piece of data from the preceding data instead of as an addition to the preceding number, leading to a misstatement of how many Judahites were under military arms. I have corrected the analysis in this edition.

None of the above changes in any way diminishes the main thesis of this book, that David was widely despised by the Israelites and had to impose his will on the people by military force.

Gary Greenberg
2008

King
David
Versus
Israel

CHAPTER 1

Good David
and Bad David

But the word of the Lord came to me [i.e., David], saying,
Thou hast shed blood abundantly, and hast made great wars:
thou shalt not build an house unto my name, because thou hast shed
much blood upon the earth in my sight. 1 CHR 22:8

$\mathcal{M}$odern impressions of King David depict him as a young boy of unsurpassed courage, a pious and humble man who triumphed over many
adversities, a goodly king whose heart was with the Lord and compared
to whom all other monarchs fall short. He is portrayed as the progenitor
of a dynasty that would one day rule over the kingdom of God on earth.
Many see in him history's first renaissance man: a poet of uncommon wit
and intelligence, a musician of national renown, a diplomat of consum-
mate skill, a politician of great wisdom, a brilliant military strategist, a
master of martial weapons, a theologian who defined the basics of Jewish
thought, and an inventor of Judaism's religious practices and institutions.
These views have a long pedigree.

Following strict biblical chronology, King David came to the throne
at about 1061 BCE, but the biblical data presents many problems, including textual contradictions and problematic synchronization with the dates
of known events from non-biblical records. Most scholars propose moving the start of his reign forward about fifty or sixty years, somewhere
between about 1010 and 1000 BCE.

David's predecessor on the throne was Saul, the first king of Israel,
and David's successor was Solomon, his son. By convention, biblical
scholars refer to the period from Saul through Solomon as the United

Monarchy. It is usually thought of as ancient Israel's golden age and the three kings, according to the biblical chronology, had a combined reign of about one century. (Technically, as discussed in later chapters, there were four kings in this period. Saul was succeeded by his son Eshbaal as king over Israel while David ruled only in Judah. Following a two-year civil war David defeated Israel and became its king, reuniting Judah and Israel under his sole rule.)

David and Saul came from different families and rival political entities that shared territorial borders, Saul from the tribe of Benjamin and David from the tribe of Judah. When David succeeded to the throne, he founded a family dynasty that lasted over four hundred years, perhaps longer than any other known royal family. Although David's kingdom split in two after the death of Solomon, Israel in the north and Judah in the south (mirroring the earlier political divisions between Saul and David), his descendants on the throne of Judah outlasted the more popular and prosperous northern kingdom by almost one hundred and fifty years.

His dynasty ended in 587 BCE when Babylon captured the Judaean capitol of Jerusalem and destroyed the great Temple of Solomon, but Hebrew prophets believed and predicted that a future descendant of David would once again rule over the kingdom of God (See, for example, Jer 23:5). Christians saw the fulfillment of that promise in Jesus Christ while Jews continue to await the arrival of the Messiah.

In the second century CE, after the Romans banished the Jewish people from Palestine, the Hebrew academy in Babylon emerged as the intellectual and spiritual center of Jewish culture throughout the Diaspora. For almost a thousand years a leader believed to be a descendant of David presided over that institution. As Christianity took hold in Europe, the ideology and theology surrounding King David inspired many Christian monarchs and religious leaders and triggered many political and religious struggles between Christian kings and the Popes.

These views of King David, burnished over millennia by armies of theologians and religious teachers, have made David the most beloved character in all of Jewish scripture, and, theologically, the most important. But how much do we really know about this man?

Archaeological Sources for David's History

Historically, we have not a shred of archeological or textual evidence contemporaneous with David showing that either he or his son Solomon ever even existed, let alone what kind of men they were. Neither David, nor Solomon, nor the kingdom of Israel over which they ruled, appear in any of the records recovered from the time of their reigns—not in Canaan or from the many nations and peoples with whom they interacted or over whom they allegedly ruled.

The earliest reference to directly mention David's name dates to sometime in the ninth century BCE. Found on a stone monument at Tel Dan, in the far north of ancient Israel, the partially readable Aramaic text appears to describe a victory by a king of Aram over both an Israelite and Judahite king, and also makes reference to a "House of David." Dating to at least a century after David's death, it doesn't directly prove that David existed, only that a House of David, whatever that was, did. But it provides strong circumstantial evidence for David's existence as it seems to imply the existence of a dynasty named after King David within one to two centuries after the time he may have ruled.

Kenneth Kitchen, a prominent Egyptologist, claims to have found an Egyptian text that contains the geographical name "The Heights of David" as one of the territories conquered by Pharaoh Sheshonk during his invasion of Judahite territories. His claim is controversial and his reading of "Heights of David" is widely challenged, but if he is correct, and the reference is to David, then the text would date to shortly after the reign of Solomon, because Pharaoh Sheshonk is identified with the biblical Pharaoh Shishak, who invaded Judah and Israel while Solomon's son was on the throne of Judah.

One other inscription, also dating to sometime in the ninth century BCE, notes the payment of three shekels to the House (or Temple) of Jahweh, which may be a reference to the Temple of Solomon, but might just refer to a local shrine or altar.

While there are other inscriptions from the ninth century BCE and later that shed light on biblical history, they do not directly or even indirectly corroborate the existence of David or Solomon. This lack of evidence, however, should not be too surprising in that the time frame set by the bible for the United Monarchy falls into a historical dark age throughout the ancient Near East. From about 1100 to 900 BCE we lack substantial material evidence throughout the region, from Greece to Egypt to Canaan to Mesopotamia, and historians have a good deal of trouble filling in the gap with substantive analysis.

Prior to the time of David, we have only one direct reference to Israel or biblical matters. It appears on an Egyptian stele erected at about 1220 BCE by the Pharaoh Merneptah, son of Ramesses II. Generally known as the "Israel Stele" or "Merneptah Victory Stele," the monument contains references to a number of military campaigns. Tucked away at the end is a victory hymn indicating that Merneptah defeated several powerful Canaanite peoples, and alleging that Israel is "desolated and has no seed." Despite the references to numerous victories in the hymn, the consensus holds that the claims were fictitious and served only to praise Merneptah as a great leader.

It's universally accepted among Egyptologists that the stele's reference to Israel grammatically distinguishes it from the rest of the nations mentioned. Where the stele uses hieroglyph determinative signs to identify the other nations as people from a particular land, it designates Israel only as a people, unconnected to any territory. For this reason, many scholars believe that the Israel mentioned on the Merneptah stele depicts biblical Israel at a time not long after the Exodus from Egypt, and have dated the departure to sometime during the preceding sixty-six-year reign of Ramesses II. (This author has previously argued that the Exodus occurred a bit earlier, at about 1315 BCE, during the co-regency of Ramesses I and Sethos I, the grandfather and father respectively of Ramesses II.

See my book *The Moses Mystery*, later reprinted as *The Bible Myth* and subsequently reissued as *The Moses Mystery*.)

OTHER SOURCES FOR DAVID'S HISTORY

The absence of archaeological or epigraphical evidence for the time of David and Solomon leaves the bible as our earliest, and for all practical purposes, only, meaningful source of information about their reigns. The biblical accounts of the United Monarchy come from 1–2 Samuel, 1–2 Kings, and 1–2 Chronicles. From a historian's point of view, these biblical records present some difficult problems.

The books of Samuel (which contain the stories of Saul and David) and Kings (which tell of the transition from David to Solomon) are believed to be primarily the work of a single author or school of writers, who began the historical account with the Book of Deuteronomy, and continued through the biblical books of Joshua, Judges, Samuel, and Kings. Scholars refer to this set of biblical books as the Deuteronomist history, and the author or authors as the Deuteronomist or Deuteronomists.

The Deuteronomist history probably took near-final shape during the reign of King Josiah of Judah (639–609 BCE), with a small addendum tacked on to cover the brief post-Josiah period leading to the capture of Jerusalem, and some possible additional editing in later years.

1 and 2 Chronicles, which also present a history of the United Monarchy, belong to a later literary cycle, and are generally dated to sometime after the Persians defeated Babylon and liberated Judah (539 BCE).

Other than the Deuteronomist and Chronicles histories of David and Solomon, we have no other significant historical source, and it is these books that planted the seeds from which sprouted David's glowing reputation over the centuries. (Throughout the biblical period and into modern times, most religious followers of the Jewish scriptures have believed that the book of Psalms derives from David, and that work also contributed to his reputation and image, but few if any serious biblical historians believe that David wrote more than a few, if any, of the Psalms.) But the books of Samuel and Kings were written more than three hundred years after David's reign and Chronicles perhaps another century or two after Samuel and Kings, and all of the works are heavily biased in favor of David and Solomon. For the historian, therefore, the factual reliability of the bible for this period presents a number of difficult problems, not the least of which is the lack of contemporaneous corroborating evidence.

Interestingly, though, buried deeply within the Deuteronomist history we find another very different picture of David, far more negative and derogatory than the present view. Portions of this other Davidic image are sometimes explicitly set forth, such as in the story of how he arranged to kill Uriah the Hittite in order to cover up his adulterous affair with Uriah's wife, Bathsheba, a crime so heinous that even biblical authors commented on it. For example, 1 Ki 15:5 says "David did that which was right in the eyes of the Lord, and turned not aside from any thing that he commanded him all the days of his life, *save only in the matter of Uriah the Hittite*" (emphasis added). On other occasions, some of David's alleged terrible sins are either dismissed as untrue, glossed over, explained away, covered up by obfuscation, or misrepresented as the acts of others. It is sometimes necessary to read between the lines to extract the truth.

THE NEGATIVE IMAGE OF DAVID IN THE BIBLE

At the head of each chapter, I have placed a biblical quote that preserves accusations against David in connection with that chapter's subject matter, and have collected these quotes together in Appendix A. While the collection is not exhaustive, it does reflect the hostility toward David's reign that existed among some of his enemies, and it might be useful to scan through them before continuing.

A careful reading of the biblical sources shows that David was never the widely popular monarch depicted in popular images and religious texts. On at least two occasions, popular rebellions nearly cost him his crown. One, led by his son Absalom, arose in David's southern home base of Judah and temporarily drove him out of Jerusalem. The other came from the north, led by followers of the House of Saul who held David responsible for Saul's death and many other wrongs.

The same studies will also show, contrary to the biblical image and popular belief, that Saul was not a manic-depressive paranoid, imagining false schemes by David to steal his throne, but a popular and well-balanced king who accurately understood what David was about and who took responsible actions to curtail David's treasonous and disloyal behavior to Israel.

In this book, I intend to examine this other history of David. This examination will show that David was a corrupt and ambitious mercenary who committed treason against Israel by working with its enemies to seize the throne from King Saul; an ambitious and ruthless politician who initiated, sanctioned, or condoned murder and assassination as a way to eliminate political rivals, royal or otherwise; a Philistine vassal who used an army of malcontents to terrorize and conquer the Kingdom of Judah while Saul was still on the throne; a usurper who went to war against Israel after Saul's death and imposed himself as king over the nation of Israel by military force; a cruel and unjust tyrant who used foreign mercenaries to centralize power under his direct control and who oppressed the people of Israel with high taxes and forced labor; a military imperialist who waged wars of conquest against his neighbors and exposed the peaceful Israelites to military counter-attacks that left many dead, wounded, or widowed; and the beneficiary of tales and legends that made him the doer of other peoples' heroic deeds, such as the false claim that the youthful David slew the Philistine giant Goliath when in fact the original story told of a soldier in David's army doing the deed long after David had become king.

THE BIBLICAL DEBATE OVER DAVID

Scholars have long noted what appear to be many "apologetic" portions of the David history in 1 and 2 Samuel, stories and comments designed to rebut or refute charges made against David by others, or to account for incriminating pieces of evidence (such as David having possession of Saul's crown and bracelet almost immediately after Saul is killed). I prefer to think of the Book of Samuel as the equivalent of a criminal defense lawyer's summation on behalf of a client, occasionally trying to explain away criminal evidence, citing testimony by character witnesses, impugning the integrity of hostile witnesses, and sometimes taking facts out of context or changing the order of events.

The central debate in the bible over King David revolves around his relationship to the House of Saul. From the northern Saulide perspective, David was thought to have betrayed King Saul by aligning himself with Israel's enemies in an effort to unseat Saul and take control over his kingdom. Subsequently, according to the northern accusations: David had Saul murdered; he waged war against the House of Saul after the king's death to prevent Saul's rightful heir from taking the throne; he authorized the murder of Abner, Saul's cousin and general of the Israelite army; he authorized the murder of Eshbaal, Saul's successor as king over Israel; he imposed his will over Israel by force after Eshbaal's death; and after becoming king, he carried on a systematic extermination of the House of Saul.

To this Saulide litany can be added some additional accusations of wrongdoing that can be corroborated by the biblical accounts, including: the adultery with Bathsheba; arranging for the death of Uriah, Bathsheba's husband; the failure of David to punish his son Amnon for raping Tamar; the general lack of justice from David's court, which resulted in the alienation of his home base in Judah; the murders of Absalom and Amasa by Joab, David's closest and most trusted aide; the taking of a census in Israel, a sin so theologically horrible that the Chronicler, a fanatical pro-David author, wrote that Satan himself incited David to conduct the numbering of the people (1 Chr 21:1); and David's support for Solomon over Adonijah as successor on the throne, Adonijah being the rightful heir by the then-current standards.

While much of the evidence against David has no doubt been suppressed, some of it has survived in the biblical texts (for reasons explained below). It includes: the acknowledgement that David served a Philistine king and offered to join with him in the fight against Saul and Israel; the admission that David had good relations with Nahash, the king of Ammon, a man defeated by Saul and Israel's bitter enemy; Samuel's endorsement of David as Saul's replacement while Saul lived; indications that David became king over Judah while Saul still ruled over Israel; David's possession of Saul's crown and bracelet immediately after Saul died; a full account of the Bathsheba and Uriah story; an account of the rape of Tamar by David's son Amnon and David's reaction; accounts of the murders of Abner, Amasa, and Absalom by Joab; the immediate appearance in David's court of Eshbaal's assassins with the murdered king's head; the execution of several of Saul's children by hanging; the story of Absalom's revolt against David's failure to provide justice in Israel; an account of David's census sin; and the story of Solomon's succession to the throne.

In response, the Deuteronomist historians argued that: God took the throne away from Saul and gave it to David so Samuel was justified in endorsing David as king over Israel; while Saul was alive David remained loyal to king and country but Saul had a paranoid and unjustified fear that David sought to displace him as king; twice David had the opportunity to kill Saul and failed to do so; David joined with Israel's enemies only because Saul drove him out of Israel and hunted him down and David needed protection from Saul's unwarranted persecution; Joab acted independently and without authorization in his various acts of murder; King Saul committed suicide after being wounded in battle and it was only by coincidence that someone found Saul dead and brought the crown and bracelet to David; David did not authorize the assassination of Eshbaal and he put the murderers to death; David loved his children too much and couldn't bring himself to punish them for wrongdoing, even when one of them rebelled against him; God wanted Saul's children executed in order to end a famine caused by wrongdoing in Saul's lifetime; David was not responsible for ordering the census in that God wanted it done as a punishment for Israel's wrongdoing; and David may have been unfairly taken advantage of by Solomon's supporters while he was sick and dying.

Before we begin our analysis of the charges, counter-charges, and evidence, let us first look at how evidence of David's wrongdoings came to survive in biblical accounts designed to present him as the ideal king.

WHY THE NEGATIVE IMAGE OF DAVID SURVIVED

Why do some negative images of David appear directly in the biblical text while others are so deeply buried, obscured, or hidden from view? To answer that question we must know something about the political and religious issues that divided Israel in the time of David and how the biblical stories came to be written. We will examine those issues in more detail in the subsequent chapters, but let me briefly summarize the political and religious schisms as they appear in the biblical accounts.

Prior to the institution of monarchy in Israel, the nation was governed by a priesthood centered in the city of Shiloh, located approximately in the central portion of Israel in the territory of Ephraim (later to become the capitol of the kingdom of Israel after the break with Judah). Many Israelites came to believe that the priesthood had become corrupt and demanded that a king be appointed to give them judgments and to defend them against aggressors. This caused a significant religious and political feud to break out between the Shiloh priesthood and other institutional forces in Israel.

The leader of the Shiloh priesthood at this time was Samuel. The pro-king, anti-priesthood faction supported Saul, a popular military hero. After much debate between the two sides, the pro-king faction won out and Israel chose Saul as its first king. This constituted a major blow to the influence of Shiloh and cut into the many valuable perks they received for exercising judgments and guiding Israel's religious affairs.

Samuel, in an attempt to preserve Shilohite influence, proposed a compromise, suggesting that it would be proper for Israel to choose a king provided that the king would submit to the will of God as determined by the priesthood. This compromise failed to take hold when Saul appeared to ignore Samuel's advice. As a consequence, Samuel denounced Saul and charged that God had taken the kingdom from Saul and his descendants. The Shilohite prophet then sought out an ally to replace Saul as king who would follow the guidelines of the priesthood. That ally was David.

During Saul's reign, David of Judah had become a popular military hero among the Israelites, perhaps even more popular than Saul. The king perceived David as a threat to his rule (rightly or wrongly to be discussed in later chapters) and to his family dynasty and sought to kill him. David fled from Saul's camp and carved out an outlaw existence as Saul chased after him. What David did during this period will also be the subject of later chapters.

When Saul died in battle against the Philistines, civil war broke out between the forces of David and the House of Saul. After a period of conflict that saw David's chief opponents assassinated, David became king over a united Israel and Judah. As part of a political and religious compromise by David, the Shiloh priesthood had to share the role of chief priest with another religious faction that also supported David. In the meantime, the remnant of the House of Saul circulated the idea that David had been responsible for killing Saul and his sons and other opponents of David.

When David died the Shiloh priesthood backed the losing side in the struggle to succeed David, and when Solomon became David's successor the Shilohites were removed from power. This led them to once again look for an ally and they settled on a northern hero named Jeroboam. Solomon tried to kill Jeroboam, but the king's rival fled to Egypt. When Solomon died Jeroboam returned to Israel and led the northern kingdom out of the coalition with Judah, splitting the nation into two rival kingdoms, each vying for domination over the other.

Again the Shilohites were disappointed. Jeroboam refused to recognize the authority of the priesthood and allowed almost anyone who wanted to become a priest to become one. Shiloh denounced Jeroboam and sought a new northern alliance.

Geo-political realities and some archaeological evidence indicate that the northern kingdom of Israel was the larger and more prosperous of the two Hebrew kingdoms. It served as a center of anti-Judah, anti-David, and anti-Solomon propaganda. The most influential of these intellectual forces, based on literary analysis of the Deuteronomist history, appears to have been the northern Shilohite prophets. But the Shilohites had a difficult position to defend among their northern colleagues.

Having worked with, supported, and endorsed David as king, the Shilohites had to defend themselves against northern attacks associating them with the crimes some influential northerners believed David had committed against the House of Saul. This required that the Shilohites tread a narrow path between the hostilities separating north and south. On the one hand they wrote about the weaknesses of David that demonstrated the need for a king to submit to God's will. On the other hand they erected an elaborate and sweeping defense against the anti-Saul crimes attributed to David, especially where the Shilohites were thought to have a role. As a by-product of the defense, it became necessary to cite some of the anti-David evidence that had to be refuted. In other instances they tried to recast old stories in a new light.

The literary layers of the Deuteronomist and Chronicles histories show that a variety of written accounts circulated throughout ancient Judah and Israel, some from the Judahite scribes defending David and/or Solomon, some from proponents of the Shilohite and northern prophets, some from those hostile to David and/or the Shilohite priests, and others from those hostile to Solomon. The Book of Chronicles, for example, cites such works as Samuel the Seer, Gad the Seer, and the Prophecy of Ahijah (a Shilohite priest). These works would have been well known to the intelligentsia in Israel and Judah.

With Israel in the north having the larger and more prosperous culture, David's reputation no doubt suffered from widespread antagonism to his reign from that community, as did that of the Davidic dynasty that followed in its wake and challenged the north for domination over the two kingdoms.

In 722 BCE, however, political realities changed. The Assyrians defeated and destroyed the northern kingdom of Israel. Some refugees fled south to Judah. The remainder (as corroborated by Assyrian records) were forcibly removed from their homeland and dispersed into the Assyrian empire, never to be heard from again.

The survival of Judah and the Davidic dynasty over Israel had the immediate effect of giving Judah the propaganda advantage over Israel. Not only did the center of anti-David and anti-Judah writing disappear, the survivors who escaped the Assyrian onslaught and relocation had to dwell under Judahite rule, further curtailing northern propaganda. In addition, the survival of the Davidic dynasty signaled that God preferred Judah to Israel, a point that may not have been lost on the northern refugees. This led to an enhancement and rehabilitation of David's reputation.

About a century after the disappearance of Israel, the Deuteronomists produced a history of Israel beginning with Moses in the Book of Deuteronomy and continuing through the books of Joshua, Judges, Samuel, and Kings.

The inclusion of many of the negative materials in the Deuteronomist history strongly suggests that David's reputation must have still suffered significantly from the negative legacy passed on from the north. It's most likely that many of the facts underlying some of the charges against David were well known, to northerner and southerner alike, although disagreements over what those facts implied would have remained a lively source of debate.

At the same time, the Deuteronomists shared the Shilohite idea that a king's first duty was to God and that the king must yield to God's word. The Deuteronomists, functioning within a Davidic dynasty, had two major problems to tackle. As with the Shilohites, they needed to defend David against those charges that undermined his legitimacy as king and that also led to a divided kingdom, while at the same time demonstrating that even a good king had weaknesses that required him to be guided by the word of God.

In that context, they adopted many of the Shilohite arguments defending David against northern accusations and integrated them into their history of David's kingdom. At the same time, they preserved examples of how David's personal weaknesses led to wrongdoing when he failed to consult with the men of God. So, charges that David assassinated Saul and other political opponents were challenged with contrary evidence, while personal failings, such as in the incident with Bathsheba and Uriah, were kept as illustrations of how even a good king needs guidance from the prophets and priests.

In the Deuteronomist history of the kings that ruled over Judah and Israel, several key themes emerge. These include the central role of the Temple in Jerusalem, adherence to the Laws of Moses, God's punishment of Israel when it strays from these principles, and evaluation of how well particular kings followed God's word and how well Israel did under those kings that walked in David's way. The northern kings of Israel invariably received poor grades while the southern kings of Judah received mixed reviews. The Deuteronomists considered David to be the role model compared to whom other kings were to be measured.

Perhaps twenty to thirty years after the Deuteronomist history of David had been written, the Hebrew nation suffered another blow. In 587 BCE Babylon captured Jerusalem, destroyed Solomon's temple, and carried off many of the elite citizens of Judah to Babylon. Such a defeat carried with it an implication that God had deserted Judah because Judah had abandoned God.

Some seventy years later, Persia defeated Babylon and liberated the Jewish people. In the Persian period the Jews began to believe in such ideas as the coming of God's kingdom on Earth, which would be ruled over by descendants of David. Sometime after the Persian liberation of Israel, how long after we can't say for sure but within a century or two, Chronicles appeared, presenting a history of the United Monarchy that portrayed David as the great heroic king of the Jews.

The Chronicles history almost completely whitewashed whatever remained of David's negative reputation, scrubbing out details that would reflect badly on their hero, adding material that would enhance his reputation, and occasionally contradicting the Deuteronomist version of events. For historical sources, the Chronicler often relied on the Book of Samuel, often sharing identically worded passages. But, the writing of Chronicles was also influenced by other source materials.

We should note that where the Deuteronomists were concerned with a theology that subjected the king to the word of God, the Chronicles theology saw David as the man chosen by God to forever lead the Israelites. It is probably fair to say that the cleaned-up image of David in Chronicles played a major role in transforming him into the all-purpose hero that transcended some of the hesitations present in the Deuteronomist account.

Subsequent to the writing of Chronicles Israel passed through a conquest by Greece, a period of liberation under the Maccabees, and then Roman domination. In the Roman period a messianic view of David's return took hold, continuing the trend of glorifying David and influencing the development of Christianity.

From then on, David's reputation flourished as his sins were ignored.

THE ARGUMENT AHEAD

Because of the lack of contemporaneous corroboration, some scholars consider the biblical history of the United Monarchy useless for determining what happened and argue for a very late writing for all of the biblical accounts, sometime well after the fifth century BCE. Most, however, find that literary and stylistic analysis of the bible, together with some of the corroborating archaeological and epigraphic finds and parallels, enables various textual strands and threads to be separated from others, occasionally providing chronological clues and sequences in their assembly. The political contexts and conflicts within many of these strands suggest that they must have been written within certain historical time frames as opposed to others, and indicate that some of the Davidic history may have been written close to, or not long after, David's reign, while other pieces appear to have been written much later.

This is not the place for a detailed scholarly analysis of the arguments involved. Many lengthy and complex treatises have been written on the subject and there is still a wide range of disagreement over what conclusions can be drawn. Therefore, let me set out my own perspective.

I am one of those who believe that there are many political layers of text in the histories of David, some of which, in context, would only have been written to serve certain political purposes, and that they would only have been relevant in certain historical circumstances. In my view, much of the Davidic history underlying the biblical sources was written during or shortly after the United Monarchy and reflected either accusations of wrongful conduct committed by various political factions or responses by those accused of such actions. The body of writings produced a mixture of truth, falsehood, and ambiguity. This collection of writings circulated throughout Israel and Judah, and the pros and cons were well-known by the educated elite through the centuries.

Over time, rival factions continued to argue and debate these issues, picking and choosing what they thought would enhance their own point of view, and applying personal political spin to make their case. By accident of history the particular texts that have been preserved in the bible, though reflecting the biases of the particular authors, maintained many of the opposing traditions. This no doubt occurred because polemic necessities often required that the writers cite the particular charges they wanted to refute.

For most of the last two thousand years, theologians, Christian and Jewish, ignored, dismissed, or reinterpreted those portions of the bible that showed David in a negative light. Driven by the idea that David was God's chosen king, a man after God's heart whose descendant would one day rule God's kingdom on Earth, efforts were made to purge all inconsistent images from the public mind. Even where the biblical authors acknowledged David's misdeeds, as in the Bathsheba affair, new extra-biblical ideas were introduced. One theologian, for example, concluded that David was morally right in killing Uriah, Bathsheba's husband, because Uriah disobeyed the king's command to return to his home and have relations with his wife. This general approach elevated David's reputation to its present misleading heroic status.

In the last century, however, a number of scholars belonging to what is called the Literary-Critical school of biblical analysis have taken a fresh look at the biblical stories of David, often examining some of the negative images in the bible, and frequently trying to unravel the written skeins that weave through the biblical texts. While for the most part they still give David the benefit of the doubt wherever possible, they have uncovered many useful insights into the origins of the biblical texts and the meanings of various puzzling passages. In many instances they are forced to admit, contrary to the popular impression, that much of David's image is mere myth, based on royal propaganda and inconsistent with the underlying truth. Unfortunately, these views are restricted mostly to scholarly journals. Such scholars rarely express such contrary opinions to the general public.

In the chapters that follow we will examine various claims and arguments made by different factions, rise above the special pleadings, and reconstruct a reasonably accurate history of King David and the United Monarchy. The history revealed will radically disagree with traditional religious teachings and standard academic treatments. It will show that David, Solomon, and the priest Samuel were not the heroic figures we thought they were, and it will rehabilitate the reputations of many of those falsely accused of wrongdoing, such as Saul, Absalom, and Jeroboam. By careful reading and logical analysis, we will separate much historical fact from a good deal of biblical fiction.

CHAPTER 2

Make Us a King

In those days there was no king in Israel: every man
did that which was right in his own eyes. JUDG 21:25

*I*n the beginning of the eleventh century BCE, while Israel still had no
king, the most important man in Israel was Eli, the chief priest at Shiloh
and chief judge of the people. The bible says he held that position for forty
years and died at the age of ninety-eight, probably not long before the birth
of David (1 Sam 4:15–18). Under Eli's leadership, the administration of
justice and religious practices had become corrupt, and this betrayal of
trust weakened the people's faith in the ability of the priestly class to gov-
ern their nation (1 Sam 2:22–24). Under Samuel, Eli's successor and protégé, the corruption continued, leading to a confrontation between the
people at large and the priestly class over a change in the form of government. The public demanded that a king be appointed to lead Israel rather
than have the nation continue under priestly rule (1 Sam 8:1–5). Samuel
unhappily yielded these powers to the newly chosen king, Saul, but a
breach between Saul and Samuel eventually led the priest to back David
against Saul in a struggle to regain authority for the Shiloh priesthood.

Shiloh served as the cultic center of Israel at this time and housed
the Ark of the Covenant, Israel's most sacred icon, and this gave the
Shiloh priesthood a strong hold over the minds and loyalties of many
Israelites and politically powerful factions. According to 1 Sam 1:9 and
surrounding verses, Shiloh had a temple structure at the site, although
on many other occasions, the pro-Jerusalem Deuteronomist historian
makes repeated claims that Solomon was the first to erect a temple as a
home to the Ark and the temple was in Jerusalem. The Solomonic claims
have to be considered very cautiously, considering the pro-Jerusalem bias

19

of the Deuteronomist. According to Jeremiah, the seventh century BCE Jerusalem prophet, Shiloh was where God first established his name (i.e., established a temple) but he destroyed it because of wickedness (Jer. 7:12).

Archaeological evidence indicates that at about this time the city served as a large administrative center with pillared buildings, numerous storage silos, and several indications of cultic use. (See ABD, s.v. "Shiloh" for a discussion of the archaeology of Shiloh.) Although no specific building identified as a temple has been discovered there, the nature of the other structures is not inconsistent with the possibility that the complex hosted such a building. In line with Jeremiah's claim that God destroyed Shiloh for its wickedness, the archaeological data shows that the city was in fact destroyed at about the middle of the eleventh century, although a small population continued to inhabit the site afterwards.

The destruction of Shiloh in the middle of the eleventh century is not explicitly mentioned in the bible, but circumstantial evidence in the bible seems to support the archaeological findings. According to the biblical account, in Eli's last days, the middle of the eleventh century, the Philistines captured the Ark of the Covenant during battle and held it for seven months (1 Sam 6:1). When Israel recovered the Ark, the priests brought the icon to a different city, eventually placing it in the city of Kiriath-Jearim near Saul's capitol (1 Sam 7:1).

In addition, from that time on, we no longer hear about the city of Shiloh as a functioning location. This suggests that the Philistine forces sacked the city and destroyed it, consistent with the archaeological evidence and Jeremiah's claim. These correlations indicate that there is some degree of historically reliable data in the early stories, but separating the fact from fiction is far from easy and the subject of enormous and constant debate in the world of biblical scholarship. In any event, the destruction of Shiloh may have helped undermine the authority of the Shiloh priesthood and contribute to its reputation as corrupt.

According to the biblical account in the opening chapters of 1 Samuel, Eli had two sons who also worked as priests at Shiloh, Hophni and Phinehas. The priests at this time all came from the tribe of Levi, and like several earlier Levites, including Moses, the names of these sons are Egyptian in origin and may reflect a cultural connection to Egypt in earlier times (as claimed in the Exodus story).

Enter the young Samuel. Prior to his birth, his mother Hannah had been unable to have children for a long time and on an annual pilgrimage to Shiloh she prayed for a child. In her petition, she promised God that if he gave her a child she would give him back to the Lord and "there shall no razor come upon his head" (1 Sam 1:11). Eli told her that God would grant her petition and soon after she gave birth to Samuel. In appreciation, she kept her vow and brought the child to Shiloh to train under Eli.

In the meantime, Eli's two sons became corrupt, even demanding sexual favors from the women who came to worship, and the people of Israel were troubled (1 Sam 2:22–25). As Samuel grew up under Eli's care and learned to perform religious tasks in service of God, the infamy of the chief priest's children spread far and wide throughout Israel. When Eli finally heard what was being said of them he warned his sons to change their ways or face the wrath of the Lord, but Hophni and Phinehas ignored him (1 Sam 2:25). Shortly after the warning, a prophet (whose name, strangely, is not given) came to Eli and brought condemnation from God.

The prophet told Eli that God had previously promised that the priest and his descendants would provide Israel's religious leadership forever, but that his failure to stop the corruption of his children terminated the covenant (see 1 Sam 2 for the full account). He accused Eli of honoring his sons more than God and of having become fat from the offerings that belonged to the Lord. As punishment, the prophet advised Eli that God would raise up a new priest to lead Israel. Furthermore, he predicted, Eli's house would eventually disappear. As a sign that this would come to pass, the prophet predicted that Eli's two sons would both die on the same day (1 Sam 2:34).

After the prophet's warning, God appeared to Samuel and reiterated his condemnation of Eli (1 Sam 3:11–14). Samuel conveyed the message to Eli, who responded that the Lord should do what he believes right. Subsequently, Samuel's reputation as a man of God soared "and all Israel from Dan even to Beer-Sheba knew that Samuel was established to be a prophet of the Lord" (1 Sam 3:20. Dan and Beer-Sheba represented the northern-most and southern-most points in Israel.).

Although the words uttered by the prophet against Eli were couched in ancient idiom and slightly ambiguous, as most omens are, the meanings were reasonably clear and the various events came to pass, but not all at once.

During a battle with the Philistines, the enemy captured the sacred Ark of the Covenant, a sign that God was no longer with Israel, weakening the authority of the Shilohite priesthood entrusted with its care. Also, Eli's two children were both slain in the battle, and when Eli learned of their death he keeled over and died. This did not end the priestly line of Eli, however, and the most important part of the prophecy, the replacement of Eli's house with a new priestly family, did not occur until the reign of Solomon.

The legitimacy of Eli's line takes on political importance in the struggles to define religious practices under David's monarchy and in the contest to succeed David on the throne. The last known priests associated with Eli were Abiathar, a loyal follower of David, and his son Ahimelech. When David became king the role of chief priest was divided in two, Abiathar and his son on one side and Zadok, from a different line, on the other (2 Sam 8:17). This triggered a battle for religious domination between the rival families.

When the question of succession to David came up, Abiathar sided with the legitimate heir, Adonijah, while Zadok sided with the usurper Solomon. On Solomon's ascension to the throne, the king removed Abiathar from office and made Zadok the sole priest (1 Ki 2:27). The Zadokites served continuously in Jerusalem, at least through the monarchical period and perhaps long afterwards. The term Sadducees, used for an orthodox Jewish faction in the time of Christ, means "Zadokite," but there is no explicit genealogical evidence connecting David's Zadok with the namesake of the Sadducees.

The theological connection between the rise of the Zadokites under Solomon and the simultaneous termination of the Elides, strongly suggests that the story of the corruption of Eli and his children may have been fictional propaganda designed to justify Solomon's actions in banishing the Shilohite priest from Jerusalem. In that regard, we should note that Samuel's children were also pronounced corrupt, but Samuel was associated with the legitimacy of David's kingship, and there is no corresponding condemnation against him as there was against Eli.

The captured Ark remained with the Philistines for about seven months, and during its stay the Philistines experienced deadly plagues. Afraid that the hand of the God of Israel had been responsible, the priests determined that the Ark should be placed in a cow-drawn cart along with some specially designed golden jewelry as an offering, and let loose. If the cart went to the city of Beth-Shemesh, they would know that the Israelite God was responsible for the disease; if it went elsewhere, that would be considered a sign that the incidents were just a random accident.

The cows pulled the cart to Beth-Shemesh, alerting the Philistines to the nature of their problem, but the people of Beth-Shemesh had some difficulties with the Ark's presence. The Levites removed the Ark from the cart and placed it on a large stone, but, allegedly, the people of the city looked inside the chest and angered God. He therefore killed large numbers of the town inhabitants for their sin. As a result, the people sent the sacred icon to the town of Kiriath-Jearim, where it remained according to the biblical account until the time of David.

With Eli's death Samuel, David's patron and sponsor, became chief priest, prophet, and judge of Israel. Nevertheless, the Philistines continued to oppress the Israelites for another twenty years. Samuel attributed the tyranny of the Philistines to the abandonment of God, and told Israel that if they put away their foreign idols, God would deliver them from their oppressors. This they did and Samuel led Israel against the enemy and defeated them, recapturing many of the cities taken over by their oppressors.

Although 1 Sam 7:13 says that after this battle the Philistines no longer bothered Israel while Samuel was alive, such claims are contradicted shortly afterwards in 1 Sam 9:16, which says that the Philistines were still oppressing Israel in the time of Samuel.

The First Request for a King

After Samuel defeated the Philistines, the story jumps an uncertain number of years into the future, when Samuel had become an old man. At this point, he appointed his sons to assist him in the judging of Israel. But these sons had become corrupt and took bribes and gave bad judgments (1 Sam 8:1–3). This angered the people of Israel, and a delegation of elders approached Samuel and demanded that he appoint a king to judge them "like all the nations" (1 Sam 8:5).

Here the claim is that the role of the king is to issue judgments, and the bible notes the uniqueness of Israel's pre-monarchical status. On a philosophical level, Israel is facing the question of how to administer a system of justice. Although the people request that Samuel appoint the king, in fact, as we learn later, it is the people, or at least influential elements of the general population, who will choose the king and Samuel's role is simply to consecrate the choice.

This constituted a fundamental policy shift. The judicial function had been handled by a self-appointed priestly elite without any role for the people in the selection process. The priests determined who would do the judging and when to remove a judge. Now, a non-priestly coalition demanded a separation of powers. It wanted to choose a judge from outside the priesthood and it wanted the priestly elite to confirm its choice. In a sense, the priests were given the role of the United States Senate, to advise and consent on appointments, and to keep an eye out for wrongdoing, while the elders, an informal group representing the people at large, were to function like the House of Representatives, reserving the right to impeach the judge for wrongdoing and asking the Priest/Senate to decide the issue of removal. The bible doesn't say how the elders were chosen but the implication is that they formed some sort of council made up of the oldest members of the political subdivision.

This, of course, did not sit well with Samuel and the priesthood. The transfer of functions and authority to a king meant a loss of resources, patronage, and perks. Samuel was not pleased and went off to commune with God.

According to 1 Sam 8:6, Samuel complained to God that the request for a king was a rejection of Samuel's leadership, but God told him the situation was much worse than that, "for they have not rejected thee, but they have rejected me, that I should not reign over them" (1 Sam 8:7). The words attributed to God accurately described the nature of the conflict between theocracy and democracy. The elite priests held their position by virtue of being God's spokespersons and handing down God's teachings. An elected king didn't have the same relationship to God that a priest had.

God then instructed Samuel to listen to the people but to first tell them what it would be like if they chose a king to rule over them. Because Samuel's speech constitutes what I believe to be the first written philosophical tract on the rights of the individual against an all powerful state, a document as significant and powerful as the Declaration of Independence, his words bear repeating in full. Whether they are actually the product of Samuel's time or whether, as I think, they reflect a post-Solomonic attack on the United Monarchy, is a separate issue that doesn't detract from the primacy of these words in the history of political liberty. Here is what Samuel said:

> This will be the manner of the king that shall reign over you: He will take your sons, and appoint them for himself, for his chariots, and to be his horsemen; and some shall run before his chariots. And he will appoint him captains over thousands, and captains over fifties; and will set them to ear his ground, and to reap his harvest, and to make his instruments of war, and instruments of his chariots. And he will take your daughters to be confectionaries, and to be cooks, and to be bakers. And he will take your fields, and your vineyards, and your oliveyards, even the best of them, and give them to his servants. And he will take the tenth of your seed, and of your vineyards, and give to his officers, and to his servants. And he will take your menservants, and your maidservants, and your goodliest young men, and your asses, and put them to his work. He will take the tenth of your sheep: and ye shall be his servants. And ye shall cry out in that day because of your king which ye shall have chosen you; and the LORD will not hear you in that day (1 Sam 8:11–18).

Note the breathtaking sweep of the charges. In broad terms it attacks what in those times could reasonably be termed the military-industrial complex, the turning of resources over to the state war machine. In specifics, it condemns military conscription, forced labor, the taking of private property for public purposes, and taxation. In this last regard Samuel talks about a stifling tax rate of 10 percent, mild by modern big government standards.

While the text indicates that this speech was made by Samuel, there are some reasons to think that the speech may have been made about a century later by another Shilohite priest, in connection with Jeroboam's successful revolt against Solomon's successor. We will deal with Solomon and Jeroboam in more detail in Chapter 16. For now I will just comment on the chronological context of this speech.

The problem is that Samuel describes the sort of political oppression that will come from choosing a king. One would expect, therefore, that these predictions would be borne out in the reign of the king to be appointed, Saul. But there is no evidence in the bible that Saul engaged in the oppression purportedly predicted by Samuel. Despite the propagandistic attacks on Saul for his opposition to David, there is nothing to indicate that he was a bad or unpopular king. Although he had some lands and property, he possessed them before he became king, and there is no biblical claim that he enriched himself. The house he lived in seems to be rather spartan in terms of royal wealth and power. He engaged in no imperialistic battles, acting only to defend Israel against enemy attacks.

More importantly, there is no apparent evidence that Saul was unjust. His sins were limited to his rivalry towards Samuel and David. Even the extremely pro-David author of Chronicles finds nothing negative to say about Saul's rule, other than quoting David as saying that Saul failed to consult the Ark for advice. Nothing about Samuel's speech applied to Saul, so he must not have been the target of the attack.

Only under David do we begin to see the abuses mentioned in Samuel's argument. It is David who transformed Israel into an imperialist war-power and fought wars of conquest, and David who launched major building projects and expensive bureaucracies. Under Solomon, Israel remained a powerful military force with large chariot reserves, but under David the country had expanded as far as it could. He could not take it any further. So Solomon concentrated on consolidating control over the foreign territories, often through treaties of marriage. Samuel's speech, then, can be seen as an attack on the excesses of the Judaean Royal family.

It is only with Solomon's death, however, that the question of a public choice comes up again. As we will see in Chapter 16, the Shilohite priests turned against Solomon and encouraged a man named Jeroboam to lead a revolution against the king. Although Jeroboam failed to unseat Solomon, when Solomon died Jeroboam returned to lead opposition to Solomon's son and successor, Rehoboam, who publicly threatened to run a government more harsh and cruel than his father (1 Ki 2:11). This resulted in a public debate over whether or not the Israelites would accept Rehoboam as king, and it is in this context that the anti-monarch words attributed to Samuel seem to make the most historical sense. Following the debate, Israel, consistent with the warning, split away from the Davidic dynasty and set up a rival government.

As to the date of authorship, it makes little historic sense for this document to have been written much after the time of Solomon. While the Deuteronomistic historian wanted the king subordinated to the word of God, he did not want to eliminate the institution of monarchy. Similarly, in the post-monarchist period, the leaders still looked forward to a restoration of the Davidic throne, so they had no desire to attack the institution of monarchy per se. Samuel's speech, however, attacks the institution itself. Since the attack comes from the Shiloh priesthood, urges the rejection of a king, and describes a monarch very much unlike Saul, Rehoboam appear to be the most likely candidate as the oppressive ruler that should be rejected by Israel. And Israel rejected him. Since Shiloh ceased to be an important political force not long after Solomon's death, the only context in which this document fits is one close in time to the end of the United Monarchy.

Whether or not Samuel made this specific argument, he failed to sway the people against kingship. In fact, the people asked that the new king also be given other priestly duties. Not only did they want the king to judge them, they wanted the king to go out before them and defend Israel against its enemies (1 Sam 8:20). The transfer of military authority from the priesthood to the monarchy further diminished the power of Shiloh. Samuel saw that he lost the debate and gave the people what they wanted.

THE FIRST ELEVATION OF SAUL

Once Samuel acceded to the popular will the focus shifted to who would become king. At this point the bible introduces us to Saul, who belonged to the tribe of Benjamin and whose father was "a mighty man of power." The introductory verses tell us that Saul was:

> A choice young man, and a goodly: [sic] and there was not among the children of Israel a goodlier person than he: from his shoulders and upward he was higher than any of the people (1 Sam 9:2).

Benjamin was the smallest of the tribes and located strategically between Judah and Ephraim, the two chief political rivals within Israel at this time. Benjamin contained the city of Jerusalem but we are given to believe that the city remained in non-Israelite hands until David became king and captured the city from the Jebusites (see Chapter 8).

The biblical account of Saul's elevation to kingship and subsequent fall from grace reflects a tension between competing and conflicting source documents. The story contains many apparent duplications of events and explanations, often with contradictory elements. The problems derive from disagreements among several sets of accounts, traditions, and legends—one group portraying Saul as a popular hero and beloved king, another reflecting the opposition of the Shiloh priesthood to the institution of kingship, and a third representing the Davidic opposition to Saul. A careful reading of these conflicting materials suggests that they reached their final form only after several stages of redaction and alteration in accord with the views of later editors sometime after the fall of the northern kingdom in 722, perhaps as late as the post-Exilic period in the fifth century BCE.

When we first meet Saul, he is a young man working on the family estate (1 Sam 9:1–2). When some of his father's asses disappear, he and a servant set out to find them. They traveled for three days throughout Ephraim and Benjamin but without any luck. Saul was ready to give up but his servant noted that there was a man of God in a nearby city and perhaps he would use his ability as a seer to help locate the missing animals. Saul at first balked at the idea, saying that he lacked anything to give the man as a fee for his services. But the servant had some money with him and said that it should be enough.

At this point the editor adds an explanatory note saying that in those olden days people used the word "seer" to describe what people in the editor's time referred to as "prophet" (1 Sam 9:9). This little note indicates the editor relied on an earlier written source for this story, one that was sufficiently old such that the term "seer" had become somewhat archaic when the editor was writing. In that regard, we should also recall that the Chronicler relied in part on a written text known as Samuel the Seer (1 Chr 29:29) and he almost certainly wrote after the editor who inserted this little note, suggesting that these older sources continued to circulate even after the Deuteronomist had finished his version of the history.

When Saul and his servant arrived at the house of the man of God, the previously unnamed prophet turned out to be Samuel. By coincidence, Samuel had just received a word from God the day before saying that the Lord would send a man from Benjamin to him and that this man should be anointed to be *nagid* over Israel so that he could deliver Israel from the Philistines (1 Sam 9:16). The Hebrew word *nagid* means "chieftain," "governor," or "leader." KJV translates the word as "ruler." In biblical usage *nagid* refers to someone who has been singled out for special attention and is mostly used to refer to a king-designate. That a *nagid* would deliver Israel from the Philistines contradicts the earlier claim that Samuel had already put an end to Philistine aggression against Israel during his lifetime.

As the story in 1 Sam 9 unfolds, Samuel invites Saul into his house for a meal, tells him that the asses had been found, and then informs him he is to become leader over Israel. At the meal he gave Saul the special portion of meat reserved for the most eminent of persons. Saul, stunned by the news, responded that it seemed inappropriate for someone like him, from the smallest clan of the smallest tribe, to receive such honor. Subsequently, Samuel and Saul had private conversations, and Samuel gave his protégé a set of signs that would occur and a list of instructions. Two of his observations require special note.

When Saul set out on his return path Samuel told him he would come near a Philistine garrison and meet a company of prophets. At that point the spirit of the Lord would come over him and he would prophesy along with them. When this occurs, Samuel added, you must then go to Gilgal and wait seven days for me, at which time we will offer burnt sacrifices and I will give you further instructions.

All of Samuel's predictions came true, including Saul's sharing in the prophetic spirit. About that experience, the bible alleges that a proverb arose in Israel: "Is Saul also among the Prophets?" (1 Sam 10:11). Like many elements in Saul's story it duplicates later events. After Saul became king, there was another incident, when he was chasing after David, where he fell into ecstatic prophetic mode and again the text says that as a result of this later incident it became a saying: "Is Saul also among the Prophets?" (1 Sam 19:24).

Despite the inconsistent origin of the proverb, the repetition makes clear that such a saying was part of the Saulide tradition partially embedded in 1 Samuel. Its importance lies in what the proverb implies. It derives from the tension and division between Saul and the prophets. Saul was thought of as hostile to the prophetic class, and if there was anyone unlikely to act like a prophet it was Saul. His functioning in prophetic mode is an extraordinary event and suggests that the incident served as a moral lesson, to wit, God will ultimately decide your fate and your role in life.

Saul's First Sin

The instruction to Saul presents a difficult problem. Saul was to wait at Gilgal for seven days so that Samuel could make a burnt offering and give further instructions. Saul's alleged failure to wait for Samuel became the basis for Samuel's challenge to Saul's right to have his descendants rule in dynastic succession. Unfortunately, severe inconsistencies in the biblical account make this claim hard to follow.

Although Saul was to wait for Samuel at Gilgal right after his ecstatic experience, the Gilgal incident for which Samuel condemns Saul took place long after Saul became king, at least a year later and perhaps much longer. (See 1 Sam 13. The textual transmission is corrupt as to the time frame in all extant biblical sources.) Saul, in fact, went home and never mentioned to his father what Samuel told him.

According to the later account about Saul at Gilgal, the Philistines had attacked the Israelites and the people panicked, scattered, and went into hiding. Saul brought some "trembling" troops to Gilgal "and he tarried seven days, according to the set time that Samuel had appointed; but Samuel came not to Gilgal; and the people were scattered from him" (1 Sam 13:8). After Samuel failed to appear at the promised time, Saul made burnt offerings. Samuel immediately appeared thereafter, as if he had been hiding behind a tree or rock watching to see what Samuel would do.

Samuel confronted Saul over the sacrificial procedure and Saul properly replied that Samuel failed to be where he should have been and that to keep the troops together it was necessary to make a sacrifice to God before the battle (1 Sam 13:11–12). Despite his own failure to keep his appointment, Samuel condemned Saul and advised him:

> Thou hast done foolishly: thou hast not kept the commandment of the LORD thy God, which he commanded thee: for now would the LORD have established thy kingdom upon Israel for ever. But now thy kingdom shall not continue: the LORD hath sought him a man after his own heart, and the LORD hath commanded him to be captain [i.e., nagid] over his people, because thou hast not kept that which the LORD commanded thee (1 Sam 13:13–14).

Resolving the chronological discrepancy between Samuel's initial directive back when Saul was his guest and Saul's alleged failure to comply with God's word on the battlefield long after he became king proves instructive as to how the biblical editors altered and distorted earlier source materials, and illustrates how politics influenced the writings.

At the heart of the solution is the recognition that Samuel was not the man of God that Saul met and who forecast that he would become king. Samuel's instruction to wait at Gilgal for seven days occurred after Saul had become king and had already been engaged in battle with the Philistines.

That Samuel wasn't the original man of God can be seen from the biblical context. When Saul and his servant were searching for the asses, the servant mentions only that a man of God lived in the city. The man was unnamed and apparently his name was unknown to either the servant or Saul. Yet Samuel was the most powerful and influential figure in all Israel, from the same geographical vicinity as Saul. If he were the man of God, his name would have been known to Saul and the servant. It is also implied initially that the man of God lived in that city. Yet, when Saul searches him out, the name still goes unmentioned by any of the parties Saul talks to. One of the residents informs him that the man of God was just there for a day to attend to a sacrifice. Only after Saul meets the man of God does he learn that the man is Samuel.

In the original source story, Saul would have met a man of God while searching for the asses and the man would have only foretold that one day Saul would become *nagid* over Israel. There would have been no anointing at that time and no instructions to meet up later. And, in line with folklore traditions, the prophet would have given Saul a series of signs to watch for as proof that the prophecy came from God. The story itself would have been a popular legend about Saul that belonged to a larger collection of stories about his heroic deeds before becoming king.

Prophetic sources, anxious to subordinate the king to religious authority, altered the story to make Samuel the man of God. But this resulted in transferring part of the confrontation between Saul and Samuel from the battle with the Philistines to the house of the man of God. In the original account, Saul would already have been king when Samuel instructed him to wait at Gilgal so that the prophet could make a burnt offering prior to the counterattack against the Philistines. This was a traditional part of battle preparation and Samuel as chief priest would have been expected to make the sacrifice in such a threatening situation. Samuel, however, seems to have withheld his support, perhaps to undermine Saul's authority and force the newly appointed king to submit to priestly authority.

Saul, opposed to Samuel in the first place, decided that as nagid he also had the authority to make burnt offerings prior to battle, a direct challenge to Samuel and the Shilohite priests. Samuel, no doubt sulking Achilles-like in his tent, rushed out to denounce Saul when he heard what happened. Saul appropriately rebuked Samuel for not being there to perform his duty, and the prophet replied with a condemnation of Saul's kingship. As a side note, despite Samuel's claim that Saul would have no successor from his family, one of Saul's children did succeed him on the throne, albeit for a short time (see Chapter 7).

This alternative reconstruction of the two stories radically contradicts the Shilohite version that made Samuel responsible for Saul's elevation. That this is the case can be seen from a second allegation in the bible about how Saul became king, one which is also chronologically inconsistent with the Shilohite version. It involves a battle between Saul and the Ammonites, allegedly after Saul had become king. Let's put these events into context.

THE SECOND ELEVATION OF SAUL

According to the biblical account, after Samuel secretly anointed Saul, he called a meeting of the people to meet their demand for a king. Instead of simply announcing, however, that the Lord had spoken to him and designated Saul to be king, he went through the charade of holding some undescribed form of a lottery, first choosing the tribe of Benjamin, then the family of Saul, and then finally Saul himself. But Saul, perhaps reflecting his modesty and piety, did not come forward. He was hiding out and messengers had to find him and bring him forward. Samuel then declared him God's chosen and presented him with a book of rules and regulations that he was expected to follow, the contents of which the text fails to set forth. But some "wicked people," according to 1 Sam 10:27, opposed Saul's elevation and despised him. Saul, however, took no action against them.

No sooner did Saul assume authority than we learn that Nahash, king of the Ammonites, encamped his troops outside the non-Israelite city of Jabesh-Gilead, on the east side of the Jordan River. The inhabitants requested a peaceful resolution and the Ammonite king advised them that there could be no peaceful resolution unless everyone agreed to have their right eyes put out as a reproach to Israel. (In a Dead Sea Scroll known as 4QSam, which contains portions of the oldest known copy of the Book of Samuel, the text includes some additional material that indicates that Nahash had previously attacked the Israelite tribes of Reuben and Gad and gouged out the right eyes of those Israelites, too. Which version of the story is the original is subject to debate.)

The people of the town asked for time to think it over and Nahash agreed. They then sent messengers to Saul and asked for help. The news outraged Saul and he told the messengers that Israel would assist them. He took an ox, hacked it into pieces, and sent the parts throughout the country along with a message saying that this is what will happen to you if you don't join together and stop the Ammonites.

Saul raised a large volunteer army and launched a surprise attack that destroyed most of the Ammonite troops. Jabesh-Gilead developed a strong attachment to the House of Saul, and biblical tradition shows a close bond between the Benjaminites and the people of Jabesh-Gilead, possibly reflecting the historical authenticity of Saul's conquest.

When Saul returned from his victory, Israel was joyous and went to Samuel to demand that Saul's opponents, those wicked people who opposed his elevation to the kingship, be executed. But, in merciful mode, Saul said that no one should be punished and that Israel should enjoy what God had given it. Then we have a very strange comment in the text. Samuel said to the people:

> Come, and let us go to Gilgal, and renew the kingdom there. And all the people went to Gilgal; and there they made Saul king before the LORD in Gilgal; and there they sacrificed sacrifices of peace offerings before the LORD; and there Saul and all the men of Israel rejoiced greatly (1 Sam 11:14–15).

Saul had already been publicly elevated to the kingship prior to the battle. Why was it necessary to go back and renew his kingship? For a partial explanation, we go to 1 Sam 12:12–13, where Samuel, as part of a long speech, says:

> And when ye saw that Nahash the king of the children of Ammon came against you, ye said unto me, Nay; but a king shall reign over us: when the LORD your God was your king. Now therefore behold the king whom ye

have chosen, and whom ye have desired! and, behold, the LORD hath set
a king over you.

As the passage indicates, Saul didn't become king until after he
defeated the Ammonites, and his elevation was the result of popular
acclamation. The priests and prophets didn't choose him; the people
did by their vocal support. The return to Gilgal, therefore, was not for
a renewal of the kingship; it was for the granting of kingship. In this
regard, we should note that Saul's name in Hebrew means "the one
asked for, or requested" (ABD, s.v. "Saul [Person] A. Name and Family Background").

This second story of kingship should be read in connection with our
reconstructed version of Saul's initial visit to the man of God. The man of
God, who I suggested was not Samuel, prophesied that Saul would become king, and when Saul defeated the Ammonites, Israel saw in him a
military savior who could better defend them than the corrupt and inef-
fective priesthood. The people made Saul king and the Shiloh priests who
previously ruled the country opposed his elevation.

The earlier claim that wicked people opposed Saul's kingship, and the
subsequent claim in the second story that the people demanded the death
of those wicked opponents, might properly be read as an identification of
the Shiloh priests as Saul's wicked opponents. After all, they were the
chief source of opposition to Saul. Therefore, it was the Shiloh priests
that the people wanted to execute and whom Saul spared. Saul's mercy
may have been tempered by effective politics. Such an act of destruction
could have led to civil war.

The first story of kingship, where Samuel selected Saul by lottery
and gave him a book of rules and regulations, can therefore be rejected
as unreliable propaganda and belongs with the false substitution of
Samuel for the man of God. It was part of an attempt to subordinate
the king to the rule of religious authority. For this same reason, the
Shilohite speech attacking the institution of monarchy was transferred
from its original place as an attack on Solomon's son Rehoboam and
put in the mouth of Samuel.

SAUL'S SECOND SIN

Having lost the argument over Saul's elevation to the throne and being saddled with the reputation of administering a corrupt priesthood, later editors attempted to rehabilitate Samuel's reputation by giving him another grand speech. He began with what can be called his "I am not a crook" speech, challenging anyone to come forward with a claim that he stole anything from anybody, and an offer to make restitution if he did:

> Whose ox have I taken? or whose ass have I taken? or whom have I defrauded? whom have I oppressed? or of whose hand have I received any bribe to blind my eyes therewith? and I will restore it you (1 Sam 12:3).

Not surprisingly, no one accused God's chief spokesman of wrongdoing, and Samuel called upon Saul, in his new capacity as judge, to bear witness to Samuel's innocence. (There is no indication, however, that he ever did anything to make good on the corrupt judgments made by his sons.)

Samuel followed his acquittal on theft charges with a short recital of history in which Israel in the past continuously did evil and suffered punishment. Next he admonished everyone to follow God's law. As a reminder of his link to God and the importance of his words, Samuel summoned forth a rain and thunder storm. The storm, he told them, was a sign of their wickedness in choosing a king and rejecting the rule of God. He then says, in effect, they still have him to teach about right and wrong, and if Israel does what he says, everything will be okay. "But if ye shall still do wickedly, ye shall be consumed, both ye *and your king*" (1 Sam 12:25, emphasis added).

Samuel's speech constituted an admission that the pro-king, anti-Shiloh faction had won out; but he still argued that the king could legitimately serve only as long as he followed the law as interpreted by the Shiloh community. The conflict between Shiloh and the popular will, however, was substantial, and an irreparable schism soon developed over the terms of battle against the Amalekites, one of Israel's traditional enemies.

There is no archaeological evidence outside the bible for the existence of the Amalekites. Biblical tradition makes them descendants of

Esau, Jacob/Israel's brother. They are depicted as a somewhat aggressive nomadic group given to marauding and looting. They inhabited a large swatch of territory running from the Edomite lands in southern Jordan to the borders of Egypt. The Book of Numbers accuses them of unprovoked attacks against Israel during the flight from Egypt (Num 14:45; see also Ju 6:3).

After his half-hearted concession to Saul, Samuel announced that God remembered the assault on Israel by the Amalekites (some three hundred years earlier) and now wanted revenge. He said God wanted Saul to lead an attack against the Amalekites and "utterly destroy all that they have, and spare them not; but slay both man and woman, infant and suckling, ox and sheep, camel and ass" (1 Sam 15:3).

Saul gathered an army and administered a stinging defeat to the Amalekites, but he did not destroy everything as Samuel directed. He and the people had spared the Amalekite king and the best of the cattle (1 Sam 15:9). When Samuel arrived at the camp he was furious to learn that not everything had been destroyed as God commanded and he demanded an explanation. Saul told him of the people's will, and then added that the people wanted to sacrifice the best animals to God (1 Sam 15:15). At worst, then, Saul's violation of God's instruction was only a matter of time delay. The animals were to be destroyed, but in a sacrifice, not immediately after capture.

Nevertheless, Samuel seized on this failure to follow the letter of God's (i.e. Samuel's) instruction as a literal violation of God's law and declared that God had ripped the kingship away from Saul and given it to "a neighbor of thine, that is better than thou" (1 Sam 15:28). The neighbor, of course, turns out to be David. As a final act, Samuel has the Amalekite king brought forward and hacked into pieces (1 Sam 15:33). The text then claims that Samuel never saw Saul again (1 Sam 15:35).

The story as presented constitutes pro-David propaganda. Indeed, not only weren't the Amalekites wiped out as implied in the story, they continued to harass and menace the Israelites all through Saul's reign. They even attacked a city owned by David in his outlaw days and kidnapped his wives. David chased after them but even he didn't eliminate them, as hundreds fled on camels (1 Sam 30:17). If Saul was under God's command to destroy the Amalekites as revenge for the attacks during the Exodus period, then David should have been too, and he also failed.

The dispute between Samuel and Saul clearly shows a continuing split between the priests of Shiloh and non-priestly elements of the general population. We also have indications of a serious religious split between the followers of Saul and the Shiloh priesthood.

In the argument between Saul and Samuel over the Amalekites, Saul twice makes a curious reference to God. In the first instance, he says the people wanted "to sacrifice unto the Lord, *thy* God" (1 Sam 15:15, emphasis added). And in the second instance, after Samuel has rejected him, he says, "turn again with me, that I may worship the Lord *thy* God" (1 Sam 15:30, emphasis added). On both occasions, where we would expect him to refer to "our God" he indicates that the deity is the one Samuel worships, implicitly a different deity than the one favored by Saul and his followers. The nature of this disagreement is not made explicit, but implicitly it suggests the continued recognition of Canaanite religious practices among the Israelite peasantry, a factor that must have at least partially fueled the resentment against the anti-Canaanite Shilohite religious authority. This usage may also reflect an early Israelite division between those who worshipped a deity named Jahweh and those who represented a different deity named Elohim, before the two names became identified with the same god.

Despite Samuel's attack on the legitimacy of Saul's kingship, the monarch continued to rule Israel for many years after and remained a popular hero. He brought a substantial degree of peace to the countryside by holding off Israel's enemies and, other than his two alleged sins against God's words and his opposition to David, there is no report in 1 or 2 Samuel of his being a bad or unjust king. Chronicles adds only the Davidic charge that Saul failed to consult the Ark (1 Chr 13:3). Certainly if he were known for being an unjust or cruel monarch his opponents would have flogged such behavior as evidence that he rejected God's law. The absence of such charges offers vivid proof that Saul was a good and popular king.

THE SECRET ANOINTING OF DAVID

Samuel had been thoroughly humiliated by Saul and the Shiloh reputation remained in disrepair among the Israelites. That Samuel and Saul never met again suggests that the breach between the Shiloh priests and the new monarch had become irreparable. Shiloh needed a new ally and it found one in the territory of Judah, in the city of Bethlehem, in the House of Jesse, father of David. But there is some question as to when this alliance was formed. Was David a child as the biblical account has it, or was he already an adult in the king's court?

The bible says that God told Samuel to stop brooding over Saul, go to the house of Jesse, and get ready to anoint a successor that he has chosen among the sons. When Samuel arrived at Jesse's house "the elders of the town trembled at his coming, and said, Comest thou peaceably?" (1 Sam 16:4). The text does not explain why the elders should fear Samuel or what it would mean if he didn't come peacefully, but the context is evident. Though defeated, Shiloh was not broken and it had its own military forces. Civil war may have been in the air, and the elders may have feared a military raid. However, Samuel announced his peaceful intentions, saying he had come to do sacrifice, and "sanctified Jesse and his sons" (1 Sam 16:5).

Jesse had seven or eight sons (compare 1 Sam 16:10–11 to 1 Chr 2:13–15) and David was the youngest, still a child not yet of a warrior's age. By some mystical process, Samuel divined that the boy should be the successor and secretly anointed him as Saul's replacement. At that moment "the Spirit of the Lord came upon David from that day forward" and "the spirit of God departed from Saul, and an evil spirit from the Lord troubled him" (1 Sam 16:13–14). It will be some twenty years later, however, before David becomes king over all of Israel, and then only after Saul dies and Saul's son has ruled another two years.

Contextually, the secret anointment of David presents a problem. Samuel has already publicly stripped Saul of his legitimacy, claiming that God himself removed the kingship from the monarch. Only a short while earlier Samuel had vehemently opposed the institution of monarchy altogether. He had called it wicked and a rejection of God's rule. He even brought a storm down upon the people to emphasize the evil act involved. Why, then, is he seeking a new king to anoint, and a secret anointment at that? He should be campaigning against kingship.

The answer, of course, is that the incident is fictitious, at least as it regards David as a young child. It is an attempt to provide cover for David, who spent many years in opposition to Saul and who tried to take the throne away from him. As will be argued in later chapters, after David became a popular military hero in Israel, the Shiloh priests formed an alliance with David in an effort to wrest the throne from Saul.

The anointment of David serves as an introduction to the famous story of David and Goliath, which we shall examine in detail in the next chapter. There we will see that the Goliath story was one more fictional attempt to build up a false background for the young David.

CHAPTER 3

Who Killed Goliath?

Elhanan son of Jaare-oregim, the Bethlehemite,
killed Goliath the Gittite, the shaft of whose spear
was like a weaver's beam. 2 SAM 21:19, RSV

*D*avid's long-held reputation for unsurpassed courage and steadfast devotion to God rests primarily upon the biblical story of his battle with the Philistine giant Goliath (1 Sam 17), which tells how the young David, trusting in the Lord's protection, slew the most powerful warrior in all of the Philistine army.

But elsewhere in the biblical text we find traces of a different story about who killed this enemy of Israel, and it wasn't David. Further, an examination of the David and Goliath story shows evidence of having been tampered with by substituting a young David for the original hero. When we put the pieces together we see that the account of this famous confrontation was a fraud perpetrated by Judaean scribes anxious to rescue David's sagging reputation.

Portions of the original source story that inspired the Davidic legend appear in 2 Sam 21:15–22 and tell of a group of heroes that belonged to "the Thirty", King David's elite fighting corps, a kind of Arthurian round table whose members went about fighting giants and performing other great deeds (2 Sam 23:18). In this other Goliath story David had already become an old and enfeebled king, and the man who slew the Philistine warrior was named Elhanan.

This second story, which diminished David's claim to fame, must have been in wide circulation long after David's death because as late as the writing of Chronicles in the post-Exilic period (in the fifth century BCE or later) we find a Chronicles editor (perhaps the original author)

41

desperately trying to protect David's heroic image by radically altering this rival account through textual omissions and factual changes. The chief liberty taken was to change Elhanan's victim from Goliath to Goliath's brother (1 Chr 20:5). With the translation of the bible into English, several versions (including the King James Version) relied on the Chronicler's deception to deliberately mistranslate the Hebrew text in 2 Sam 21:19, the earlier pre-Chronicles version citing Elhanan as Goliath's killer, so that it, too, would show the victim to be the giant's brother rather than the giant supposedly slain by David.

In this chapter we will first look at some of the textual and logical problems with the story of David and Goliath, and then we will review the alternative version of the story in which Elhanan is responsible for Goliath's death. Then we will partially reconstruct the original story of Goliath, place it in a larger literary context, and show the manner in which biblical scribes transformed it from a tale about other heroes of David's old age to one about a heroic young David.

INTRODUCING DAVID

We first meet the character of David in the biblical chapter immediately preceding the story of his confrontation with Goliath. To appreciate some of the inconsistencies presented by the story of David's confrontation we need to first take a closer look at how he is introduced to the reader.

According to 1 Sam 16:1, God determined that Saul was no longer fit to rule and sent Samuel to Bethlehem in search of a successor, someone that the Lord himself would choose. The journey brought the prophet to the house of Jesse and his eight sons, the youngest of whom was David, a sheepherder. Although Samuel, judging initially only on the appearance of physical strength, thought that one of David's older brothers would surely be the chosen one, God advised him:

> Look not on his countenance, or on the height of his stature... for the Lord seeth not as man seeth; for the man looketh on the outward appearance, but the Lord looketh on the heart (1 Sam 16:7).

David was the last of the sons to be inspected by Samuel, and it was this child that God appointed to replace Saul. Consequently, the prophet secretly anointed David as the king's successor.

After the anointment of Jesse's young son, the bible tells us that the Lord's spirit departed from Saul and entered upon David (1 Sam 16:13–14). Next, God caused Saul to suffer fevers that could only be assuaged by soothing music (1 Sam 16:14–17). It should not come, therefore, as too much of a surprise that David also had a splendid reputation for musicianship and that he was summoned to the king's court to play for the suffering Saul. The young boy's melodic art worked well upon the king and he became a favorite of the monarch (1 Sam 16:23), who designated David as his personal armor-bearer (1 Sam 16:21). Whenever Saul felt melancholy, the youth came to play for him.

There is also a puzzling passage in this introduction. When Saul seeks out someone skillful in music, one of his courtiers describes David as "the son of Jesse the Bethlehemite, that is cunning in playing, and a *mighty valiant man, and a man of war,* and prudent in matters, and a comely person, and *the Lord is with him*" (1 Sam 16:18, emphasis added). It seems somewhat strange to see this untested child-sheepherder described as "a mighty valiant man, and a man of war" without any prior indication that this is the case. Certainly, based on Samuel's initial reaction in meeting David and his brothers, the prophet knew of no such reputation. Also, there is no basis for any public claim that the Lord was with David, since his anointment by Samuel occurred in secret and no public evidence of the Lord's support had yet been presented. These special characteristics described by Saul's courtier before they are publicly known obviously stem either from later additions to the story by a careless pro-David redactor anxious to conform the written history to the desired image or represent traces of the original story before it was altered to fit propagandistic purposes.

As we look into further aspects of David's encounter with Goliath, it will be necessary to recall that in this first introduction 1) we are given the names of David's father and older brothers, 2) we are told that they came from Bethlehem, 3) Saul has been told who David's father is, and 4) David had a close personal relationship with Saul prior to his battle with Goliath, serving as his armor bearer and court musician.

GOLIATH ENTERS THE SCENE

With David's arrival at Saul's court, the bible turns to the story of Goliath (1 Sam 17). The account begins with the Philistines and the Israelites each poised upon opposite sides of a valley, ready to engage in combat. Suddenly, the Philistines sent out a champion named Goliath, who challenged the Israelites to a one-on-one battle, winner take all (1 Sam 17:9). The standard Masoretic Hebrew text gives the Philistine's height as "six cubits and a span" (1 Sam 17:4), approximately nine and a half feet. However, the Septuagint Greek version as well as an earlier Hebrew fragment of this same story found among the Dead Sea Scrolls gives the height as "four cubits and a span" (1 Ki XVII:4, Septuagint version), which is about six and a half feet, still tall for the average Near Eastern and Mediterranean resident but not so improbable as we had been given to expect.

Goliath is not only large, but he comes encased in massive amounts of heavy armor, with a shield carrier walking before him. Among his weapons we discover a spear, the staff of which is described as "like a weaver's beam" (1 Sam 17:7 Revised Standard Version). The meaning of this phrase long puzzled religious scholars, but in recent years it has been recognized as descriptive of a Mycenaean spear dating to the late second millennium BCE. This ancient weapon had a rope loop attached to the front of the shaft near the spear-point that served as a throwing aid. The image was like a threaded beam used in a weaver's loom.

The phrase "weaver's beam" appears only three more times in the bible (1 Sam 21:19, 1 Chr 11:23, 1 Chr 25). Twice it is used with regard to the weapon carried by Elhanan's opponent and once in connection with one of David's other warriors, Benaiah, who seized such a spear from an Egyptian giant of five cubits height (taller than Goliath, per the Septuagint version of the text) and slew him with it. Since that sort of weapon had disappeared from use early in the first millennium BCE, when the biblical stories started to appear in their earliest forms, and because the Philistines did have Mycenaean roots, the description of the spear has been taken by some scholars as an indication that the original Goliath story must have originated either prior to or not much later than the time period associated with King David.

As the Goliath story unfolds, the giant comes forth every day for forty days, each time arrayed in full battle gear, and shouting out his challenge to the Israelites. But all of Israel was "dismayed and greatly afraid" (1 Sam 17:11) and no hero would stand up for the Lord.

ANOTHER INTRODUCTION OF DAVID

After introducing Goliath, the story suddenly switches to a second introduction of David. Once again we are told that he was the son of "that Ephrathite of Bethlehem-Judah, whose name was Jesse, and he had eight sons" (1 Sam 17:12), of whom David was the youngest. We are also told that David tended sheep while his three eldest brothers were off fighting with Saul against the Philistines. Next, we are told that Jesse sent David to the battle site to bring some corn (i.e., grain), bread, and cheese for the captains of the army.

Note the problem here. We have already met David in the previous biblical chapter, learned about who his family was and where they were from, and left him as an armor-bearer in the court of King Saul. Now, we are introduced to him again, as if we had no idea who he was from the previous verses, and we find him not with Saul at the battle site but at home, still tending sheep. This is a clue that the Goliath story had been inserted into an existing history of King David and that perhaps the original hero of this story was not originally the David introduced earlier.

A later redactor, apparently aware of this awkward reintroduction, attempted to rehabilitate the story's credibility by adding a verse immediately after the second introduction saying that David had left Saul's court and went home to feed the sheep (1 Sam 17:15), a game but not very convincing solution. David's large family had several available sons to attend to the farm and it seems unlikely that in a time of battle, with David assigned to be the king's armor bearer, David's father would pull David home to feed the sheep. Indeed, in this time of battle, if an extra hand were desperately needed at home, David's important role as both King's armor bearer and Court musician soothing Saul's tormenting headaches would likely result in the monarch sending a servant in David's place to help out.

When David arrived at the battle site he heard Goliath's stentorian demands and observed the fear among the Israelites. He then heard the soldiers talking about the great rewards that would accrue to the slayer of the Philistine.

> [A]nd it shall be, that the man who killeth him, the king will enrich him with great riches, and will give him his daughter, and make his father's house free in Israel (1 Sam 17:25).

This sounded like an enormous opportunity to David and he immediately inquired if he had heard correctly. The soldiers repeated what had been said earlier.

One of David's brothers saw him making inquiry of the reward and chastised him for leaving the sheep back home, accusing him of abandoning his task so that he can come and watch the fighting, a strange charge to hurl at someone supposedly appointed to be the king's armor-bearer. David showed no regret and responded angrily, "What have I done? Is there not a cause?" (1 Sam 17:29). He then continued to inquire about the rewards. As David navigated through the crowd, complaining about the Philistine's insults against the "armies of the living God" (1 Sam 17:26) and again verifying the existence of a reward, his words found their way to Saul, who sent for him (1 Sam 17:31). When he appeared before the king, David offered to fight Goliath.

Here again, we have a problem with the flow of the story. To begin with, David is a youngster, and whatever boasts he might make, they would be a child's boasts to an audience of Israelite soldiers. It is unlikely to be taken seriously with word being brought to the king. Also, David has already been identified as a personal intimate of Saul, his musician and armor-bearer. He needs no introduction or invitation to visit the king's tent. Additionally, it is somewhat shocking to see how much attention David pays to the offer of a reward when we are given to believe his motivation is solely love for and faith in the God of Israel. These points present further clues that the original hero of this story was not the young David secretly anointed to be king, but someone older and of a warrior class, someone who might be tempted into dangerous combat by the offer of a large enough prize.

DAVID CONFRONTS GOLIATH

After David volunteered to fight the mighty Goliath, Saul questioned the ability of "but a youth" to successfully challenge this "man of war from his youth" (1 Sam 17:33). The boy then boasted of a prior incident in which a lion and bear grabbed one of his sheep and he single-handedly slew both, grabbing the lion by his beard in the process. His success, he argued, was due to divine guidance and the Lord, who, he said, "will deliver me out of the hand of the Philistine" (1 Sam 17:37).

Unbelievably, this child's story sounded pretty convincing to Saul, and he placed the whole fate of Israel on David's scrawny shoulders (1 Sam 17:46). This was, after all, supposed to be a winner-take-all battle.

Saul fetched his own personal armor for David's protection, but after trying it on and feeling its heft the boy warrior shed the heavy skins, choosing instead to rely on his sling and a few stones. As David arrived within earshot of the Philistine giant, the two potential combatants exchanged insults, David threatening to feed the Philistine's carcass to the "fowls of the air and to the wild beasts of the earth" (1 Sam 17:46). Finally, David ran towards Goliath, grabbing a stone from his bag, loading it into the sling, and hurling the missile directly at the heavily armored warrior's forehead, causing the Philistine to fall dead upon his face. Goliath must have previously removed his "helmet of brass" so that David might have a less obstructed target.

David took Goliath's sword and with it chopped off the dead Philistine's head. Afterwards, "David took the head of the Philistine and brought it to Jerusalem; but he put the armor in his tent" (1 Sam 17:54). This particular verse presents further difficulties with David's encounter. The more important problem is the bringing of Goliath's head to Jerusalem. Why would David do that? At this particular time, Jerusalem was in the hands of the Jebusites, enemies of Israel. It is not until David became king over all of Israel that the Israelites captured the city and David made it his capitol. This strongly suggests that the original version of this story took place at a time when David was already king, which, as we shall soon see, was the case.

The lesser problem with the passage is that it matter-of-factly describes David as already having his own tent, without any explanation of how this child so quickly acquired such an important and luxurious facility at the battle campsite. He had, as you recall, just arrived on the scene after feeding his sheep. This discrepancy might be explained away by saying that he was given the tent after his heroic act, but no such claim appears in the text. This suggests that the original hero of the story was already a high-ranking soldier in a military environment.

Although not mentioned in the story of David's slaying of Goliath, we learn later that the sword of Goliath, unbeknownst to David, had come to be placed in an Israelite sanctuary in the city of Nob (1 Sam 21:9). We will return to this matter later when we discuss the other story of Goliath's death.

THE MYSTERY KILLER

Perhaps the most puzzling passage in the entire David and Goliath saga occurs in 1 Sam 17:55. Right after David beheads Goliath, Saul turns to Abner, captain of the Israelite host, and asks, "Whose son is this youth?"

Abner replies, "As thy soul liveth, O king, I cannot tell."

Consequently, David is summoned before Saul, Goliath's head still in his hand, and the king inquires, "Whose son art thou, thou young man?" (1 Sam 17:58).

The youth replied, "I am the son of thy servant Jesse the Bethlehemite" (1 Sam 17:58).

These conversations present several difficulties. They suggest that neither the king nor his chief military officer knew which Israelite had just slain Goliath, presumably because they were too far from the battle scene to make out the features. Indeed, when Saul addresses David and asks who his father is, he addresses the boy as "thou young man," a phrase suggesting a lack of familiarity with the person before him. Yet, as we saw from the first introduction of David, Saul would already have known who David was because the boy served as his musician and armor-bearer. Also, we were told earlier that Saul personally sent David out to fight with the Philistine warrior, even offering his personal armor to the young boy.

Lest it be argued that the passage only indicates that Saul did not know who David's father was, recall that the king had already been told that the boy was the son of Jesse prior to his arrival at court. Further, it seems unlikely that David could perform these vital services for Saul and the king would have no idea who David's father was.

Saul's unfamiliarity with the identity and background of the killer of Goliath suggests that David's placement within the story was artificial and that the king (whoever it was at the time) did not know who went out to fight with the giant.

Once Goliath was slain, fear gripped the Philistines and they fled from the scene, with the Israelites in hot pursuit. Somehow everyone forgot that this was a winner-take-all battle in which the Philistines agreed that if Goliath were slain "then will we be your servants" (1 Sam 17:9). This suggests that the original story was not about a winner-take-all battle.

THE MYSTERIOUS GIANT

Before looking at the other biblical claim about who slew Goliath, one further observation about David's encounter should be noted. Throughout the story, the name Goliath appears only twice and on all other occasions the enemy soldier is simply referred to as "the Philistine" or "the

Philistine of Gath," and on both occasions, some scholars believe, the appearance of the name Goliath has the sense of an insert into an existing text. This is especially obvious with regard to the second instance.

On the first occasion that Goliath's name appears, we are told, "There went out a champion out of the camp of the Philistines, named Goliath of Gath, whose height was six cubits and a span." (1 Sam 17:4). On the second occasion, the text says, "And as he [David] talked with them [his brothers], behold, there came up the champion, the Philistine of Gath, *Goliath by name*" (1 Sam 17:23, emphasis added). The problem with the second statement is the use of the phrase, "Goliath by name," which implies that we did not previously know the name of this Philistine. Yet, we had already been given his name just a few verses earlier. The phrase serves no logical literary function and disrupts the smooth flow of the story. This suggests that in the course of editing and transmitting the story from one editor to another, this second reference to Goliath may have been inserted earlier in time than the first reference to Goliath, in which case it would make sense to use the phrase "Goliath by name" as it would be the name's first appearance. This, in turn, implies several layers of editing and rewriting before the story achieved its present form.

The Second Slaying of Goliath

Let's turn now to the second story about the slaying of Goliath, which appears in 2 Sam 21. Since it is brief and almost never presented in routine biblical histories of ancient Israel, I will set it forth in its entirety and then comment on it. The passage here is from the King James Version. Pay particular note to the words I placed in bold italics. They do not appear in the original Hebrew text and the KJV translators simply added them in to protect David's reputation and to eliminate an obvious contradiction in the supposedly inerrant bible:

> Moreover the Philistines had yet war again with Israel; and David went down, and his servants with him, and fought against the Philistines: and David waxed faint. And Ishbibenob, which was of the sons of the giant,

the weight of whose spear weighed three hundred shekels of brass in weight, he being girded with a new sword, thought to have slain David. But Abishai the son of Zeruiah succoured him, and smote the Philistine, and killed him. Then the men of David sware unto him, saying, Thou shalt go no more out with us to battle, that thou quench not the light of Israel. And it came to pass after this, that there was again a battle with the Philistines at Gob: then Sibbechai the Hushathite slew Saph, which was of the sons of the giant. And there was again a battle in Gob with the Philistines, where Elhanan the son of Jaare-oregim, a Bethlehemite, slew *the brother of* Goliath the Gittite, the staff of whose spear was like a weaver's beam. And there was yet a battle in Gath, where was a man of great stature, that had on every hand six fingers, and on every foot six toes, four and twenty in number; and he also was born to the giant. And when he defied Israel, Jonathan the son of Shimeah the brother of David slew him. These four were born to the giant in Gath, and fell by the hand of David, and by the hand of his servants (2 Sam 21:15–22).

As indicated in the opening verse, David had grown faint in the course of battle. Then follow accounts of four individual battles between four of David's soldiers and four sons of an unidentified giant from the city of Gath, the place where Goliath came from. In the middle of the story, one of the biblical redactors, concerned that David's image as tired and weak might undermine his heroic reputation, adds the claim that the soldiers begged David not to go into battle lest he be killed and the light of Israel be quenched. Finally, even though David obviously had nothing to do with defeating the four Philistine warriors, their deaths are attributed jointly to both David and his servants, again a scribal attempt to shore up David's less than heroic image in this battle.

The King James English translation, whose editors were anxious to avoid the contradiction between Samuel and Chronicles, identifies one of these sons of the giant as "the brother of" the Goliath that had a spear, the staff of which was like a "weaver's beam," i.e., brother of the Goliath slain by David. The problem with this identification is that the words "the brother of" appear only in the English translation, not in the underlying Hebrew text. They were deliberately added by the translators. Other more recent translations, such as the New Revised Standard Version (NRSV), give the correct wording and name this son of the giant as Goliath. Therefore, we have a clear cut biblical claim that Elhanan slew Goliath, not the brother of Goliath, and this Goliath carries the same distinguishing weapon as the Goliath in the earlier story, a spear with a staff like a weaver's beam.

The author of Chronicles, devoted passionately to protecting King David's reputation and seemingly aware that David was not widely recognized as the slayer of Goliath, even among the Judaean remnant returning from exile in Babylon, felt it necessary to alter the story as it appears in 2 Sam 21. Although in 1 Chr 20:4–8 he quotes almost verbatim from 2 Sam 21, indicating that he had before him either the text of Samuel or a source common to both him and the author of Samuel, he left out several important details and made some alterations in order to rehabilitate his favorite king.

The most significant change is that he actually says that the person killed by Elhanan was not Goliath but Goliath's brother, Lahmi (who is nowhere else mentioned). It was reliance on the Chronicler's assertion that enabled the King James translators to plausibly add "the brother of" into the English translation of 2 Sam 21:19.

Another important difference between Samuel and Chronicles is that the Chronicler omits the first of the four battles with the sons of the giant. The Chronicler does so because in this battle, the first of the giant's sons carried a sword that was thought to have killed David (2 Sam 21:16) and the Chronicler could not allow such a slanderous insult to remain against his beloved David. In a similar vein, the Chronicler also omitted from the story the claim that David had grown faint.

Finally, there is one last change made by the Chronicler. In Samuel, the second and third battles with the sons of the giant took place in a vicinity called Gob, not otherwise known in the bible. The Chronicler changed the site to Gezer, a Philistine stronghold (1 Chr 20:4). The significance of this change will become apparent shortly.

WHO IS ELHANAN?

In 2 Sam 21:19, the slayer of Goliath is identified as Elhanan, the son of Jaare-oregim, a Bethlehemite. The father's name means "Jaare the weaver," reminding us of the description of Goliath's spear like a weaver's beam. In Chronicles, the slayer of Goliath's brother is identified as Elhanan the son of Jair. Jaare and Jair are variations of the same root name, so there is no significant difference between the two patronyms. One describes the father's profession, the other doesn't. (Many scholars believe the description of Elhanan's father as a weaver is simply a transcription error somehow derived from the reference to "weaver's beam" in the same sentence.) But, 2 Samuel also makes reference to a second Elhanan, this one the son of Dodo of Bethlehem and a member of David's elite fighting group known as the Thirty (2 Sam 23:24, 1 Chr 11:26). Are these two Elhanans one and the same, despite the different names for the father? The context suggests that they are.

The three other warriors who fought alongside Elhanan against the sons of the giant all belonged to David's special combat unit, the Thirty, many of whom are described in the bible as engaging in grand heroic deeds. (2 Sam 23:39 gives the total membership of the Thirty as thirty-seven.) So it is hard not to assume that Elhanan son of Jaare-oregim was a member of this special warrior class. Since the only Elhanan mentioned among this group's membership (2 Sam 23, 1 Chr 11) is Elhanan son of Dodo, we should assume that he and the other Elhanan are one and the same. The three different names for the father suggest some confusion in the textual transmission of the story. It is somewhat ironic, therefore, that given this surfeit of patronyms, Saul asked after the identity of the slayer's father.

The name of Elhanan's father, Dodo, may have accidentally contributed to the idea that David was the actual slayer. In Hebrew, at about the time the Deuteronomists produced the Book of Samuel, David is spelled DWD and Dodo is spelled DWDW. Both characters come from Bethlehem. It doesn't take a great leap of imagination for Hebrews in later times to hear a story about how "the son of" DWDW of Bethlehem slew Goliath and confuse that reference with a heroic "King" DWD of Bethlehem. Many religiously orthodox scholars have gone so far as to suggest that Elhanan the son of Dodo and David were one and the same person. In fact, the name David may not be the king's original name. In Hebrew, DWD means "beloved" and may be an adopted throne name or a nickname applied to the king at a later time. But if David and Elhanan the son of

DWDW were one and the same, it doesn't explain why the latter would be listed as just one of King David's thirty-seven best soldiers.

THE ISRAELITE SANCTUARY AT NOB

I mentioned earlier that the sword of Goliath, unbeknownst to David, had been deposited in an Israelite sanctuary at Nob. (Such a lack of knowledge seems at least a bit incredible.) When David fled from Saul's wrath he took temporary shelter at the Nob sanctuary and asked if they had any weapons for him (1 Sam 21:8). They gave him the sword of Goliath (1 Sam 21:8). Later, Saul punished the sanctuary by ordering the priests executed (1 Sam 22:18). Eighty-five priests were struck down but one escaped, Abiathar, who joined David's rebel band and became chief priest at Jerusalem during David's reign (1 Sam 21:20). (Solomon removed him from office when Abiathar backed one of Solomon's rivals for the succession to David.)

The location of Nob is uncertain, but according to Neh. 11:32, it was located in the Saulite territory of Benjamin, close to Jerusalem, but it appears to have been an important religious sanctuary at one point, making it a pivotal battleground in the struggle between Davidic Judah and Saulite Benjamin for control over Israel. The iconography associated with Nob appears to have close but contradictory relationships with aspects of the story of Elhanan and the war against the four sons of the giant, and may represent a distortion of the original historical events associated with that site.

The first of the four battles occurred between the Philistine Ishbibenob, who was "girded with a new sword thought to have slain David," and Abishai, the Israelite who slew him. The passage raises some interesting issues. First, it appears to belong to a truncated account, in that it refers to the existence of "the" giant, as if we should know who he was, but whose identity isn't given in the story. Second, Ishbibenob had a sword thought to have killed David. Third, the Philistine's name (which translates as "His dwelling is in Nob") indicates that he comes from the city of Nob, which is where Goliath's sword supposedly reposed, and may indicate that the sanctuary at Nob was under Philistine control at the time of this confrontation. Fourth, the Chronicler was so offended by the description of this battle that he omitted it from his own retelling. These clues indicate that Nob was the home of some special sword somehow connected to David's image. Whether it was the sword taken from Goliath by David or some other sword remains to be seen.

The second and third battles took place at Gob, this third confrontation being the encounter between Goliath and Elhanan. Although Goliath is identified as the son of a giant, he, himself, is not specifically described as a giant. The Chronicler transferred both battle sites to Gezer, a Philistine stronghold.

The city of Gob is unknown outside of these two biblical mentions. In Hebrew, "G" and "N" have a near-identical appearance and I strongly suspect that originally "Gob" was actually "Nob" and there was a subsequent error in transmission. I believe too that in the Chronicler's copy of the 2 Samuel text the error in transmission had not yet occurred and it still retained the name Nob. Because the site was so sacred to the mythology of David, the Chronicler felt it necessary to transfer the battles to a different location. He may have even been familiar with an earlier version of the story that questioned the connection between David and Nob, and made Nob a Philistine sanctuary.

The fourth battle took place at Gath, Goliath's home city, but it was fought between David's nephew, Jonathan son of Shimeah, and an unidentified Philistine of great stature, with six fingers on each hand and six toes on each foot.

RECONSTRUCTING THE "DEATH OF GOLIATH" STORY

The pro-David story of Goliath's death and its aftermath provides some interesting contrasts with the anti-David story about Goliath's demise in the war with the four sons of the giant of Gath.

+ In the pro-David story, David slew Goliath, the giant from Gath; in the anti-David story, Elhanan killed Goliath, "the son of" the giant from Gath.

+ In the pro-David story, David is a youth when Goliath falls; in the anti-David story, David is an old enfeebled king when Goliath dies.

+ In the pro-David story, the battle involves a single giant named Goliath; in the anti-David story, the battle is with four sons of a giant, one of whom is named Goliath.

+ In the pro-David story, a sword thought to have killed Goliath was stored at a sanctuary at Nob and later carried by David; in the anti-David story, the brother of Goliath, from the city of Nob, carried a sword thought to have killed David.

+ In the pro-David story, Saul's allies killed the inhabitants at Nob; in the anti-David story, David's forces destroyed the Philistine enemy at what appears to have been the sanctuary at Nob (the name later transmitted as Gob, either due to a copyist's error or an attempt to cover up an embarrassing fact).

While we cannot reconstruct the original story precisely, we can suggest what its contours may have been. Long after David became king, he waged a war against Philistines in the vicinity of Nob, which may have been subject to Philistine control at the time and probably housed a Philistine sanctuary. Ishbibenob, a Philistine warrior, brandished a sword before the Israelites and claimed to have killed their king with it. He then challenged the Israelites to send out a champion for one-on-one combat (but not for a winner-take-all battle). Because David was old and unable to appear on the battle front to counter Ishbibenob's claim, rumors of the king's death spread rapidly and demoralized the troops.

In the meantime, Ishbibenob continued to challenge the Israelites to send out a hero, but no one wanted to face the man that struck down God's favorite. David then offered a reward to whoever would slay the braggart. Abishai, one of David's closest allies and most famous warriors, who rode with David even in the outlaw days, went to do battle with the Philistine and killed him. The tide turned and Israel renewed its attack with ferocity. Other Israelites fought famous battles with other Philistines.

As in the David story, when the Philistine hero fell the Philistine army retreated and the Israelites rode out after them, slaughtering the enemy as they fled. After the battle, David seized the sanctuary at Nob from the Philistines and, in typical Judaean fashion, slaughtered the enemy priests that maintained the cult site. Afterward, David commemorated this victory by establishing an Israelite sanctuary at Nob and placed Ishbibenob's sword inside, the one thought to have killed David, as a reminder that God favored David with victory. The sword became a sacred icon.

The use of the term "giant in Gath" was almost certainly a poetic metaphor for the militarily powerful Philistine city of Gath. One of the five chief cities of Philistia, Gath figures most prominently throughout the story of David. Similarly, the reference to the four sons of the giant probably referred to four divisions of Philistine troops from the same city. The four Israelite warriors who fought the sons of the giant, members of the Thirty, probably served as the captains over four corresponding Israelite divisions. Over time the metaphor became confused with the fact and the four Philistine hordes metamorphosed into four sons of a giant from the Philistine city of Gath.

REPLACING ELHANAN WITH DAVID

Unfortunately for David, as we will see in chapter 5, in his early years as an outlaw David closely allied himself with the Philistines of Gath in his efforts to unseat Saul. A story about brave Israelites defeating Philistine monsters from Gath while an elderly David stood on the sidelines couldn't have done much to bolster the heroic image of this king. Also, the story of Elhanan and his allies takes place sometime in the last years of David's reign. All that follows the event are a story about David's sinning against God and bringing punishment down on Israel (see Chapter 13) and David's death, not a very glorious finale to his supposedly glowing career. It became necessary to rehabilitate David's reputation, and Judaean scribes attempted to counter the anti-David imagery with pro-David propaganda.

One scribe added a line to the end of the tale about the war against the sons of the giant that attributed the victory to the hand of David.

Other scribes tried to make David himself the hero of the battle with the giants, and to counter the enfeebled image of the elderly king they made him a young vital warrior. Along the way the four sons of the giant were transformed into a single behemoth. As Goliath was the only one of the four sons of the giant who came from Gath, he came to be identified as "the giant in Gath" rather than the son of the giant. The confusion between David (DWD) and Elhanan the son of Dodo (DWDW) aided in this transformation.

In the course of retelling the story in later years, the ordinary sword seized by Abishai from Ishbibenob, which the Philistines erroneously thought had killed David and which was placed in the captured Philistine sanctuary of Nob as a symbol of David's power, became the sword David seized from Goliath. The story-tellers then had David take this "Goliath" sword from Nob during his outlaw days. As part of the propaganda wars between Israel and Judah, David's murder of the Philistine priests captured at Nob became a slaughter of Israelite priests by Saul.

The story of David and Goliath, complete with its introduction of David as the son of Jesse, would have originally been an independent tale separate and apart from other stories about David's rise to power over the House of Saul. Subsequently, as the final versions of Samuel came to be written, this story was clumsily inserted into the existing text, which explains why there was a second but inconsistent introduction to David in the Goliath story. Although the editors failed to smooth out the inconsistencies between the two introductions, at least one sharp-eyed scribe recognized the problem of David being at his father's house instead of with Saul on the battlefield, and added in the explanation that David went home for a visit.

There can be little doubt that the association of David with the slaying of Goliath was a late invention, clearly derived from the earlier tale about Elhanan and his allies. The efforts of the Chronicler to rewrite the story of the battle with the giants—misidentifying Goliath as Goliath's brother, omitting David's weakness, cutting out the story of the sword thought to have killed David, and moving the battle from Nob to Gezer—

show that despite the disappearance of the kingdom of Israel, David's image continued to suffer badly among many Hebrews and even in this post-Exilic stage major rehabilitation efforts were needed.

This deterioration in David's reputation may have been triggered in part by the earlier Babylonian defeat of the Kingdom of Judah and the resulting termination of the Davidic dynasty. The destruction of David's line signaled that God no longer favored Judah and that David may not have been as favored by God as the Hebrews had been led to believe. Perhaps, in the Hebrew mind of that time, the anti-David stories that circulated in the northern kingdom had the ring of truth.

CHAPTER 4

A Failed Coup

Then Saul said unto his servants that stood about him,

Hear now, ye Benjamites; will the son of Jesse give every one

of you fields and vineyards, and make you all captains of thousands,

and captains of hundreds; That all of you have conspired against me,

and there is none that showeth me that my son hath made

a league with the son of Jesse, and there is none of you that is sorry

for me, or showeth unto me that my son hath stirred up my servant

against me, to lie in wait, as at this day? 1 SAM 22:7–8

*T*he biblical account of David's days at Saul's palace (primarily in 1 Sam 18–20) lays the foundation upon which David's advocates try to cover up their young hero's sins against Saul and Israel. It portrays Saul as a dangerous paranoid who foolishly believed, despite numerous witnesses to the contrary (including his own children), that David sought to seize the kingship from him. Based on this erroneous fear, Saul tried to murder David, who, with the help of Saul's children, fled from the palace and had to live off the land while Saul hunted him down. The pro-David forces then blamed Saul's efforts to catch David as a justification for what appears to be his rather nefarious actions, such as David's alliance with the Philistine king of Gath.

The pro-David defense depends, in large part, on dropping context, rearranging the sequence of events, and distorting the clear meaning of various passages. This corrupted biblical account contributed substantially to one of the most successful hoaxes in all of history. To this day, standard popular histories of the United Monarchy routinely dismiss Saul as a manic-depressive not quite up to the task of kingship, and they effusively praise David for his grace under pressure and his loyalty to Saul despite the king's malevolent behavior towards him.

In this chapter we will look more closely at the biblical account of David's days at Saul's court. We will examine what it actually says about the events in question, reconcile several inconsistencies, and then, placing the events in their political and logical context, we will reconstruct the original historical account of what happened between David and Saul. As we unravel the defensive skein we will see that David, in league with Samuel and the Shiloh priesthood, and with the aid of Saul's son Jonathan, attempted to overthrow Saul by force of arms. The revolt failed, and David fled from Saul's court, seeking protection from the Philistines of Gath, Israel's chief enemy (and, presumably, the home city of Goliath). In the next chapter, we will examine what happened after David escaped.

Let's begin with a brief summary of events as related in the biblical account. As with so many of the stories about David and Saul, we will find several instances in which different versions of the same event appear as separate successive occurrences. We will also notice abrupt breaks in the story and odd inconsistencies in the resumed narrative. In addition, there is evidence that the sequence of events related has been altered to cover up the truth.

The Biblical Account of David's Days with Saul

As we saw in the previous chapter, the bible presents two inconsistent versions of how David came to Saul's court. One told of how the Lord inflicted an evil spirit on Saul, requiring him to seek out a talented musician as the only remedy to soothe his fevers; the other, embedded in the Goliath story, told how David came to the Hebrew camp and, learning of Goliath's boasts, found his way into Saul's presence. Since the Goliath tale is a late and false insertion into the biblical text, we can eliminate its implications from our discussion. This leaves us with Saul summoning David to court so that he may ply his musical skills to the king's benefit. This particular David is "a son of Jesse the Bethlehemite, that is cunning in playing, and a mighty valiant man, and a man of war, and prudent in matters, and a comely person, and the LORD is with him" (1 Sam 16:18). He is not quite the unsophisticated, inexperienced naïf depicted in the Goliath account. Upon arriving at the court, he is already a man of some military skill and reputation.

Almost immediately upon taking up residence in Saul's entourage, David formed a tight bond with the highly popular warrior Jonathan, Saul's son and apparent heir to the throne. We are told that:

> The soul of Jonathan was knit with the soul of David, and Jonathan loved him as his own soul. And Saul took him that day, and would let him go no more home to his father's house. Then Jonathan and David made a covenant, because he loved him as his own soul. And Jonathan stripped himself of the robe that was upon him, and gave it to David, and his garments, even to his sword, and to his bow, and to his girdle (1 Sam 18:1–4).

An immediate favorite at the court, David soon demonstrated himself to be a clever and effective soldier, and Saul "set him over the men of war" (1 Sam 18:5). David quickly became popular throughout Israel and in Saul's council. After some undefined period of time, David's reputation for combat surpassed even that of Saul. When Saul traveled through the cities of Israel, the women came out to sing, dance, and play instruments, but the words of the song didn't please Saul, for they sang:

> Saul hath slain his thousands, and David his ten thousands (1 Sam 18:7).

The implications of these lyrics weren't lost upon the king. Saul had become ruler of Israel because of his military prowess, and now his chief military officer eclipsed his reputation. Saul recognized that David's popularity threatened to undermine the foundation of his kingship:

> And Saul was very wroth, and the saying displeased him; and he said, They have ascribed unto David ten thousands, and to me they have ascribed but thousands: and what can he have more but the kingdom? And Saul eyed David from that day and forward (1 Sam 18:8–9).

The very next day, Saul had one of his headaches, described as "the evil spirit from the Lord" (1 Sam 18:10), and he took a javelin and hurled it at David. Although the text only describes one toss of the spear, it also says that David twice managed to sidestep Saul's missile (1 Sam 18:11). Saul interpreted David's agility as a signal that the Lord abandoned him for his popular rival (1 Sam 18:12). In order to put distance between them, he appointed David captain over a "thousand" (1 Sam 18:13. The Hebrew word often translated as "thousand" may simply mean a large military unit.). David continued to perform well and act wisely, and his reputation flourished (1 Sam 18:16).

The appointment of David over a "thousand" provides something of an ambiguity in the flow of events. Earlier David was said to be "over the men of war." This later appointment sounds as if it was a demotion, but there doesn't appear to be any contextual support for such an interpretation. I strongly suspect that this passage comes from a separate textual strand about the conflict between David and Saul, and that it may have been inserted into the main strand out of chronological order. Saul would have initially placed David in charge of a smaller unit before placing him over all the men of war. His popularity should have led to an elevation rather than a demotion.

David's celebrity continued to soar, threatening Saul's hold on the monarchy. So, he conceived a plan to get rid of the threat. He offered David the opportunity to marry his eldest daughter, asking only that David go out and be valiant against the Lord's enemies. The biblical text quotes Saul as saying, "Let not mine hand be upon him, but let the hand of the Philistines be upon him" (1 Sam 18:17). Although David protested that he and his family were too insignificant in Israel to merit such honor, the arrangement fell through when at the appointed time the daughter married someone else (1 Sam 18:19).

This scheme to have David killed at the hands of the Philistines seems rather odd and misconceived, evoking the sense of a late invention by one of the anti-Saul biblical sources. David was already engaged in constant combat with the Philistines; that's how he became so popular. What would marrying Saul's daughter change? Also, it is inconceivable that the daughter would marry someone else at the appointed time if Saul wanted her to marry David. That's not how marriage worked in those days.

That the story may just be an alternate version of a similar story is suggested by the fact that immediately after this marriage fell through, Saul's other daughter, Michal, declared her love for David, and Saul conceived a new plan to eliminate David (1 Sam 18:20–21). When the groom-to-be proclaimed himself too poor to afford a dowry, Saul offered instead to let Michal marry her love if he would simply bring him one hundred Philistine foreskins, a task that Saul hoped would lead to David's death at the hands of Israel's enemy (1 Sam 18:25). Naturally, David exceeded expectations and brought back two hundred foreskins (1 Sam 18:27. KJV indicates that two hundred Philistines were killed; NRSV indicates only one hundred.). David and Michal became engaged, and Saul became more afraid than ever (1 Sam 18:27–29).

These two marriage stories present something of a problem. In each David claims to be just a poor little country boy. In fact he comes from an extremely rich family. According to the Book of Ruth, which contains stories about David's ancestry, David's father Jesse was the grandson and heir of Boaz, who according to the bible was a wealthy landowner in Bethlehem (Ruth 2:1).

Nevertheless, David's popularity continued to grow as he repulsed new attacks by the Philistines. So, Saul called a meeting of his councilors, including his son Jonathan, and asked them to kill David (1 Sam 19:1). Jonathan, however, warned his good friend David and told him to hide out while he tried to assuage his father (1 Sam 19:2). Jonathan confronted Saul and argued that David had committed no sin against Saul, and that he had achieved only good things for Israel in his battle against the Philistines. Saul listened to Jonathan and relented, promising "as the Lord liveth" (1 Sam 19:6) he would not slay his son's good friend. Jonathan then brought David back to court where he resumed his place of honor (1 Sam 19:7).

Following David's return to the court, his heroic deeds continued to earn him praise throughout the country, and Saul's headaches returned (1 Sam 19:8–9). Once again David played music to sooth the king, and once again Saul heaved a javelin at David. Well practiced at this maneuver by now, David sidestepped the spear and fled from the house (1 Sam 19:10).

This incident probably reflects another version of the earlier javelin attack, but the biblical editors inserted it as if it were a separate and distinct incident. In both instances, the tossing of the javelin takes place immediately after a claim that David had done well against the Philistines and while David is playing music.

Saul then ordered a watch on David's house with instructions to kill David in the morning (1 Sam 19:11). But Michal warned her betrothed of the plan and he fled during the night (1 Sam 19:12). Michal then set up a decoy image in the bed. In the morning, Saul sent his messengers to fetch David, but Michal delayed their efforts by claiming he was sick. When Saul learned of what happened and inquired of his daughter, she told him that David claimed no ill intent towards Saul (1 Sam 19:17).

In the meantime, David fled to Samuel's hometown of Ramah where Samuel took him under his wing and brought him to nearby Naioth where a company of prophets sheltered him (1 Sam 19:18). When Samuel learned of David's whereabouts, he sent messengers to demand the refugee be returned (1 Sam 19:20). But when Saul's envoy met up with Samuel and his company of prophets, the messengers were overcome with the spirit of God and began to prophesy, apparently a sign that David was under divine protection (1 Sam 19:20).

Three times this happened, and on the fourth occasion, Saul himself led the march to Naioth (1 Sam 19:21–23). Along the way, he, too, was overcome by the spirit of the Lord, and began prophesying, and when he got to Naioth, he stripped naked before Samuel and continued in a prophetic mode (1 Sam 19:24). The biblical editor gives this story of Saul's prophesying as an alternative to the earlier story discussed in chapter 2 to explain the origin of the ancient saying, "Is Saul also among the Prophets?" (1 Sam 19:24).

Despite Saul's efforts, David escaped from Naioth and suddenly, in a very strange encounter that we will have to discuss in more detail below, he appears with Jonathan and asks why his friend's father wanted to kill him (1 Sam 20:1). Jonathan appears shocked by David's allegation and claimed that he had never heard any such plan from his father and that his father wouldn't keep such a secret from him (1 Sam 20:2). But David explained that Saul knew how much his son liked David and probably withheld the information from him (1 Sam 20:3).

Jonathan's reaction is inexplicable given that we have been previously told that Jonathan was not only present when Saul asked his servants to kill David, but Jonathan explicitly urged Saul to drop the plan (1 Sam 19:1). In addition, there was the second plan to kill David that was thwarted by Michal. And let's not forget the two javelin hurling incidents that David must have surely told his best buddy about. It seems obvious that this strand must come from a different source than the earlier stories about Saul's efforts to kill David.

Jonathan's lack of knowledge about Saul's plan strongly suggests that the several stories about Saul's efforts to kill David are all variations of a single incident. The redactors simply compiled the incidents from various sources and treated them all as if they were separate and distinct events. The particular story that follows after David's inquiry is, as we shall soon see, the one that comes closest to the original historical situation.

After the exchange between the two friends, we are given an even stranger piece of information. Despite Saul's just-reported efforts to seize David from Samuel at Ramah, we are told that David was expected to sit at Saul's dining table three nights in a row for a new moon festival (1 Sam 20:5). Jonathan says that he wants to sound his father out, and the two of them come up with a plan to explain David's absence (1 Sam 20:6–7). They agreed that Jonathan would tell Saul that David's family called him back to Bethlehem for an annual sacrifice. If Saul didn't become angry, they would know David was safe; otherwise, the king's deadly intentions would become clear.

As they worked out the details of their strategy, Jonathan extracted a promise from David, a promise that plays an important role in David's later defense but the plain meaning of which seems to suggest the very opposite of what David's defenders allege. I will discuss it further below, and simply set it forth here:

And thou shalt not only while yet I live show me the kindness of the LORD, that I die not: But also thou shalt not cut off thy kindness from my house for ever: no, not when the LORD hath cut off the enemies of David every one from the face of the earth. So Jonathan made a covenant with the House of David, saying, Let the LORD even require it at the hand of David's enemies. And Jonathan caused David to swear again, because he loved him: for he loved him as he loved his own soul (1 Sam 20:14–17).

On the first night of David's absence Saul made no mention, thinking David ill (1 Sam 20:26). On the second night Saul became curious and asked after the missing guest (1 Sam 20:27). Pursuant to plan, Jonathan informed Saul that David had to meet with his family for an annual sacrifice, and that Jonathan granted him permission to do so (1 Sam 20:28–29).

Saul became furious and said:

Thou son of the perverse rebellious woman, do not I know that thou hast chosen the son of Jesse to thine own confusion, and unto the confusion of thy mother's nakedness? For as long as the son of Jesse liveth upon the ground, thou shalt not be established, nor thy kingdom. Wherefore now send and fetch him unto me, for he shall surely die (1 Sam 20:30–31).

Who and what might Saul mean when he refers to Jonathan's mother as that rebellious woman? We will soon explore the likely answers to those questions. For now, we just observe that Jonathan got the message. Saul wanted David dead. By a prearranged signal he warned his friend of what loomed ahead (1 Sam 20:35), and David fled to the sanctuary at Nob (1 Sam 21:1).

When David arrived at the sanctuary, Ahimelech, the priest in charge, became frightened and allegedly asked David, "Why art thou alone, and no man with thee?" (1 Sam 21:1). David replied that Saul sent him on secret business and that he was to meet up with some others at an appointed meeting place (1 Sam 21:2). He then asked the priest for five loaves of bread. The priest responded that they only had hallowed bread at this time and inquired if David and the other men were clean or had at least kept away from women. David said that they had all been kept from women for three days.

David then asked for some weapons, saying that in his haste he had forgotten to arm himself (1 Sam 21:8). Interestingly, the only weapon on the premises, according to the priest, was the sword of Goliath of Gath captured by David (1 Sam 21:9). While this conversation was going on, by coincidence, a man named Doeg the Edomite, a chief servant of Saul, happened to be present (1 Sam 21:7).

David took the sword of Goliath and made straight to the Philistine city of Gath, where he asked to join up and serve Achish, king of Gath, one of Israel's most dangerous enemies. This is the first of two biblical incidents in which David attempts to serve Achish, and it contains a rather astonishing phrase:

> And the servants of Achish said unto him, *Is not this David the king of the land?* (1 Sam 21:11, emphasis added).

What would lead these Philistines to think of David as king of the land? We'll examine this question further below. For now, we'll note only that the king's advisors didn't trust David, who then feigned madness and was dismissed by Achish as a loony (1 Sam 21:13–15).

In the meantime, Saul raged at his council, accusing them of disloyalty and of supporting David:

> Then Saul said unto his servants that stood about him, Hear now, ye Benjamites; will the son of Jesse give every one of you fields and vineyards, and make you all captains of thousands, and captains of hundreds; That all of you have conspired against me, and there is none that showeth me that my son hath made a league with the son of Jesse, and there is none of you that is sorry for me, *or showeth unto me that my son hath stirred up my servant against me*, to lie in wait, as at this day? (1 Sam 22:7–8, emphasis added).

At this time, Doeg the Edomite told Saul of what happened at the sanctuary at Nob (1 Sam 22:9). The king demanded that the priests be brought to him. When the king asked Ahimelech why he aided David, the priest responded that as far as he knew, the king had no more loyal supporter than David, and why should they have suspected any wrongdoing (1 Sam 22:14–15). Saul accused Ahimelech of conspiring with

David against him by providing food and weapons and enquiring of the Lord for him, and he ordered the priest and all his house put to death (1 Sam 22:13, 16).

None of the Israelites, however, would carry out his command (1 Sam 22:17). So Doeg agreed to do the deed, and slaughtered eighty-five priests. He then set out and destroyed the city of Nob, killing all the inhabitants, including women, children, and oxen. But one priest escaped, Abiathar, who joined up with David, and when David became king over Israel he made Abiathar one of his two chief priests (1 Sam 22:18–20).

Let us now examine this biblical account and put events and incidents in their proper political, chronological, and logical context, to see what actually took place.

HISTORICAL CONTEXT

There are certain events that form the backbone of the conflict between David and Saul, but, despite the order in which these stories are presented, there remain questions about the chronology of these events.

At the center of the dispute, the bible explicitly tells us that Samuel and Saul had a falling out; that Samuel denounced Saul and declared that the kingship had been taken from him and given to someone else; and that Samuel anointed David as Saul's replacement. The story implies that David was a young child when Samuel secretly anointed him, but we will challenge that claim during our analysis. Nevertheless, enmity between Samuel and Saul, and Samuel's desire to put someone else on the throne of Israel, are among the main tenets of the biblical story.

We must also keep in mind that Samuel still led a powerful and influential institution, the Shiloh priesthood. Often overlooked in this context is that this priesthood also functioned as a warrior class. These priests are Levites, and the bible gives several indications that the Levites were a militaristic force. In the Book of Genesis, Levi and Simeon, two of Jacob's sons and the founders of the tribes with those names, violently attacked the men of Shechem and put to death a large number of the male inhabitants in revenge for the rape of their sister Dinah by Shechem's prince (Gen 35:25). Elsewhere in Genesis, during Jacob's final speech, Levi and Simeon are again attacked for their violent behavior in other matters (Gen 48:5–7). In the biblical accounts of Israel's Exodus from Egypt, the tribe of Levi acts in militaristic fashion on several occasions. After Aaron fashioned the golden calf, for instance, the Levites killed three thousand men as punishment (Ex 33:28). In addition, the priesthood guarded and defended Israel's most sacred icon, the Ark of the Covenant.

Saul, then, had good reason to fear that Samuel would take whatever opportunity he had to stir up resentment against him and promote some popular hero as an alternative. And Saul knew that Samuel had military forces and moral influence at his disposal to be placed in support of an opponent. With David's rising popularity, Saul would naturally expect Samuel to use this as a lever to remove him from his office.

Another factor that has to be taken into account is that David came from Judah, and throughout the biblical accounts of the United Monarchy under Saul, David, and Solomon, Judah and Israel are constantly depicted as separate, large, political entities, although theoretically joined together in alliance around common principles. Judah, therefore, could be expected to line up militarily behind one of its own in a battle for control of the kingship, and provide a large army in the process. In fact, as we shall see in the next chapter, that is precisely what it eventually did.

Against this background, the biblical account shows David under the protection of Samuel just before Jonathan proclaims that he has no knowledge of any plans by his father to kill David. Then, immediately after Jonathan warns David that his father really does want to kill him, David flees to Nob, where, supposedly, the remnant of the House of Eli, Samuel's patron, has taken up residence (1 Sam 19:11), and where David receives the sword of Goliath. For some strange reason, we are told, the priests were frightened by seeing David arrive alone. What is it about his being alone that might have frightened them so? That is one of the many questions we will now explore.

DAVID'S ANOINTMENT

At the end of 1 Sam 15, just before the story of David's anointment by Saul, we are told:

> Then Samuel went to Ramah; and Saul went up to his house to Gibeah of Saul. And Samuel came no more to see Saul until the day of his death: nevertheless Samuel mourned for Saul: and the LORD repented that he had made Saul king over Israel.

The very next set of verses says:

> *And the LORD said unto Samuel, How long wilt thou mourn for Saul, seeing I have rejected him from reigning over Israel?* fill thine horn with oil, and go, I will send thee to Jesse the Bethlehemite: for I have provided me a king among his sons. And Samuel said, How can I go? if Saul hear it, he will kill me. And the LORD said, Take an heifer with thee, and say, I am come to sacrifice to the LORD. *And call Jesse to the sacrifice,* and I will show thee what thou shalt do: and *thou shalt anoint unto me him whom I name* unto thee. And Samuel did that which the LORD spake, and came to Bethlehem. *And the elders of the town trembled at his coming, and said, Comest thou peaceably?* And he said, Peaceably: I am come to sacrifice unto the LORD: sanctify yourselves, and come with me to the sacrifice. And he sanctified Jesse and his sons, and called them to the sacrifice (1 Sam 16:1–5, emphasis added).

The transition from the end of Samuel 15 to the beginning of Samuel 16, by itself, creates uncertainty as to how long a period lapsed before Samuel went to Jesse's house to consecrate David. The verses indicate that after the break between Saul and Samuel, they never saw each other again, and that Samuel appears to have been waiting for some period of time after the break before going to David's house. How long a time passed between the break and the anointment? We have to rely on textual context for the answer.

The biblical editors clearly want us to think that the event occurred early in Saul's reign, while David was still a child. They place the event before the confrontation with Goliath, which describes David as an untested youth with no apparent military experience. There are several difficulties with this scenario.

To begin with, we have already seen that the story of Goliath was a late insert into an already existing text, and it cannot be relied upon for contextual chronology. In addition, we have two different versions of how David came to Saul's court. One depicts him as a child, which derives from the Goliath account; the other shows that he was already a man with a reputation as a valiant warrior.

One of the problems with the story of David's anointing is that there is never any public proclamation by Samuel as to that fact, not even after Saul died (1 Sam 15:35, though ambiguous, seems to indicate that Samuel outlived Saul). What was the purpose of anointing the child if there was not to be any public proclamation?

Anointment was a serious matter. As we are told in later episodes involving David and Saul, it is a crime against God to slay one of his anointed (1 Sam 26:9). Even though Samuel had declared that God had taken the throne away from Saul and given it to someone else, Saul remained protected by Samuel's original anointment of him as king (1 Sam 26:9). If Saul had been hunting David down and trying to kill him, what better protection could David have than for Samuel to publicly announce that David had been anointed by God to become king? At the very least it would cause Saul to rethink his plans to kill a popular hero who has been anointed.

Many biblical scholars believe that the story of David's anointment had been added to the text simply as a way to associate David with the prophetic leaders of Israel and validate his reign. I would like to suggest another theory.

I propose that Samuel did publicly proclaim David as the anointed king, but not when David was a child. The evidence here and following, suggests that Samuel had formed an alliance with David, a popular war hero whose reputation rivaled Saul's, and that a coup had been planned to place David on the throne. David had been seeking support from various leaders and, contrary to the biblical claim, did not join up with Samuel to flee Saul's wrath, but rather joined with Samuel to initiate plans to seize the throne from Saul.

The plan called for David and Samuel to go to Bethlehem in Judah to anoint David as king where he would receive the military support of Judah. An armed escort to take David and Samuel to Bethlehem had been stationed at Nob, and there may have been some cooperation from the Philistine king of Gath in this escapade. Events were to come to a head during the three days of the full moon festival.

The coup failed, however, when Saul learned what was going on and set up a blockade at Ramah, preventing Samuel and David from leaving, and demanding that David be turned over at the start of the new moon festival. David managed to get Jonathan, a coconspirator, to arrange for him and Samuel to receive safe passage through the troop lines. They escaped to Nob. Samuel and the support troops retreated while David fled to Gath.

When the story of David was reedited in later times, probably in the late fifth century BCE, the break between Saul and Samuel and the anointment of David were moved back in time to the beginning of Saul's reign and David's youth, disassociating either of them from any coup attempt. They also tried to cover up the coup by distorting the record, claiming that David fled from Saul to Samuel because of the king's irrational fear.

Let's look at some additional evidence for this theory.

The Festival at Bethlehem

When I summarized the story of David's stay at Saul's court, I observed that a particular meeting of David and Jonathan seemed to be a rather odd and inconsistent insertion into the biblical narrative. The meeting occurred after David had fled to Samuel's hometown and came under the prophet's protection.

On four occasions Saul's troops confronted Samuel's prophets and demanded the surrender of David, but on each occasion the priests refused and the spirit of God came over Saul's forces, causing them to prophesy. On the last occasion, Saul himself succumbed to the spiritual assault. While the text states that holy spirits stopped Saul's forces, the more likely interpretation is that Samuel's warrior-priests stood behind these mystical forces. While blood does not appear to have been shed, and Saul's forces chose not to physically confront the priests at this time, we can assume that Saul now knew that David and Samuel were allied together.

The scene suddenly shifts to a secret meeting between David and Jonathan, with David saying that Saul wanted to kill him and Jonathan professing no knowledge of such a scheme. Jonathan's lack of knowledge strongly implies that all the earlier stories about Saul's efforts to kill David are really just different variations of the same story. Otherwise, how could Jonathan not know about some of the earlier schemes, when on one occasion Saul directly asked him to kill David, and on another his sister helped David escape?

In this particular narrative, David and Jonathan prepare a plan to find out what Saul's intentions are. That night a new moon festival is to take place, lasting three nights. David, despite Saul's failed efforts at retrieving him from Samuel's camp, is, for some reason, expected to be at Saul's table during these three nights. The two friends agree that if Saul asks about David's absence, Jonathan should tell him:

> David earnestly asked leave of me that he might run to Bethlehem his city: for there is a yearly sacrifice there for all the family (1 Sam 20:6).

On the first evening, Saul simply assumed that David was ill. On the second night he made inquiry as to David's whereabouts. Jonathan replied:

> David earnestly asked leave of me to go to Bethlehem: And he said, Let me go, I pray thee; for our family hath a sacrifice in the city; and my brother, he hath commanded me to be there: and now, if I have found favour in thine eyes, let me get away, I pray thee, and see my brethren. Therefore he cometh not unto the king's table (1 Sam 20:28–29).

At this point, Saul exploded in anger at Jonathan. The story as given presents some problems, but before reconstructing what should be the original set of events, I want to note some other problems.

We were originally told that after the break between Samuel and Saul, the two men never saw each other again. Yet, when Saul went to fetch David from Samuel's protection, the two men were in each other's presence (1 Sam 19:24). The logical chronological implication is that the break between Samuel and Saul occurred after David fled to Samuel's town, not much earlier as the biblical text would have us believe.

The event precipitating the break was Samuel's efforts to deprive Saul of the throne by declaring the king in violation of God's law and insisting that the Lord had given the kingship to another. As we noted in chapter 2, the chronology associated with this event was confusing and had the sense of being inserted in the wrong location.

Finally, after denouncing Saul, Samuel is directed to go to the House of Jesse in Bethlehem to anoint one of his sons as the new king. When the prophet says that Saul will kill him for such an act, a deception is planned. Samuel should announce that he is going to Bethlehem for the purpose of making a sacrifice at which the House of Jesse was to be invited.

Here we see the original story starting to unfold. David had met with Samuel for the purpose of being installed as king. The ceremony was to take place in Bethlehem. Saul had sent troops to Samuel demanding that David be turned over. Samuel refused, and Saul gave him an ultimatum. David was to return to the king's house by the new moon festival or there would be war. David and Samuel needed to go to Bethlehem, where David's family and community would offer him more protection, and there he was to be anointed. When Jonathan told Saul that he gave David permission to go to Bethlehem, the king knew what was at stake. David was going to declare himself king in opposition to Saul, and he had the backing of Samuel. The potential of civil war filled the air and Saul lashed out at Jonathan, who had been duped into giving David permission to go.

That Perverse Rebellious Woman

When Saul learned of Jonathan's betrayal, he shouted out:

> Thou son of the perverse rebellious woman, do not I know that thou hast chosen the son of Jesse to thine own confusion, and unto the confusion of thy mother's nakedness? For as long as the son of Jesse liveth upon the ground, thou shalt not be established, nor thy kingdom (1 Sam 20:30–31).

Saul's speech suggests that not only does the trip to Bethlehem indicate that David plans to be king, but it also implies that Jonathan foolishly failed to see that David had no intention of letting Jonathan become king. In addition, Saul attacked Jonathan's mother as that "perverse rebellious woman." Who is this woman and what role does she play?

The bible identifies Jonathan's mother, and the mother of all of Saul's children, as Ahinoam (1 Sam 14:49–50). Strangely, when David embarks upon his outlaw career after fleeing from Saul, he somehow acquires a wife named Ahinoam, whom the text simply identifies as a Jezreelite. No other background is given. These are the only two Ahinoams mentioned in the bible, and it seems more than mere coincidence that Saul denounces his wife as a "perverse rebellious woman" in league with David, and shortly thereafter David appears with a wife having the same name.

Jonathan's Covenant

On several occasions the bible reminds us of the close relationship between David and Jonathan, and how Jonathan aided David when Saul sought to kill him. One particular passage, however, is troubling. While David and Jonathan plot to make excuses for David's absence, Jonathan says:

> But if it please my father to do thee evil, then I will show it thee, and send thee away, that thou mayest go in peace: and the LORD be with thee, as he hath been with my father. And thou shalt not only while yet I live show me the kindness of the LORD, that I die not: But also thou shalt not cut off thy kindness from my house for ever: no, not when the LORD hath cut off the enemies of David every one from the face of the earth (1 Sam 20:13–15).

Jonathan, in this passage, has basically said to David, if I do you this favor, please don't kill me later on, and please don't kill my family. David agreed (1 Sam 20:17). This promise is often part of the litany about the friendship of David and Jonathan, and it serves later as the excuse for David to save one of the members of Saul's house from execution. As will be shown later, rather than showing kindness, David took that child as a hostage and kept him under house arrest to prevent any uprisings by Saul's family.

Implicit in this request is the recognition by Jonathan that if Saul persists in his antagonism towards David there will be a war between the two sides. Although Saul's son clearly implies that should such a war break out he will have to remain loyal to his own family, he expresses the hope that David will understand and not kill him and his family if his good friend should win out.

Jonathan's remarks have a somewhat whiny and effete tone about them. This contrasts sharply with the frequent depiction of Jonathan as a brave and heroic warrior, and appears somewhat artificial. A later scene presents the more likely scenario that Jonathan deliberately conspired with David against his father in the hope that the young rebel would oust the king. The incident, which takes place after David has fled from Saul's court, can be found at 1 Sam 23:16–18:

> And Jonathan Saul's son arose, and went to David into the wood, and strengthened his hand in God. And he said unto him, Fear not: for the hand of Saul my father shall not find thee; and thou shalt be king over Israel, and I shall be next unto thee; and that also Saul my father knoweth. And they two made a covenant before the LORD: and David abode in the wood, and Jonathan went to his house.

Putting this passage in its narrative chronological context, it appears right after Saul has planned to hunt David down in his hiding place. The meeting between David and Jonathan occurs in the very next verses, with Jonathan knowing where David was hidden and meeting him there. Since some of the next verses show that David moved his troops from his stronghold into another location while Saul rode to David's hideout, we can reasonably assume that Jonathan warned David about his father's plans and told him to move out.

From these various passages we see that Jonathan, though feigning loyalty to his father, consistently supplied David with military intelligence about Saul's actions in the hope that David would defeat Saul and reward Jonathan with a high position in the new administration.

Since Jonathan held the position of heir-apparent to Saul, one wonders why the king's son would form an alliance with his father's enemy in return for being appointed to the number-two position in the new administration. One very likely answer is that there was bad blood between Saul and his son. According to the biblical account, on two occasions the king sought his son's death.

The first incident, in 1 Sam 14, is rather odd, and is sandwiched between the two stories in which Samuel denounced Saul for violating God's instructions. It follows after Jonathan's successful forays against the Philistines.

While Saul's son was away from the base camp, the king directed that no soldier should have anything to eat before evening, and he placed a curse on anyone who violated the directive. The men found honey everywhere but restrained themselves from eating it because of the king's command. But Jonathan, unaware of the instruction, tasted some honey. This led to some form of revitalization of the warrior and "his eyes were enlightened."

Some of the Israelites informed Jonathan about his father's ban on eating, and Jonathan criticized the king's directive as very unwise, arguing that the army would be more effective if it had first eaten. The soldiers then defeated some Philistine forces and ate the cattle "with the blood."

This eating of meat with blood not only violated Saul's edict but also constituted a great sin under Israelite law. When Saul learned what happened, he built his first altar for the purpose of sacrifice. After the offerings, he inquired of God whether he should attack the Philistines, but received no answer.

He took this as a sign that a great sin remained unpunished and promised to get to the bottom of it, even if it meant that he or his son Jonathan were to blame. He called for the casting of lots, with himself and Jonathan on one side, and the people of Israel on the other. The lot showed that the people were innocent.

The priests then cast a second lot, choosing between Saul and his son, and the lots identified Jonathan as the wrongdoer. Jonathan confessed to eating the honey and Saul ordered that he be put to death. But the people rebelled against Saul's order saying that Jonathan had been a valiant warrior who had brought great victories to Israel and should be spared. Saul relented.

It's hard to know what to make of this story. The ban on eating was an aspect of priestly direction, a form of personal sacrifice to call the Lord down in your favor. The story, as mentioned above, appears between the two events that divided Saul and Samuel. This incident is of the same nature. It depicts a schism between priestly directives and the democratic will. As on the other two occasions, Saul rejected religious law and put the will of the people first.

Jonathan's actions reflected the casual disregard that many Israelites appeared to have for the role of the priests and it no doubt exacerbated the feud between Saul and Samuel. Still, Saul's initial willingness to carry out the execution of his son may well have left Jonathan with much anger towards his father.

Additionally, right after Jonathan advised his father that he gave David permission to go to Bethlehem, Saul hurled a javelin at him (1 Sam 20:33). It's tempting to read into this latter incident the possibility that Jonathan participated in a palace coup in support of David and the report of Saul's reaction is a truncated account of his efforts at putting down the rebellion within his own house. But that may be reading too much into what may also have simply been an act of justifiable anger.

In either event, the bible portrays Jonathan as a young headstrong individual, haughty, proud, and rebellious, whose actions consistently caused Saul embarrassment. Anger at his father may well have provoked his later support for David's rebellion. Jonathan may also have been impatient, as youths often are, and foresaw many long years in Saul's shadow, with his father keeping him on the outskirts of power.

One other very likely possibility was that Jonathan had determined that David might win the struggle for power and he wanted to remain in good stead with the winning side, whichever it might be. So he played both ends against the middle, loyalty to Saul's house in public while supporting David in private. Jonathan's frequent claims that David would become king should be seen in the light of his military assessment of the situation rather than any divine religious or spiritual insight.

The Priests at Nob

We are given to believe that the priests at Nob and their community are the last descendants of the House of Eli, the judge-priest whose corrupt sons caused a curse to be placed on the family (1 Sam 22:16). According to the curse, the House of Eli was to be eliminated. In the story of Saul's destruction of Nob, all the priests but one, Abiathar, were killed, making the escaped priest the last descendant of the House of Eli, and the curse was now almost complete.

Nob is virtually unknown throughout the biblical text. It appears for the first time only when David arrives there in his flight from Saul and asks for bread. He also obtains the sword of Goliath at Nob, where for the first time we learn that it had been placed there. After Doeg the Edomite destroyed Nob, there are only two other direct mentions of Nob, and they are of almost no significance, each appearing among a long list of cities well after the collapse of the United Monarchy.

In the previous chapter we talked about the sanctuary at Nob in connection with the Goliath story. We saw that Nob initially appeared to be a Philistine sanctuary rather than a Hebrew one. The question raised here is: what are these Hebrew priests doing at Nob? Why aren't they at one of the main sanctuaries guarding the Ark of the Covenant, as Eli's house was bound to do?

The presence of the sword of Goliath also presents a problem. On the one hand, since the Goliath story is a late edition, it could suggest that the entire Nob incident was a very late addition to the biblical text and had nothing to do with the original story. On the other hand, we did note the likelihood that there was some sort of special sword there, an icon, but that it was captured from the Philistines, in which case the renaming of it as the "sword of Goliath" may be the only late addition to the story, leaving the original episode more or less intact.

Another explanation for the "sword of Goliath" being at the sanctuary is that the term is a metaphor for an armed Philistine guard under the leadership of Goliath or another soldier from Gath. As we observed in the previous chapter, the battle with Goliath actually occurred in David's last years, and the reference to the giant from Gath may have been a metaphor for the Philistine army. In that later story about Gath, we saw that three of the four Philistine giants had associations with Nob, and the fourth was Goliath, whose sword we now find at Nob. These facts suggest that Nob may have been a Philistine sanctuary during Saul's reign and that Philistine troops may have been posted there to aid David.

In addition to connecting this city to the Philistines of Gath, we also note that immediately after David fled from Nob, he went to the Philistines at Gath to seek employment. This helps us bring the story into better focus.

When David arrived at Nob, the chief priest was frightened by the fact that David arrived alone. Why should that scare the chief priest unless he had some special reason to think that David would have an armed escort with him? The likely answer is that the priests at Nob were there at Samuel's direction to provide additional support for David's coup. David's arrival without any other supporters (although I suspect that Samuel may have been with him) would have indicated that the coup had collapsed, a frightening event indeed for these rebels.

The priests at Nob may have also had a temporary alliance with the Philistines at Gath to allow the priest-warriors to hide from Saul by remaining secreted in this Philistine shelter. Certainly the Philistines would welcome a friend on the throne of Israel instead of their implacable foe. This would probably explain why David's first action after leaving Nob was to go to Gath and seek shelter from Saul.

In any event, Saul's indictment of the priests charged that they provided weapons and supplies to David's forces, although the biblical text alleges that the priests gave little more than bread and a sword to him. Yet, it makes little sense for David, who had ample time to lay in provisions and arms while Jonathan helped arrange his escape, to have arrived at the shelter without either. What the priests provided was far more than a couple of loaves of bread and a sword. The biblical account provides a distorted account in order to minimize priestly involvement in the coup and to cast Saul in bad light. But Samuel's patrons knew full well what he and David would have been up to.

Saul was almost certainly correct in charging the priests with treason. The failure of some of his officials to carry out the order of execution may reflect David's deep penetration into the court's inner circle, just as Saul had charged. Saul's swift action against the priests no doubt helped to quickly subdue the revolt.

King of the Land

When David fled to Gath, at least on the first occasion according to the bible, the Philistines ask, "Is not this David the king of the land?" This is certainly a strange phrase to use about someone such as the David depicted in this biblical episode. And when David asked to join up with them they indicated a lack of trust in him, at which time David feigned mental illness, and the Philistines dismissed him.

Throughout the story of David and Saul, the two of them appear as mighty enemies of the Philistines. One of the Philistine nobles even recalls the song about Saul slaying his thousands and David slaying his tens of thousands (1 Sam 21:11). No matter how loony David appeared to them, under normal circumstances they would never have let him go. They would have lopped off his head and hung his body out to dry, as they did with Saul and Jonathan after the Philistines found them dead on the battlefield.

That they let him go suggests a different scenario. David had a secret alliance with the Philistines, who gave him covert support in an effort to overthrow Saul. When one of the Philistines asked if this David was king of the land, he was obviously remarking on what appeared to be the failed attempt to overthrow Saul. David's subservient relationship with the Philistines will be discussed in the next chapter.

SUMMARY

We have looked at a number of pieces of evidence concerning a failed coup by Samuel and David to replace Saul. Some of the evidence in isolation is weak but when taken together with the various clues, I believe a rather compelling case can be made for this conclusion.

The biblical chronology is deliberately vague as to when Samuel and Saul had an irreparable schism. Samuel tried to have Saul removed from the throne and went to Bethlehem to anoint a rival king. While the biblical editors tried to create the impression that the event was early in Samuel's reign, the evidence suggests otherwise.

Since after the break between the king and the prophet they never saw each other again, the confrontation between Samuel and Saul at Ramah, where Samuel gave David shelter, suggests that this is about the time when the two men reached an impasse in their relationship. After the break, Samuel arranged a trip to Bethlehem under the pretense of going to Jesse's house to arrange a sacrifice, where he intended to anoint a new king. Since this event is now dated to after the time Samuel gave David shelter, David's ruse about going to Bethlehem to conduct a sacrifice at the House of Jesse, would seem to correspond in time to Samuel's trip, indicating that Samuel and David had planned a deceptive trip to Bethlehem to crown David king.

Jonathan's lack of knowledge about any plan by Saul to kill David strongly suggests that the earlier stories about Saul's homicidal intentions were just variations of a basic story about Saul's reaction to David's failed coup. The real confrontation began after Jonathan told Saul that David was going to Bethlehem.

Saul accused his wife of being a "perverse rebellious woman" (1 Sam 20:30–31) in league with David, and soon after David left the court he acquired a wife with the same name as Saul's rebellious wife, and these are the only two women in the bible with that name.

The powerful and influential House of Eli, a group of warrior priests, is strangely lodged at the city of Nob, a city never before heard of but which may have had a strong connection to the Philistines at Gath. When David arrived there alone, the priests become afraid. Immediately after he left the sanctuary, David headed straight to the city of Gath to seek service in the Philistine army. One of the nobles inquired if this David is the king of the land.

Although David should be bitterly hated by the Philistines for his leading role in the Israelite army, and taken into custody, beheaded, and displayed for all to see, the Philistines simply allowed him to walk away.

Taken together these facts strongly suggest that 1) Samuel planned to take David to Bethlehem and anoint him king; 2) The Philistines of Gath allowed Samuel to hide a military attachment in the city of Nob; 3) David met up with Samuel at Ramah but Saul threw a roadblock around the city and demanded that David be turned over by the beginning of the new moon festival; 4) David conned Jonathan into letting him and Samuel escape; 5) Although the two co-conspirators escaped, Saul's blockade and military preparedness nipped the coup in the bud; 6) The king executed any captured participants; 7) David fled first to the Philistine sanctuary at Nob and then to the Philistine city of Gath, where he would have been protected by Israel's enemy.

In retrospect, the only headache Saul had was David's ambition.

CHAPTER 5

The Outlaw King

And Achish believed David, saying, He hath made
his people Israel utterly to abhor him; therefore he shall be
my servant for ever. 1 SAM 27:12

*W*ith David on the run from Saul and his departure from Gath, the biblical action shifts from Saul's court to the southern territories in and around Judah, documenting David's exploits there as Saul tries to catch him. The fugitive immediately headed toward Adullam, a territory near Gath, southwest of Jerusalem and Bethlehem, where he might find allies and sympathizers to hide and protect him from the king. There his family joined him and he quickly gathered an army of about four hundred soldiers. The bible describes his troops:

> And every one that was in distress, and every one that was in debt, and
> every one that was discontented, gathered themselves unto him; and he
> became a captain over them: and there were with him about four hundred
> men (1 Sam 22:1–2).

The four hundred rapidly grew to six hundred (1 Sam 23:13), a fairly substantial military force even for a moderately large city in the ancient Near East, let alone someone without a political or territorial base. The assembly of such a large army in such a short time reinforces the earlier argument that David and Samuel planned to go south and crown David king, from which platform they would lead an armed uprising to displace Saul. The biblical editors must have been painfully aware of how this would have looked to the Israelites and they were careful, therefore, to paint David and his troops as defenders of Israel's interests against its enemies, and depict David as loyal to Saul even though he was on the outs with the king.

To do this required that the editors rearrange the evidence, misrepresent the facts, and change the sequences of events. Fortunately, their efforts were less than perfect and a number of damaging pieces of evidence managed to escape the redactors' heavy hands. A careful analysis of the biblical texts will show that David allied himself with various enemies of Israel in an effort to forcibly remove Saul from the throne and establish himself as the new king. We will also see that David, as a vassal of the Philistines, seized control over Judah, pulled the region out of the Israelite confederation, and had himself declared king of the southern portion of Saul's kingdom at least five years before Saul's death.

An Alliance with Moab

When Saul became king he quickly took arms against Israel's enemies:

> So Saul took the kingdom over Israel, and fought against all his enemies on every side, against Moab, and against the children of Ammon, and against Edom, and against the kings of Zobah, and against the Philistines: and whithersoever he turned himself, he vexed them (1 Sam 14:47).

Ammon, Moab, and Edom formed an arc south of Israelite territory on the Jordanian side of the kingdom. Moab lay between the other two, situated to the east of Judah on the Jordanian side of the Dead Sea. These three nations could be relied upon to ferret out weaknesses in Saul's military situation and to assist anyone presenting the Israelite king with serious problems. David knew this and it is not surprising, therefore, that in one of his first actions he secured an alliance with Moab.

According to the biblical account, as soon as David assembled his troops he traveled to Moab and placed his family under the protection of the king (1 Sam 22:3–4). Most biblical commentators and scholars pay little attention to this incident, mostly dismissing the significance of it by noting that David's great grandmother, Ruth, was a Moabitess, and ancient traditions may have entitled David to place his family under the king's protection. Overlooked are the very important military and strategic advantages to David and to Moab in this arrangement.

First, and most important, David's action guaranteed a mutual nonaggression pact between the two sides. As long as David's family remained in Moab, he couldn't attack Moabite troops, even if they raided Israelite territory. By the same token, Moab would not attack territories loyal to David.

Second, David now had an incentive to keep Israelite troops from attacking Moab, and could provide a buffer zone that would force Saul to go through Ammon in order to get at Moab. The reason David could establish a buffer zone is that David remained a popular hero among Israelites and, as we saw, could rally substantial military support from Judah. Saul had to be careful to avoid antagonizing David's allies by plunging his kingdom into direct military confrontation with other Israelites. Saul needed to capture David with the least possible public relations damage.

Evidence in the biblical account that David did set up such a buffer zone can be found in 1 Sam 22:5, which says:

> And the prophet Gad said unto David, Abide not in the hold; depart, and get thee into the land of Judah. Then David departed, and came into the forest of Hareth.

The prophet Gad, who also appears in one of the later stories about David, is almost certainly the title character of the Book of Gad the Seer, cited in 1 Chr 29:29 as a source of information about King David's reign. Since a copy of that book has yet to surface, we have no way of knowing if Gad himself authored such a book or someone at a much later time wrote it, putting the words in the title character's mouth. Whatever the case, the verse implies that David had a "hold," i.e., a military defensive position, and that Gad urged David to leave the "hold" and go into Judah. Contextually, since the "hold" is outside Judah, it must have been in Moab, where he had just deposited his family.

Third, Saul had to be careful not to place David's family in danger. David's family was almost certainly a major political influence in Judah, and if any harm befell them because of Saul's actions, it could generate a full-scale revolt within Israel on his southern flank. A raid into Moab could lead to just such harm. This strengthened security for David's ally.

Fourth, David could now guarantee some protection from potential Moabite targets in Judah if those villages threw their lot in with him, generating good will and needed support from wavering Judahites. Fifth, the joint alliance between David and Moab would also make it difficult for Saul to commit a large number of troops in the attempt to catch David without endangering his own front against the Moabites and Ammonites.

THE AMMONITE CONNECTION

David needed no such arrangement with the Ammonites. The biblical evidence suggests that David already had a close personal and familial relationship with the Ammonite kingdom and could count on their support and protection.

The Ammonite king at this time was Nahash, and as you will recall, Saul's stinging defeat of Nahash propelled the military hero into the kingship. The Ammonites are depicted in the bible as exceptionally cruel. They had demanded the forfeiture of an eye from other Israelites and their neighbors in order to spare the lives of those they defeated.

Textual evidence suggests that David received explicit support from the Ammonite king during his fugitive days. Shortly after David became king, 2 Sam 10:1–2 says:

> And it came to pass after this, that the king of the children of Ammon died, and Hanun his son reigned in his stead. Then said David, I will show kindness unto Hanun the son of Nahash, *as his father showed kindness unto me*. And David sent to comfort him by the hand of his servants for his father (emphasis added).

Other evidence of a strong connection between David and the Ammonite king can be found in 2 Sam 17:25, which says:

And Absalom made Amasa captain of the host instead of Joab: which Amasa was a man's son, whose name was Ithra an Israelite, *that went in to Abigail the daughter of Nahash, sister to Zeruiah Joab's mother* (emphasis added).

Although not explicitly stated, the Nahash in this passage is obviously the Ammonite king. The passage appears in context in a scene where David is fleeing for his life from Absalom and receives shelter and support from King Nahash's son (2 Sam 17:27). There are several interesting questions surrounding this passage.

First, the text identifies Joab as the grandson of King Nahash. Joab and his two brothers, Abishai and Asahel, were the three most important and valiant members of David's army. The first two are almost ever-present with David throughout his history and play leading roles in many of the stories. The third was one of the most skillful warriors in David's army. All three are the grandsons of the Ammonite king.

Second, and even more important, is the relationship between David and these two women. According to 1 Chr 2:15–17 these two women were David's sisters. Recounting a portion of David's genealogy, the text reads:

David the seventh: Whose sisters were Zeruiah, and Abigail. And the sons of Zeruiah; Abishai, and Joab, and Asahel, three. And Abigail bare Amasa: and the father of Amasa was Jether the Ishmeelite.

If Abigail and Zeruiah were David's sisters, and the two women were also daughters of Nahash, then who was David's father? All along we have been told that David was the son of Jesse of Bethlehem. If that were true, and Abigail and Zeruiah were the daughters of King Nahash, then Jesse and Nahash must have each been married to the same woman, although not at the same time. That means that either David was born while his mother was married to Nahash, or he was born after his mother left Nahash and married Jesse. In either case, Jesse must have been a figure of some major importance to be married to the former wife of a king.

In either event, David had a close affiliation with Nahash, both through his mother and his sisters, and also through his three chief soldiers. This would help explain why Nahash had been so kind to David while he was a fugitive.

Third, it is particularly interesting that the editors of both Samuel and Chronicles attempted to cover up the relationship between David and Nahash, suggesting they were aware of the problem. Samuel makes no mention that David, Abigail, and Zeruiah were siblings, thereby severing the familial connection between David and Nahash. This still left a relationship, though, between David's chief officers and the Ammonite throne. The Chronicles redactors followed a different tack. Although acknowledging the relationship between David and the two women, the Chroniclers omitted any reference to the fact that Abigail and Zeruiah were the daughters of Nahash, eliminating both the filial relationship between David and the Ammonite king and the genealogical connection of Zeruiah's three sons to the Ammonite throne.

Before moving on, I want to make note of certain literary practices in the bible involving Joab and Abishai, David's two Ammonite allies. David often had two types of problems. Whenever David needed to take hostile action to advance his power, something that would cast David in a negative light if he performed the deed or ordered it done, we often find Joab committing the act on his own initiative. Subsequently, David makes a noble speech absolving himself of blame and promising to punish Joab, although he never actually takes such action against his ally. On the other hand, whenever it would be to David's advantage to be depicted as opposing a hostile act and preventing it from happening, we find that it is Abishai who suggests that the act be done, with David explaining that it would be wrong and restraining his ally from acting. Throughout the biblical account, David frequently bemoans the troubles brought on him by the wild behavior of these two sons of Zeruiah. Their Ammonite roots no doubt helped validate David's complaint.

These stylistic patterns help us identify many of the charges made against David by his critics. Those actions for which Joab took the blame were clearly attributed to David's inner circle and a scapegoat had to be found. On the other hand, those actions proposed by Abishai and rejected by David are used to exonerate David of later accusations that he had done wrong to some party. The clearest example of such behavior involving David and Abishai occurs when Abishai has the opportunity to run Saul through and David restrains his ally and denounces the action as wrong. In this case the biblical editor is setting up a later defense against charges that David somehow physically harmed Saul, an issue we will examine in chapter 6.

THE BATTLE AT KEILAH

After leaving Moab, David went to the forests of Hereth, a place mentioned in the bible only on this occasion (1 Sam 22:5). Although we don't know its precise location, it must have been near the city of Keilah, which figures in David's next major action.

Archaeologists identify Keilah with the area now known as Khirbet Qila, south of Bethlehem and Adullam, and north of Hebron, which places David reasonably deep into Judean territory.

According to the biblical account in 1 Sam 23:1–13, David learned that the Philistines were attacking the city of Keilah and stealing the grain from the threshing facilities. David made inquiry of the Lord, presumably through a priest, and asked if he should try to rescue the town. David's men complained that it was dangerous enough just being in Judah without going against the Philistine armies. So David inquired of the Lord again and received acknowledgment that he would defeat the Philistines:

> So David and his men went to Keilah, and fought with the Philistines, *and brought away their cattle*, and smote them with a great slaughter. So David saved the inhabitants of Keilah (1 Sam 23:5, emphasis added).

After David rescued the city the bible says that Saul learned of David's presence in Keilah, which he described as a city of gates and bars, i.e., a walled city, and prepared to march after David in a lightning strike that would leave him trapped inside (1 Sam 23:7).

Somehow David divined that Saul "secretly practiced mischief against him" (1 Sam 23:9) and that the king planned to destroy the city in order to capture the fugitive. So he inquired of the Lord if it was true that Saul was coming and, if true, would the town turn him over. The Lord (through the priests) told him that Saul did indeed plan to come after him and that the town would surrender him (1 Sam 23:12).

David roused his army, which had now grown to six hundred men, and fled to a wooded area in the Wilderness of Ziph, south of Hebron and deeper into Judah (1 Sam 23:14). Here, suddenly, Jonathan appeared to warn David that Saul planned to come after him (1 Sam 23:16). We can probably safely assume that Jonathan was also the oracle that mysteriously advised David that Saul planned to come after him in Keilah.

The biblical account of the battle of Keilah depicts David as a loyal defender of Israel despite Saul's vendetta. But one puzzling passage in the story raises some doubt as to the veracity of that portrayal. In the last passage quoted above, I emphasized the phrase "and brought away the cattle." The cattle supposedly belong to the Philistines, but if this is a Philistine raiding party, what are they doing with cattle? You do not bring slow-moving, grazing beasts on a raiding party requiring swift action.

The animals must have belonged to the people of Keilah and David seized them for the purpose of feeding his troops. Far from rescuing the people of Keilah, David was the attacker. His outlaw army needed food and he seized it from the Israelite village. There was no Philistine raiding party. Somewhere along the line David's defenders invented the Philistine cover story. No wonder David feared that the ungrateful citizens would turn him over to Saul. Keilah probably sent a messenger to ask for Saul's help in breaking David's siege of the city.

THE INCIDENT AT CARMEL

After the flight from Keilah, the Book of Samuel relates the first of two important stories about how David was in a position to take Saul's life but spared him. We will treat both of these stories in the next chapter and pass over to the next major incident in sequence, events that happened in Carmel, near Hebron.

The story, which appears in 1 Sam 25, tells us about a man named Nabal, his wife Abigail, and David's interaction with these two. The bible describes Nabal as "very great" and portrays him as a man of much wealth, with extensive cattle holdings in Carmel. He is also identified as a Calebite. The text describes his wife, Abigail, as wise and beautiful.

Nabal's farm was located close to the Wilderness of Ziph, where David and his men camped out. One day, David sent a team of ten envoys to Nabal, telling them to deliver the following message:

> Peace be both to thee, and peace be to thine house, and peace be unto all that thou hast. And now I have heard that thou hast shearers: now thy shepherds which were with us, we hurt them not, neither was there ought missing unto them, all the while they were in Carmel. Ask thy young men, and they will show thee. Wherefore let the young men find favour in thine eyes: for we come in a good day: give, I pray thee, whatsoever cometh to thine hand unto thy servants, and to thy son David (1 Sam 25:6–8).

In other words, we didn't steal your sheep or kill your shepherds, so payoff us off or things won't go well with you. Essentially, David ran a protection racket.

Unimpressed, Nabal declined David's proposal and arrogantly responded:

> Who is David? and who is the son of Jesse? there be many servants now a days that break away every man from his master. Shall I then take my bread, and my water, and my flesh that I have killed for my shearers, and give it unto men, whom I know not whence they be? (1 Sam 25:10–11).

The messengers returned to David with Nabal's reply, and David's racketeering nature emerged. If Nabal won't give him the payoff voluntarily, David would seize the property by force. He ordered his troops to arm themselves and set out with four hundred soldiers, leaving the other two hundred behind to look after the other provisions (booty?) they had gathered, obviously a fairly substantial amount of property to require so many guardians (1 Sam 23:13).

As David's troops approached Nabal's farm, one of the workers advised Abigail that David's men always behaved themselves and provided protection (1 Sam 25:14–15). Further, he added, Nabal was too difficult to talk to (1 Sam 25:17). This is one of several references in the course of the story that emphasize how David did good only to be repaid with evil.

When Abigail learned what happened, she arranged for a large portion of provisions to be assembled in secret, without Nabal's knowledge (1 Sam 25:18). Mounting the goods on asses, she went out to greet David (1 Sam 25:20). When she confronted him, she made a fervent plea for mercy, flattered David, and predicted great and wonderful things to befall him. In part, she said:

> And now this blessing which thine handmaid hath brought unto my lord, let it even be given unto the young men that follow my lord. I pray thee, forgive the trespass of thine handmaid: for the LORD will certainly make my lord a sure house; because my lord fighteth the battles of the LORD, and evil hath not been found in thee all thy days. Yet a man is risen to pursue thee [i.e., Saul], and to seek thy soul: but the soul of my lord shall be bound in the bundle of life with the LORD thy God; and the souls of thine enemies, them shall he sling out, as out of the middle of a sling. And it shall come to pass, when the LORD shall have done to my lord according to all the good that he hath spoken concerning thee, and shall have appointed thee ruler over Israel (1 Sam 25:27–30).

Her speech impressed David and he accepted her offer of provisions in full satisfaction of his complaint against her husband (1 Sam 25:35). The next morning, Abigail told Nabal what had happened and "his heart died within him, and he became as a stone" (1 Sam 25:37). Although that description certainly sounded as if Nabal had become a stiff corpse, the text adds that it took ten days before he finally died (1 Sam 25:38). As soon as David heard of Nabal's fate, he asked Abigail to marry him and she did (1 Sam. 25:39–42).

On the surface, this story tells us that David was a good man who did favors for a selfish wealthy farmer and that he would have been justified in killing the farmer for not sharing his estate with David. A wise and beautiful woman talked him out of shedding blood and shortly thereafter God struck Nabal dead, protecting David from doing a bloody deed that would have been condemned by his enemies. The story ended happily with David marrying the beautiful woman. It also calls Abigail as one more witness to Saul's unreasonable pursuit of David and has her reiterate that David was destined to become king over all Israel.

As an aside, I would ask how so many people know that David is destined to become king in place of Saul or Saul's heirs unless Samuel had gone public with his anointment of David as king of Israel. Ordinarily, the son of the king would be expected to succeed his father on the throne. That would be Jonathan, a hero in his own right, and he was not someone who would have publicized his secret covenant to help David onto the throne. This is just one more indication that the biblical redactors have covered up David's aggressive pursuit of the throne and his rebellious coronation in Bethlehem as king of Israel.

David's behavior in this story corroborates the earlier thesis about what happened at Keilah. His modus operandi seems to have been to go to a location, claim to be its protector, and demand that he be given a substantial reward. If the inhabitants refused, he launched an attack against them. At Keilah, the redactors invented a Philistine raid to cover up David's true actions. Here they came up with a story that David, out of the goodness of his heart, chose to protect Nabal's workers against theft from outlaws, and it was unseemly for Nabal not to reward these actions. It doesn't seem to have occurred to the biblical editors that Nabal's large operation would have had its own guards to protect his property against theft. David's actions were superfluous and not asked for. The only thieves seeming to plague him were David and his army.

Let us now consider some of the background politics behind this story. Nabal is a Calebite and a rich powerful man. That suggests that he was a leader of the Calebite clan. The chief territory of the Calebites was Hebron and its environs (Josh14:14), not very far away from the scene of this story. Carmel would be the equivalent of a suburb. Hebron, at this time seems to be one of the most substantial cities in all of Judah.

This meant that Nabal probably controlled Hebron or had considerable influence over it. David married Nabal's wife, and, backed by his army, obviously became the owner of all that Nabal owned. He was now an influential power, if not direct ruler, over a key piece of territory. It's no coincidence, therefore, that Hebron became David's first capital, where he served as a king for seven and a half years.

His marriage to Abigail raised the stakes in his war against Saul and his claim over Judah. And it is not the first time that someone's convenient death boosted David to higher position. When David heard that Nabal died, he said:

> Blessed be the LORD, that hath pleaded the cause of my reproach from the hand of Nabal, and hath kept his servant from evil: for the LORD hath returned the wickedness of Nabal upon his own head (1 Sam 25:39).

One can't help but suspect that this speech was intended to rebut charges that David deliberately killed Nabal. And when the biblical editors add the claim that Nabal only passed away ten days after his heart died and he turned to stone, one can't help but suspect that either a bribed servant or Abigail herself deliberately poisoned him.

This brings us to the question of Abigail's identity? There are only two Abigails in the bible. One is David's sister and daughter of King Nahash; the other is Nabal's and then David's wife. This reminds us of the similar situation in which there were only two Ahinoams; one the rebellious woman married to Saul and who supported David, and the other David's wife. Can the two Abigails be the same person? Did David marry his sister? Did she help him dispose of Nabal?

The evidence does not permit a decisive answer, but more than one scholar has concluded that at the minimum they were brother and sister. Unfortunately, there is not much in the way of clues. The chief argument is the improbability that the only two Abigails in the bible are David's sister and wife. Another argument concerns some confusion over the names of the husbands of these two Abigails.

To begin with, Nabal is almost certainly not the original name of the husband of the Carmelite Abigail. The word means "fool," and in the course of the story there are some puns around his name. It is highly unlikely that the rich and powerful Calebite would go around with the name "fool." This suggests that the redactors may have wanted to cover up the identity of this husband of Abigail.

Coincidentally, there is some confusion over the identity of the other Abigail's husband. In Samuel, David's sister is married to someone identi-fied as Ithra the Israelite (2 Sam 17:25) and in Chronicles he is identified as Jether the Ishmeelite (1 Chr 2:17). One old version of the Septuagint text (Codex Coislinianus) identifies him as a Jezreelite.

Given that Nabal was a rich and powerful clan leader, it is not a large stretch to accept that he might marry the daughter of a foreign king such as Nahash of Ammon. But, that still leaves us in the realm of speculation. There is, however, good reason to think that Nabal did not die a natural death?

THE SOJOURN IN GATH

The next major event in Samuel after the incident at Carmel is the second occasion on which David had the opportunity to slay Saul but chose in-stead to spare his life. As I noted earlier both of these confrontations be-tween Saul and David will be discussed in the next chapter. Immediately following the second incident with Saul, David determined that if he re-mained within the territory of Israel and Judah, Saul would surely catch him and kill him. So, he decided to join up with the Philistines where he would be out of his tormentor's reach. He gathered up his army of six hundred soldiers and enlisted with Achish, king of Gath (1 Sam 27:203). The stratagem worked and Saul permanently abandoned his quest for the fugitive's capture (1 Sam 27:4).

David's employment by the Philistines, Israel's preeminent foe, must have been one of the most shocking developments in Israel's history. The two nations were at continuous war during the reign of Saul, and David's actions clearly constituted a form of treason and disloyalty to both his king and his country. The notoriety attached to David's behavior made it impossible for the biblical editors to cover up the fact. Instead, all they could do was blame Saul's persecution as the causative factor. For full effect, they place the countercharge directly in David's mouth when, earlier in the text, he says to Saul:

> Wherefore doth my lord thus pursue after his servant? for what have I done? or what evil is in mine hand? Now therefore, I pray thee, let my lord the king hear the words of his servant. If the LORD have stirred thee up against me, let him accept an offering: but if they be the children of men, cursed be they before the LORD; *for they have driven me out this day from abiding in the inheritance of the LORD, saying, Go, serve other gods.* Now therefore, let not my blood fall to the earth before the face of the LORD: for the king of Israel is come out to seek a flea, as when one doth hunt a partridge in the mountains (1 Sam 26:18–20, emphasis added).

The reference to serving other gods should be understood as a political rather than religious failing. It meant serving the people who worshipped the other gods, not that David actually worshipped a foreign deity. Nevertheless, this defense, that Saul made him do it, flies in the face of everything that the biblical editors have asked us to believe about David.

They told us that David had been chosen by God to become king over Israel and that David's heart was with God and that he always made inquiry of the Lord before making important decisions. They also told us that David constantly placed his fate in the hands of the deity. What, then, is David afraid of? God is on his side; God will protect him; God will make him king of Israel. He just needed to hide out, consult the Lord, and let fate take its course. Instead, he defected to Israel's greatest enemy, and did so without any indication that he first made inquiry of the Lord and that the Lord advised him to fight for the Philistines.

David apparently served Achish well, and after about a year and four months he asked that the Philistine king reward his faithfulness by giving him a town that he could own (1 Sam 27:5). His patron agreed and gave David the town of Ziklag (1 Sam 27:6). Biblical tradition places this town within the inheritance of the tribe of Simeon, although the bible describes Simeon's inheritance as a subdivision within Judah (Josh 19:19).

From Ziklag, David set out to conquer territory, and it appears that his enemies had accused him of attacking Israelite territories. His defenders, according to the biblical account, claimed that he never actually attacked Israelite cities, but after attacking non-Israelite cities, and killing all possible witnesses against him, he lied to Achish about what happened. Let's look at the specific passage in question:

> And David and his men went up, and invaded the Geshurites, and the Gezrites, and the Amalekites: for those nations were of old the inhabitants of the land, as thou goest to Shur, even unto the land of Egypt. And David smote the land, and left neither man nor woman alive, and took away the sheep, and the oxen, and the asses, and the camels, and the apparel, and returned, and came to Achish. And Achish said, Whither have ye made a road to day? And David said, Against the south of Judah, and against the south of the Jerahmeelites, and against the south of the Kenites. And David saved neither man nor woman alive, to bring tidings to Gath, saying, Lest they should tell on us, saying, So did David, and so will be his manner all the while he dwelleth in the country of the Philistines. And Achish believed David, saying, He hath made his people Israel utterly to abhor him; therefore he shall be my servant for ever (1 Sam 27:8–12).

This passage indicates that David raided Philistine territories in the region of Judah but that he lied to Achish about his activities by telling him that he raided Israelite territories. The claim that David lied about his achievements is difficult to believe. The bible twice shows that Philistine princes didn't trust David, and it is highly unlikely they wouldn't have kept a close eye on his actions and have checked out his claims. His lack of prisoners would have certainly suggested something was amiss, as the taking of prisoners for slave work was a common feature of political life in those days. Moreover, military leaders routinely employ spy networks to keep them informed as to what was happening within enemy territories. Those spies would certainly have known whether David had a good or bad reputation among the Israelites. Even more importantly, those Philistine cities would likely have been in regular contact with Achish and if they had been totally destroyed, as indicated in the passage, the king would have been aware that David had actually raided those Philistine territories.

Another strange claim of the defense is that David secretly hunted down the Amalekites, killed the people, and took possession of their cattle. In the story of Samuel and Saul we were given to believe that the

Amalekites were totally destroyed. Furthermore, one of Saul's two major sins that caused Samuel to disavow him was the failure to destroy the Amalekite cattle. Presumably that edict was still in effect. Everything belonging to the Amalekites belonged to Israel's God, and could not be distributed to the people. This defense of David implies that he committed the same sin as Saul and should be denied the throne for the same reason that Saul was.

David remained in service to Achish up until the day of the battle between the Philistines and Israel that claimed the life of Saul and his sons. Preliminary to that battle, Achish told David that he and his men were expected to fight alongside the Philistines against Saul, and David replied, "Surely thou shalt know what thy servant can do" (1 Sam 28:2).

The pro-David chorus alleges that David's reply was deceptive, that he planned to turn against Achish in battle and give Israel a significant military advantage, and then Achish would surely know what his servant could do. We have no evidence, however, that this is the case. It is a surmise that is possible from the text but nothing in context suggests that this would have happened.

In any event, Achish certainly believed David and replied, "Therefore will I make thee keeper of mine head for ever" (1 Sam 28:2). The term "head" means "a bodyguard." (See the NRSV translation of the same passage.) The story then detours for a strange episode in which Saul sought a necromancer to call Samuel up from the dead for a consultation (1 Sam 28:7). Samuel's ghost appeared and renewed the attack on Saul's legitimacy, bringing up the sin with regard to the Amalekites, and predicting that Saul and his sons would fall in tomorrow's battle with the Philistines (1 Sam 28:16–19).

As the Philistines prepare for battle against Israel, David and his men formed a guard around the king, who was in the rear of the assembly (1 Sam 29:2). Recognizing that this could give David a chance to betray the Philistines by taking out their king, the princes demanded that David be sent away (1 Sam 29:4). Despite the Philistine king's defense of David's integrity, the nobles insisted otherwise, and the king yielded. When informed of the decision, David pleaded to remain:

But what have I done? and what hast thou found in thy servant so long as I have been with thee unto this day, that I may not go fight against the enemies of my lord the king? (1 Sam 29:8).

The king reiterated his praise of David but sent him away (1 Sam 29:9).

Now, if David really intended to secretly aid Israel's army against the Philistines in what was shaping up to be a major confrontation between the two foes, and if David truly were loyal to Israel and concerned with its safety, then after being dismissed we should expect him to turn around and fight on Israel's side once the battle begins. Instead, he abandons the battle arena and makes a three-day trek with his army to Ziklag (1 Sam 30:1).

During David's journey to his home base, Saul and Jonathan fell in battle and the Philistines routed the Israelite army. We will have more to say about the return to Ziklag in the next chapter. We will only note here that the alleged departure of David from the war zone enabled him to claim that he was nowhere around when Saul died on the battlefield.

THE KING OF JUDAH

In this chapter, so far, we have followed the chronological order of events as they are laid out in the Book of Samuel, beginning with David's flight from Saul's court and continuing to the day of Saul's death. Samuel continues with an account of civil war between the House of David and the House of Saul. During this confrontation, Saul's son Ishbosheth served as king in Israel and the people of Judah chose David to rule over them. (In 2 Samuel, the name of Saul's son is given as Ishbosheth but in 1 Chr 8:33, 9:39 it is given as Eshbaal. It is widely assumed among biblical scholars that the original name was Ishbaal and that the editor of Samuel changed it because of the offensive "baal" element in the name, which may have referred to a chief Canaanite deity.) The new king of Israel was assassinated approximately two years later, after which Israel asked David to rule over them as well. As the biblical account of these events unfolds, the editors take great care to give the impression that David did not become king over Judah until after Saul died. It is here that we must challenge this editorial arrangement and demonstrate that David became king of Judah several years before the end of Saul's reign.

Let's look first at how the biblical editors arranged the evidence concerning when David became king of Judah.

They began by telling us that when David learned of the death of Jonathan and Saul he grieved deeply over their deaths. 2 Samuel 1 ends with the last lines of David's eulogy. 2 Samuel 2 follows immediately thereafter with these verses:

> And it came to pass after this, that David inquired of *the LORD, saying, Shall I go up into any of the cities of Judah? And the LORD said unto him, Go up. And David said, Whither shall I go up? And he said, Unto Hebron. So David went up thither, and his two wives also, Ahinoam the Jezreelitess, and Abigail Nabal's wife the Carmelite. And his men that were with him did David bring up, every man with his household: and they dwelt in the cities of Hebron. And the men of Judah came, and there they anointed David king over the house of Judah.* And they told David, saying, That the men of Jabesh-Gilead were they that buried Saul. And David sent messengers unto the men of Jabesh-Gilead, and said unto them, Blessed be ye of the LORD, that ye have showed this kindness unto your lord, even unto Saul, and have buried him. And now the LORD show kindness and truth unto you: and I also will requite you this kindness, because ye have done this thing. Therefore now let your hands be strengthened, and be ye valiant: for your master Saul is dead, and also the House of Judah have anointed me king over them (2 Sam 2:1–7, emphasis added).

The Italicized portion of the text suggests to the reader that David became king of Judah only after he learned of Saul's death. The evidence below will show that David became King at a much earlier point in time. That portion of the text, therefore, must have been transferred from a much earlier time in the sequence of events to its present location between the end of David's lament and the continuation of the story. The next sentence after the italicized words should have been the next event after reciting the eulogy, which in this case would have been the information to David that the men of Jabesh-Gilead had buried Saul.

The second misrepresentation occurs in the last line quoted above. David says to the people of Jabesh-Gilead, presumably for the purpose of recruiting them to his cause, that 1) Saul is dead, and 2) Judah has elected him king. The statement is calculated to make it look like David only became king after Saul died. While both statements are correct if considered separately, the second clause, as we shall see, neatly omits the fact that he was elected king long before Saul died.

There are several indications that the biblical text in question is out of sequence. To begin with, the men of Jabesh-Gilead buried Saul almost immediately after he was killed, retrieving his body in a military raid on the Philistine city of Beth-shan where it had been fastened to the wall (1 Sam 31:9–13). The biblical editors expected us to believe that David, who had close contact with the Philistine king, heard about Saul's death but knew nothing about what happened to the body, and waited until after he moved his entourage from Ziklag to Hebron before asking if Saul and his great friend Jonathan had been buried. Logic tells us that David would have inquired of his Philistine patron after Saul's body, and even if he didn't learn what happened from Achish, news of the successful raid on Beth-shan by the men of Jabesh-Gilead would have quickly spread throughout the region.

More importantly, though, we have direct evidence that the biblical editors overlooked, and which shows that David became king over Judah while Saul still ruled in Israel. According to 2 Sam 5:3–5:

> So all the elders of Israel came to the king to Hebron; and King David made a league with them in Hebron before the LORD: and they anointed David king over Israel. David was thirty years old when he began to reign, and he reigned forty years. *In Hebron he reigned over Judah seven years and six months: and in Jerusalem he reigned thirty and three years over all Israel and Judah* (emphasis added).

1 Chronicles 3:4 reiterates that David ruled in Hebron for seven and a half years and another thirty-three in Jerusalem, but omits the information that David ruled only over Judah during those seven and a half years in Hebron. This apparently deliberate omission helped the Chronicler cover up the fact of David's earlier reign in Judah while Saul ruled in Israel.

If David ruled over Judah alone for seven and a half years, and Judah and Israel combined only after that time, and the civil war lasted only about two years, then David must have been on the throne of Judah for at least five years while Saul was still king. In other words, when David asked to march with Achish against Israel, he was already king of Judah for over five years. His arrangement with Achish, therefore, signifies that he served as a vassal of the Philistines. The gift of Ziklag to David cemented the treaty between the two sides.

Scholars routinely and casually dismiss this damning passage, failing to analyze its import. They simply reject it as problematic and the likely result of some sort of error. They need to believe in the underlying biblical account, and this passage makes it impossible for them to do so.

That David ruled as king of Judah for at least five years before Saul died strongly corroborates our earlier argument that David and Samuel planned to go to Bethlehem in Judah and crown David king. This suggests that they did just that. Samuel crowned and anointed David, the newly-crowned David raised an army more powerful than anywhere else in the territory, and, piece-by-piece by force of arms and in subservience to the Philistines, he assembled a kingdom in Judah.

There is one more important piece of evidence that corroborates the argument that David became king while Saul still ruled over Israel. David sired numerous children by numerous wives. According to 2 Sam 3:2 and also 1 Chr 3:1, while David ruled in Hebron over Judah he had six children by six wives (several more were born in Jerusalem). The first child was born to Ahinoam and the second to Abigail.

(As a side note, it is worth mentioning that in Chronicles the information about David's children in Hebron is followed by the information about how long David ruled in Hebron and Jerusalem, but the information is buried in long lists of genealogical listings (1 Chr 3:4). In Samuel, the notice about his children in Hebron is separated from the notice about how long he ruled in Hebron, with the first notice appearing at the beginning of the civil war and the second appearing just after he was crowned king over Israel, two years later (2 Sam 2:11; 3:2). This suggests that one of the Samuel editors divided up this notice about events in He-bron and redistributed it for propagandistic purposes.)

One can assume that such a prolific father would likely have impreg-nated his wives shortly after their marriage. This would suggest that at the latest he became king of Judah in Hebron within a year or so of marrying Ahinoam and Abigail.

As the biblical account is presented to us, these two women first ap-pear as his wives right after the death of Nabal at Carmel. As we noted in the review of that story, Nabal was a very rich and powerful member of the Calebite clan, and the Calebites controlled Hebron; Hebron appears to have been the most important city in Judah. When Nabal died and David married Abigail, he effectively replaced Nabal in the existing He-bronite hierarchy. Given that he had a large military force behind him, we can safely assume that shortly after the marriage to Abigail, David was well situated to become ruler of Hebron, and from that position, with his Philistine backing, he became the effective king of the region.

Unfortunately, the bible is vague as to when in time Nabal died and David married Abigail. Still, it creates the strong impression that it hap-pened early in David's fugitive career. And if we are correct in our assump-tion that David's Ahinoam was originally Saul's rebellious wife, we can tie the Nabal incident to shortly after David's flight from Saul, which would strongly corroborate our claim that David fled south in order to be declared king. If David's Ahinoam was not Saul's wife, then our anchor is a little less secure as to when in his fugitive career he became king over Judah.

Although we use the term "king" here, we should not assume that David, or even Saul, at this early stage in the history of the monarchy ruled as grand monarchs. They were both more like regional chieftains, controlling an alliance of cities and villages. Still, there is a clue in Samuel that suggests the approximate extent of David's kingdom at the time of Saul's death. According to 1 Sam 30:26–31, at the time of Saul's death, these are the cities "where David himself and his men were wont to haunt": Bethel, Ramoth, Jattir, Aroer, Siphmoth, Eshtemoa, Rachal, the cities of the Jerahmeelites, the cities of the Kenites, Hormah, Chorashan, Athach, and Hebron.

These are, for the most part, places in the Hebronite section of Judah and in Simeon to the south. The only problematic names in the list are Bethel, which was by the Benjamin-Ephraim border, north of Judah, and Aroer, which is in the Transjordan. However, these may be transcription errors as the Septuagint gives a different version of this list of territories, substituting different names for those in the Hebrew version. Bethel, for instance, appears as Beth-zur, Carmel replaces Rachal (corroborating our Carmel-Hebron connection), and Beer-Sheba substitutes for Chorashan. As for Aroer, several scholars believe that it had originally been rendered as Arouel.

In substance, David controlled many of the key cities of Judah and Simeon, where this "outlaw king" could roam at will without fear of interference from Saul.

CHAPTER 6

The Suspicious Death of King Saul

The LORD hath returned upon thee [i.e., David] all the blood
of the House of Saul, in whose stead thou hast reigned;
and the LORD hath delivered the kingdom into the hand
of Absalom thy son: and, behold, thou art taken in thy mischief,
because thou art a bloody man. 2 SAM 16:8

Of the various accusations leveled against David, the most serious charge alleged that he had murdered King Saul, and, by implication, Jonathan. The most direct piece of evidence for that indictment, aside from David's position as a Philistine vassal ready to ride out with Achish against Saul, appears to be David's possession of Saul's crown almost immediately after the king had died on the battlefield. Also, the bible has two inconsistent accounts of how Saul died, suggesting that the official story may not be reliable.

In response, David's defenders inserted several stories into the bible that tended to exonerate their hero. The most successful and most effective rebuttal in the bible comes from two incidents that portray David as having had the opportunity on two prior occasions to kill Saul but refusing to do so. He didn't take Saul's life because, the bible says, 1) he was loyal to the king and had done nothing to earn Saul's hostility, and 2) it would be wrong to take the life of God's anointed representative.

In addition, his defenders claim, David had been en route to Ziklag, far from the Israelite-Philistine battlefield, so there was no way for him to be present at the location where Saul and his sons were killed. Furthermore, when he reached Ziklag he discovered that Amalekites had burned down his home base and captured his two wives and the women and children of the men under his command. Consumed with personal grief, he led his men on a successful chase to retrieve their families. It was only on his return from rescuing his family that he first learned of Saul's death. As to his possession of Saul's crown, David claimed that he received it after his return to Ziklag, when an itinerant Amalekite brought it to him from the place where Saul fell dead.

Additionally, the biblical editors claim that the God of Israel had determined that Saul and his sons should die at the time he did. In support of this claim the editors inserted a story that had the Lord declare his intention through the spirit of the deceased Samuel, which had been brought forth by a necromancer at Saul's request. If God wanted David dead at the hands of the Philistines, argues the defense, then David could in no way be responsible for that death even if he had fought by the side of Achish.

THE CONTRADICTORY ACCOUNTS OF SAUL'S DEATH

The Book of Samuel presents two stories about the death of Saul. In both accounts Saul died on Mount Gilboa, in the territory usually assigned to the northern tribe of Issachar, far away from David's home base of Ziklag. The biblical sequence of events places Saul's death after the story in which Samuel's ghost prophesied the death of Saul and his sons on the next day (1 Sam 28:19) and after David had left the Philistine camp for Ziklag (1 Sam 29:11). This sequence of events, as we shall soon see, is inconsistent with the logical chronology inherent in the biblical accounts and, below, we will reconstruct the time line. The misleading order of stories shows that the biblical editors deliberately rearranged the sequence of events at a late date in order to protect David's reputation.

The more famous of the two death stories, usually defended as the official version, tells us that Saul committed suicide because, after being badly wounded in battle, he didn't want to be captured and tortured by the Philistine enemy. In the other, an Amalekite wanderer found Saul badly wounded and, at Saul's request, ran him through so that the king wouldn't be captured.

The Suicide Story

According to the first story, in 1 Sam 31, the Philistines pressed the Israelites hard. Three of Saul's sons fell first and the Israel defense continued to deteriorate. Saul took a hit from enemy archers and believed that in his wounded condition the other side would capture him. He then asked his armor-bearer to take a sword and run him through so that "these uncircumcised" Philistines wouldn't take him alive. But his frightened aide couldn't bring himself to commit such a horrible act. So Saul took a sword and fell upon it. When the armor-bearer saw what Saul did, he did likewise. "So Saul died, and his three sons, and his armourbearer, and all his men, that same day together" (1 Sam 31:6). The only Israelites to escape death had been camped on the other side of the valley. When they learned that Saul and his sons had died, they fled from their cities and the Philistines took over the sites and moved into the abandoned homes (1 Sam 31:7).

Later, the Philistines found Saul's body along with those of his three sons. They chopped off Saul's head, stripped off his armor, displayed the items in several of the Philistine temples, and fastened Saul's body to a wall in the city of Beth-shan (1 Sam 31:8–10). When the citizens of Jabesh-Gilead heard what happened they sent a raiding party to retrieve their hero's body and bring it back to their own city, where they gave it a proper funeral (1 Sam 31:11. It was Saul's defense of the non-Israelite city of Jabesh-Gilead against David's friend King Nahash that propelled Saul into the kingship of Israel.).

This report of Saul's death suffers from the obvious defect that no witnesses remained alive to say what happened. The text says that Saul's aide and all the men that were with him died. While the biblical account provides Saul with some dignity and nobility in the manner of his death, someone made it up out of whole cloth. But who?

Despite the sympathetic portrayal, it is most likely not a product of Saul's court history. His followers blamed David for his death. Since the story shifts blame away from David, one would suspect that someone from David's coalition would be responsible. This suggests either the Shiloh priesthood or someone in David's coterie. However, the second version of the story of Saul's death involves David's court directly, so this first version may reflect a Shilohite effort to disassociate itself from any question of any involvement in the king's death, especially since the Shilohite priest Samuel had been quoted as predicting Saul's death earlier.

The Amalekite Story

The second report on Saul's death, in 2 Sam 1, occurs after David has returned from rescuing the families taken prisoner during an Amalekite raid on Ziklag. Three days after his return, the bible tells us, a man came from Saul's camp, clothing torn and dirt on his face, and traveled to David's court, where he fell to the ground and expressed his obeisance.

Upon his arrival, David asked where he came from, and he replied, "out of the camp of Israel am I escaped" (2 Sam 1:3). Next, David asked how the battle went. The visitor told his host the battle went badly and Saul and Jonathan were both dead. When David asked how the man knew this, the man replied:

> As I happened by chance upon Mount Gilboa, behold, Saul leaned upon his spear; and, lo, the chariots and horsemen followed hard after him. And when he looked behind him, he saw me, and called unto me. And I answered, Here am I. And he said unto me, Who art thou? And I answered him, I am an Amalekite. He said unto me again, Stand, I pray thee, upon me, and slay me: for anguish is come upon me, because my life is yet whole in me. So I stood upon him, and slew him, because I was sure that he could not live after that he was fallen: and I took the crown that was upon his head, and the bracelet that was on his arm, and have brought them hither unto my lord (2 Sam 1:6–10).

Upon hearing this news David and all his men were overcome with grief, ripping apart their clothing at the horrible fate that befell their beloved king (2 Sam 1:11). David then declared a period of mourning over the tragedy that befell Saul, Jonathan, and the people of Israel (2 Sam 1:12). But before doing so, David asked the man where he came from and the man informed him that he was an Amalekite. David then inquired, "How wast thou not afraid to stretch forth thine hand to destroy the LORD'S anointed?" (2 Sam 1:14).

After putting the question, and without waiting for a reply, David ordered that the stranger be put to death (2 Sam 1:15). This eliminated the only alleged witness to the demise of King Saul. Following the Amalekite's execution, David recited one of the most beautiful poems in biblical literature:

> The beauty of Israel is slain upon thy high places: how are the mighty fallen! Tell it not in Gath, publish it not in the streets of Askelon; lest the daughters of the Philistines rejoice, lest the daughters of the uncircumcised triumph. Ye mountains of Gilboa, let there be no dew, neither let there be rain, upon you, nor fields of offerings: for there the shield of the mighty is vilely cast away, the shield of Saul, as though he had not been anointed with oil. From the blood of the slain, from the fat of the mighty, the bow of Jonathan turned not back, and the sword of Saul returned not empty. Saul and Jonathan were lovely and pleasant in their lives, and in their death they were not divided: they were swifter than eagles, they were stronger than lions. Ye daughters of Israel, weep over Saul, who clothed you in scarlet, with other delights, who put on ornaments of gold upon your apparel. How are the mighty fallen in the midst of the battle! O Jonathan, thou wast slain in thine high places. I am distressed for thee, my brother Jonathan: very pleasant hast thou been unto me: thy love to me was wonderful, passing the love of women. How are the mighty fallen, and the weapons of war perished! (2 Sam 1:19–27).

It's ironic that David's lament asks that notice of Saul's death not be publicized in the Philistine cities when the first account tells us that such publication was made. The Amalekite's story also clearly contradicts the earlier version. Here Saul stood alone wounded, no armor-bearer at his side to refuse his request to run the king through. Most importantly, though, the Amalekite brought Saul's crown and bracelet to David, a long distance away from the battlefield. Why?

INDICATIONS OF ASSASSINATION

Defenders of David easily reconcile the two stories by arguing that the Amalekite lied when he said he found Saul alive and ran him through at the king's own request; he simply found the dead king's body and removed the jewelry, bringing the crown and bracelet to David for a reward. But if personal gain motivated the Amalekite, why did he travel the long distance from Mount Gilboa to Ziklag, a three-day's journey when David made the trip, in order to give the items to David when he could almost certainly have gotten a large reward by bringing it a shorter distance to someone in Saul's entourage, such as Abner, the king's general, especially since the crown belonged with Saul's house? And what would lead him to think that he should take the crown and bracelet to David in the first place, since Saul's antipathy to David had now become well-known?

Unfortunately, David executed him before he could answer those questions. Furthermore, if the Amalekite had already found Saul dead, why would he lie to David about it unless he thought David would have a favorable reaction to such a false account?

This story about the Amalekite and Saul's crown indicates that short-ly after Saul's death, David somehow came into possession of the king's crown and bracelet. Given Saul's hostility to David, and the fact that David had set up a rival kingdom while Saul still ruled, many Israelites obviously assumed that David obtained those icons by having Saul assassinated so that he could set himself up as king over Israel. The charges must have resonated strongly among the northern enemies of David and an explanation was needed. This second story serves that function, but there are some problems with this defense.

First, nowhere in the biblical account do we find David returning the crown and bracelet to Saul's family. If the items were brought to David by mistake or for foolish reasons, why wouldn't David return them to the rightful owners? If they had been returned, such evidence would have certainly appeared in the story. The failure to do so reinforces the idea that possession of the crown served as a symbol of David's claim to the throne. In support of that idea, as we will see in the next chapter, civil war broke out between the House of David and the House of Saul for the right to rule Israel, suggesting that David certainly believed he had a superior right to the throne of Israel that did the House of Saul.

As we saw in the last chapter, David had set himself up as king over Judah at least five years before Saul's death, and served as a Philistine vassal. His desire to be king over all of Israel had become common knowledge and the enmity between David and Saul had become well known. The occasion of Saul's death, despite the glorious poetry and crocodile tears, served David's interests well. It removed a major barrier to David's attempt to unite all of Israel under his rule.

This brings us to the next interesting question about how Saul died. What is an Amalekite wanderer doing way up in the north at Mount Gilboa, in the middle of a battle between Israel and the Philistines? Not only were the Amalekites a nomadic tribe of raiders from the territory of Edom, far south in Jordan, they were supposed to be bitter enemies of Israel. It was Saul's failure to slaughter every last Amalekite that caused Samuel to denounce him as a traitor to the Lord. Lone Amalekites should not be found traveling alone in Israelite territory, and they certainly wouldn't be publicizing their identities to the Israelites upon simple inquiry, especially to a leading Israelite chieftain such as Saul, as the Amalekite claimed he did in his report.

THE ZIKLAG ALIBI

Particularly strange about finding an Amalekite in David's court is that we were given to believe that David had just returned from wiping out a contingent of Amalekite raiders who had just burned down Ziklag and kidnapped his wives and his soldiers' families. That the Amalekite chose David as the person to whom he brought Saul's crown defies rational explanation unless David hired the Amalekite (and perhaps an Amalekite raiding party) to kill Saul. If true, it overcomes the alibi that David couldn't be responsible because he had been in Ziklag at the time of Saul's death.

It's interesting that the raid on Ziklag not only provided David with an alibi that placed him far from the scene of Saul's death, but that it also undercut any claim that David would have hired an Amalekite to work for him on such a deed as killing King Saul. So, the alleged raid of Amalekites on David's home base serves to undermine the accusations against David. It separates him from any alliance with the Amalekite and reinforces his alibi.

It's quite astonishing, therefore, that the fanatically pro-David editor of Chronicles omitted the Amalekite raid on Ziklag from that account of David's history. 1 Chronicles 12 begins with a notice that David kept himself close in Ziklag because of Saul's enmity, and that he gathered a large force of Israelites from many tribes, "mighty men, helpers of war," who rallied to his side. Then after these lengthy listings of the Israelites who joined up with David at Ziklag, Chronicles says:

> And there fell some of Manasseh to David, when he came with the Philistines against Saul to battle: but they helped them not: for the lords of the Philistines upon advisement sent him away, saying, He will fall to his master Saul to the jeopardy of our heads. As he went to Ziklag, there fell to him of Manasseh, Adnah, and Jozabad, and Jediael, and Michael, and Jozabad, and Elihu, and Zilthai, captains of the thousands that were of Manasseh. *And they helped David against the band of the rovers:* for they were all mighty men of valour, and were captains in the host. For at that time day by day there came to David to help him, until it was a great host, like the host of God (1 Chr 12:19–22, emphasis added).

In this passage, Chronicles tells us that David brought members of the Israelite tribe of Manasseh to join with the Philistines against Saul, and then it reiterates the skepticism of the Philistine princes about David's true intentions. It also says that David went to Ziklag, with a large army, and chased after rovers, i.e., unidentified groups of raiders. But nowhere do we find a claim that Amalekites raided David's home base and kidnapped his family. Such omission suggests that the Amalekite raid in Samuel was a late fiction added in order to bolster David's faltering reputation.

In fact, Chronicles omits the entire second Amalekite account of how King Saul died. It records only the official unwitnessed version in which

Saul committed suicide. The Chronicler must have understood how bad the second incident looked for David.

Additionally, the surrounding Chronicles passages make it clear that while Saul still ruled, David gathered a large and powerful military force from various parts of Israel, an obvious indication that David and Saul had been engaged in a military struggle for control of the kingdom.

Perhaps the most difficult issue raised by David's presence in Ziklag concerns the question of why he was in Ziklag in the first place. As noted in the last chapter, if David secretly planned to aid Israel against the coming Philistine attack, as so many of his defenders allege, why didn't he stay in the combat zone after Achish expelled him from the Philistine army? A major battle was taking shape and Israel needed all the help it could get. The very fact that David went to Ziklag proves that he wanted Saul defeated and perhaps even killed in battle. A weakened Israel would have given him a military advantage. David's arrival in Ziklag undermines the sincerity of David's display of grief when he heard the news of Saul's death. Even the Chronicler admits David left for Ziklag, which left Israel in the lurch.

To the charge that David had Saul murdered, the biblical evidence so far shows the following:

1. On the morning of a great battle between Israel and the Philistines, David inexplicably chose to abandon his nation by sitting out the battle and returning to Ziklag.
2. He left no one behind to bring him news of the battle.
3. The official story of Saul's noble death had no witnesses.
4. An Amalekite, far from his home territory, had claimed that he accidentally found Saul badly wounded and complied with Saul's request to put him to death before the Philistines captured him.
5. For no apparent logical reason, the Amalekite traveled several days to bring Saul's crown and bracelet to David, who by now was well reorganized as an enemy of Saul, when he could have much more easily have brought it to the Israelites where it naturally belonged.

6. The Book of Chronicles omits the story of an Amalekite raid on Ziklag, undercutting the claim that David was angrily fighting the Amalekites and thus unlikely to make a deal with them to be his agents.

7. David took the crown and bracelet, executed the Amalekite before he could answer troubling questions, and never returned the items to the House of Saul.

All in all, this appears to be a strong circumstantial case that David hired Amalekite assassins to do Saul in. Implicit in all of this is that if David arranged for the death of Saul, he arranged also for the death of Jonathan, who would have had a direct claim to the throne of Israel and who, as a result, might no longer be willing to be David's number two in command. It's interesting, therefore, that the only other death notice besides Saul's that the Amalekite brings back is that of Jonathan's.

THE LOYALTY STORIES

Given the strength of the circumstantial case against David, the biblical editors reinforced the Ziklag alibi by adding into the biblical account two additional stories, each showing that David had an opportunity to kill Saul but wouldn't do so because he was loyal to Saul and wouldn't strike down one of the Lord's anointed.

The first story appears in 1 Sam 23:19–24:22 and the other in 1 Sam 26. They share a number of similarities, the implications of which we shall examine below, but differ on the specific details surrounding how David spared Saul's life.

Each account begins with the arrival of a delegation of Ziphites to Saul, who inform the king that David is hiding in the hill of Hachilah, which, they tell him, is by Jeshimon. On both occasions Saul set off after David with an army of three thousand soldiers. In the first story, Saul trapped David in Jeshimon, but before he could complete the capture, messengers suddenly called him away to a battle against the Philistines and David escaped to another location. After the Philistine encounter,

Saul resumed his chase after David, seeking out the fugitive's new hideout. In the second story, the action remained at Jeshimon throughout.

The First Loyalty Story

In the story of the first encounter between David and Saul, the king went into a cave to relieve himself. By coincidence, David and some of his men were hiding inside:

> *And the men of David said unto him, Behold the day of which the LORD said unto thee, Behold, I will deliver thine enemy into thine hand, that thou mayest do to him as it shall seem good unto thee.* Then David arose, and cut off the skirt of Saul's robe privily. And it came to pass afterward, that David's heart smote him, because he had cut off Saul's skirt. And he said unto his men, The LORD forbid that I should do this thing unto my master, the LORD'S anointed, to stretch forth mine hand against him, seeing he is the anointed of the LORD. So David stayed his servants with these words, and suffered them not to rise against Saul (1 Sam 24:4–7, emphasis added).

Note here that for the first time, David's followers claim to know of a prophecy by which Saul would be delivered into David's hands. This reinforces the earlier argument that David was in open revolt against Saul and seeking the throne of Israel while Saul still lived and that Samuel openly aided David in this effort.

After David had second thoughts about his actions he and his men withdrew into the cave and Saul departed. As the king left, David called out to him and bowed down to "my lord, the king" (1 Sam 24:8). He then showed Saul the piece of his robe that had been cut off and said to him:

> Wherefore hearest thou men's words, saying, Behold, David seeketh thy hurt? Behold, this day thine eyes have seen how that the LORD had delivered thee to day into mine hand in the cave: and some bade me kill thee: but mine eye spared thee; and I said, I will not put forth mine hand against my lord; for he is the LORD'S anointed. Moreover, my father, see, yea, see the skirt of thy robe in my hand: for in that I cut off the skirt of thy robe, and killed thee not, know thou and see that there is neither evil nor transgression in mine hand, and I have not sinned against thee; yet thou huntest my soul to take it. The LORD judge between me and thee, and the LORD

avenge me of thee: but mine hand shall not be upon thee. As saith the proverb of the ancients, Wickedness proceedeth from the wicked: but mine
hand shall not be upon thee. After whom is the king of Israel come out?
after whom dost thou pursue? after a dead dog, after a flea. The LORD
therefore be judge, and judge between me and thee, and see, and plead my
cause, and deliver me out of thine hand (1 Sam 24:9–15).

David's words left Saul choked with emotion and the king tearfully
called out "Is this thy voice, *my son David*?" (1 Sam 24:16, emphasis added). Saul then acknowledged his own sinful behavior and praised David's
righteousness. Finally, he said:

And now, behold, I know well that thou shalt surely be king, and that the
kingdom of Israel shall be established in thine hand. Swear now therefore
unto me by the LORD, that thou wilt not cut off my seed after me, and
that thou wilt not destroy my name out of my father's house. And David
sware unto Saul (1 Sam 24:20–22).

The story as set forth shows David to be a righteous figure and concludes with Saul acknowledging his own wrongdoing, praising David,
predicting that David would be king, and asking David to spare his family.
The biblical editors do not tell us why Saul would think that this good,
fair, and righteous man would harm the king's family. In any event, there
are some problems with this story.

The most obvious one is that the only known witnesses to this account are David and Saul, although one of David's men in the cave might
have overheard it. Since we have no basis for believing Saul publicized the
story, we can only assume it came from the pro-David faction, leaving its
integrity somewhat in doubt.

Also difficult to accept is that David somehow slipped behind Saul while
the king squatted down to relive himself, and, prior to the advent of the scis-
sors, somehow managed to cut off a swatch of the royal robe without Saul
being aware that David was right behind him and fiddling with his clothes.

Even David's defenders must have recognized that the story didn't
quite pass what lawyers often refer to as the "giggle" test. Hence, the appearance of a second loyalty story to make up for the deficits of the first.

The Second Loyalty Story

The second story takes place at Jeshimon. In the first account, Saul had trapped David at this location, but due to a sudden Philistine attack elsewhere, Saul had to withdraw to meet the enemy while David escaped. On this second occasion at Jeshimon, David and his friend Abishai, Joab's brother, sneak into the middle of the Israelite camp and go over to where Saul and Abner were asleep. As they stand over the king, Abishai says:

> God hath delivered thine enemy into thine hand this day: now therefore let me smite him, I pray thee, with the spear even to the earth at once, and I will not smite him the second time (1 Sam 26:8).

To which David replied:

> Destroy him not: for who can stretch forth his hand against the LORD'S anointed, and be guiltless? (1 Sam 26:9).

After further reminding Abishai that "the LORD forbid that I should stretch forth mine hand against the LORD'S anointed," he decided to take Saul's spear and water jug (1 Sam 26:11). After departing the camp, David went to the top of a distant hill and called out to Abner, tweaking him for failing to effectively protect the king. Upon hearing David's words, Saul calls out, just as he did in the first incident, "Is this thy voice, *my son David?*" (1 Sam 26:17, emphasis added).

David responded:

> Wherefore doth my lord thus pursue after his servant? for what have I done? or what evil is in mine hand? Now therefore, I pray thee, let my lord the king hear the words of his servant. If the LORD have stirred thee up against me, let him accept an offering: but if they be the children of men, cursed be they before the LORD; for they have driven me out this day from abiding in the inheritance of the LORD, saying, Go, serve other gods. Now therefore, let not my blood fall to the earth before the face of the LORD: for the king of Israel is come out to seek a flea, as when one doth hunt a partridge in the mountains (1 Sam 26:18–20).

As in the first story, Saul acknowledged his sin against David and predicted that David would do great things and that he would prevail, but did not request that David spare his family. He also promised to stop hunting after David.

Although this story attempts to create a more public domain for the evidence of David's loyalty, the chief proof, the conversation between David and Abishai, still remains unwitnessed by anyone other than David and his friend. This is one of several occasions in which the biblical editors arrange for Abishai to propose some hostile action against an enemy of David, and David opposes the action on some high moral ground (see 2 Sam 16:19, 19:21). As such, it is simply a literary device to make David look good.

As to the more public aspect of the claim, it is not impossible that someone may have sneaked into the camp and stolen Saul's spear and water jug, although how easily identifiable those items might be from a distant hill, I can't say. Nevertheless, if Saul and Abner found them missing it would suggest that somebody from David's side slipped into camp unnoticed, but we have no evidence independent of David's witnesses as to who removed the property.

The Two Stories Compared

Both stories of David's loyalty share a common vocabulary to describe events, suggesting that they both derive from a common source describing a single incident and that at a later time the biblical editors treated the two variations as separate consecutive incidents. Consider the following phrasings and themes that appear in both stories—quotes from the first story in regular type and from the second story in italics:

A1. "Then came up the Ziphites to Saul to Gibeah, saying, Doth not David hide himself with us in strong holds in the wood, in the hill of Hachilah, which is on the south of Jeshimon?" (1 Sam 23:19).

A2. *"And the Ziphites came unto Saul to Gibeah, saying, Doth not David hide himself in the hill of Hachilah, which is before Jeshimon?"* (1 Sam 26:1).

B1. "Then Saul took three thousand chosen men out of all Israel, and went to seek David and his men upon the rocks of the wild goats" (1 Sam 24:2).

B2. *"Then Saul arose, and went down to the wilderness of Ziph, having three thousand chosen men of Israel with him, to seek David in the wilderness of Ziph"* (1 Sam 26:2).

C1. "Behold the day of which the LORD said unto thee, Behold, I will deliver thine enemy into thine hand" (1 Sam 24:4).

C2. *"God hath delivered thine enemy into thine hand this day"* (1 Sam 26:8).

D1. "And he said unto his men, The LORD forbid that I should do this thing unto my master, the LORD'S anointed, to stretch forth mine hand against him, seeing he is the anointed of the LORD" (1 Sam 24:6).

D2a. *"And David said to Abishai, Destroy him not: for who can stretch forth his hand against the LORD'S anointed, and be guiltless?"* (1 Sam 26:9).

D2b. *"The LORD forbid that I should stretch forth mine hand against the LORD'S anointed"* (1 Sam 26:11).

E1. "Saul said, Is this thy voice, my son David?" (1 Sam 24:16).

E2. *"And Saul knew David's voice, and said, Is this thy voice, my son David?"* (1 Sam 26:17).

F1. "After whom is the king of Israel come out? after whom dost thou pursue? after a dead dog, after a flea" (1 Sam 24:14).

F2. *"For the king of Israel is come out to seek a flea, as when one doth hunt a partridge in the mountains"* (1 Sam 26:20).

G1. "And he said to David, Thou art more righteous than I: for thou hast rewarded me good, whereas I have rewarded thee evil" (1 Sam 24:17).

G2. *"Then said Saul, I have sinned: return, my son David: for I will no more do thee harm, because my soul was precious in thine eyes this day: behold, I have played the fool, and have erred exceedingly"* (1 Sam 26:21).

H1. "The LORD judge between me and thee, and the LORD avenge me of thee: but mine hand shall not be upon thee" (1 Sam 24:12).

H2. "*The LORD render to every man his righteousness and his faithfulness: for the LORD delivered thee into my hand to day, but I would not stretch forth mine hand against the LORD'S anointed*" (1 Sam 26:23).

As ought to be apparent from the above quotations from the two stories, the phrasing, expressions, and themes are so close and unfold in such parallel fashion that they are almost certainly drawing on a common source. From that common source, two different accounts have been fashioned, changing certain story elements to fit the desired theory.

The fact that neither account makes reference to the other suggests that the two stories are each variations on a single incident. After all, you would expect that if David spared Saul's life on a first occasion, then on the second occasion one would expect David to remind the king of what had happened previously. Yet, neither story exhibits any recollection of an earlier occasion where David spared Saul.

The two loyalty stories, therefore, reduce to one original story. Additionally, we have no independent witnesses as to the key piece of evidence in each story, David's refusal to take Saul's life when given the opportunity. Removing the fluff, the stories present sheer spin, no substance.

What Really Happened at Jeshimon

In both stories the action begins at Jeshimon, but the two diverge as to what happened there. The first story says that Saul trapped David and that only because Saul's troops were suddenly called elsewhere did David escape. The second story makes no mention of Saul's superior position or David's narrow escape. Taking the two together, and reading between the lines, one gets the impression that something significant happened at Jeshimon, but that the first author thought that keeping the events at

Jeshimon would undermine David's credibility, contradicting the noble stature intended by the biblical editors.

Recognizing that originally there was only one story about this event at Jeshimon, we need to remember that it was immediately after this event that David united with the Philistines. If we look more carefully at the public conversation in the second story, we begin to realize that this story is not so much about David's loyalty to Saul as it is about David rejecting Saul's offer of peace.

David told Saul that those who spoke negatively about him "have driven me out *this day* from abiding in the inheritance of the LORD, saying, Go, *serve other gods*" (1 Sam 26:19, emphasis added). In other words, David argued that opposition to him within Saul's court has forced him, this day, to join up with the Philistines. The speech is intended to justify his break from Saul, not demonstrate his loyalty to Saul.

The king responds "I have sinned: return, my son David: for I will no more do thee harm" (1 Sam 26:21). And then adds, "Blessed be thou, my son David: thou shalt both do great things, and also shalt still prevail" (1 Sam 26:29). In other words, Saul told David, in substance, *don't join the Philistines. Let's bury the hatchet and have peace between us. You still have a great future ahead of you, and you might become king yet.* (David had been betrothed to Saul's daughter, making him a potential heir.)

Saul did not go to Jeshimon to make war with David, but to head off an alliance with the Philistines. David was at this time king of Judah, and he may have already arranged a treaty with Israel's enemy. The two sides met to see if they could negotiate a peaceful settlement. Saul may have even promised to make David his heir on condition that he abandon the kingship over Judah. While David no doubt reiterated his loyalty to Saul and Israel, he would have resisted giving up his throne. So, talks broke off. David remained a Philistine vassal, and Saul abandoned his efforts to topple his enemy.

If my theory about this is correct, it would account for the origin of the loyalty stories and Saul's kindly disposition towards David and predictions of David's becoming king over Israel. These behaviors were elements of negotiating positions, and partisans could twist them. Still,

David's withdrawal and alliance with the Philistines would have left a bitter taste in the mouths of Israelites.

The Visitation of Samuel

The final strand in David's defensive skein appears in the strange story of Saul's visit to the witch of Endor to summon forth the spirit of the deceased Samuel. The action takes place on the night before the great battle between the Philistines and Israel. According to the biblical story, in 1 Sam 28:3–25, Saul had become frightened by the sight of the Philistine army and sought the Lord's advice. But receiving no answer, neither by "dream, nor by Urim [lots], nor by prophets," he set out to consult a necromancer, the witch at Endor (1 Sam 28:6–7).

At Saul's direction the witch summoned forth the spirit of Samuel and Saul made inquiry of the ghost (1 Sam 28:14). Samuel replied:

> Wherefore then dost thou ask of me, seeing the LORD is departed from thee, and is become thine enemy? And the LORD hath done to him, as he spake by me: for the LORD hath rent the kingdom out of thine hand, and given it to thy neighbour, even to David: Because thou obeyedst not the voice of the LORD, nor executedst his fierce wrath upon Amalek, therefore hath the LORD done this thing unto thee this day. Moreover the LORD will also deliver Israel with thee into the hand of the Philistines: and to morrow shalt thou and thy sons be with me: the LORD also shall deliver the host of Israel into the hand of the Philistines (1 Sam 28:15–19).

In substance, through Samuel's ghost, the biblical editors remind us that God had taken the kingdom away from Saul and given it to his neighbor, David. In addition, Samuel predicted that the Philistines would defeat Israel, and that Saul and his sons would die on the next day. Therefore, Saul's death was God's will.

The story presents a number of interesting problems. Perhaps the most intriguing is the somewhat cryptic scenario that interprets a Philistine victory over Israel as the way in which God intends to hand over Saul's kingdom to David. This would certainly seem to be a disguised recognition that David joined with the Philistines in order to get their help in overthrowing Saul and becoming king.

Samuel's recounting of Saul's earlier sin in failing to kill off all the Amalekites suggests another disguised reference to Saul's death. A number of scholars have suggested that the verses about Saul's sin were either a very late addition to the original story, in which case Samuel may not have been the spirit that Saul consulted, or the recitation foreshadowed David's battle with the Amalekite's in Ziklag. But it seems to me that the most obvious connection is to the Amalekite who killed Saul. To wit, if Saul had carried through on God's command to destroy all the Amalekites, then this wandering Amalekite wouldn't have been around to slay Saul in the end.

If my interpretation is correct, it indicates that the association of Saul's death with an Amalekite slayer had wide circulation among the Israelites, and Saul's suicide story constituted a diversionary cover-up.

Another troubling issue concerns the chronology of events. The story of Samuel's ghost not only interrupts the smooth flow of the surrounding story passages, it presents some geographical inconsistencies. This suggests that it was added late in the game for propaganda purposes.

The bible places the story in sequence right after David had promised Achish that he would join the Philistine battle against Israel and Achish appointed David as his personal bodyguard. Then comes the story of Saul and Samuel's ghost. Immediately after we have the story about David being expelled by the Philistines and his return home to Ziklag, where he goes to retrieve his wives and family from the Amalekites. Then the bible takes us to the battle preparations between Israel and the Philistines.

The geographical inconsistency is this: at the beginning of the Samuel story, the Philistines are situated in Shunem, preparing to attack the next day. The Israelites are south of them in Gilboa. The witch is north of Shunem in Endor, which would require Saul to cross behind enemy lines to consult with her, which seems highly improbable. And finally, when the battle story resumes and David is expelled from the Philistine camp, the Philistines are camped at Aphek, which is well south of Shunem and Gilboa, close to the Philistine homeland.

The biblical sequence of events implies that the Philistines marched far up to the north to Shunem to battle the Israelites in nearby Gilboa, then, during the night, went all the way back to their home territory by Aphek, and then the next morning returned all the way back up to the north to fight at Mount Gilboa. This makes no chronological or logistical sense.

If the battle site locations can be trusted, at the very least one should expect that the Philistines started at Aphek and marched north to Shunem, where they confronted the Israelites at Gilboa. Therefore, David either departed from the Philistines at Aphek and went south, or he marched north with them to Shunem before he was expelled. This latter alternative recalls the claim in 1 Chr 12:19–20, which tells us that as David marched with the Philistines in this final battle against Saul, he was joined by members of the tribe of Manasseh, and when he returned to Ziklag, he attracted more people from Manasseh, who then helped him against the bandits around David's home territory. The significance of this information is that in order to get from Aphek to Shunem one must march almost exclusively through Manasseh, and David is specifically associated with gathering people just from Manasseh in both his march forward and his march back.

Taking the Chronicles information together with the distorted flow of events created by the insertion of the Samuel's ghost story suggests that David actually marched north with the Philistines before they asked him to leave, and the editors of the Book of Samuel inserted the ghost story where they did precisely to confuse the scenario and cover up David's actions.

Assessing the Murder Charge

We are now in a position to evaluate the charge that David had Saul assassinated.

The evidence against David can be summarized as follows:

1. In open revolt against Saul, David had become king of Judah.
2. On several occasions the biblical editors assert that Saul's reign was invalid and David was his rightful replacement.

3. David marched with the Philistines against Israel and protested his expulsion from the Philistine army.

4. After his expulsion from the Philistine army, he did not stay behind and fight for Israel.

5. Samuel the priest said that God wanted Saul and his sons to be killed.

6. Saul did not die at the hand of a Philistine.

7. The story of Saul's suicide had no witnesses and must be rejected as evidence.

8. David's defenders acknowledge that an Amalekite claimed to have killed Saul.

9. Amalekites were bitter enemies of Israel.

10. David had no compunctions against working with Israel's enemies, having been allied with Moabites, Ammonites, and Philistines.

11. David's defenders acknowledge that immediately after Saul's death the Amalekite brought the king's crown and bracelet to David.

12. It makes no logical sense for an Amalekite, based in south Jordan, to accidentally be way up north by Mount Gilboa.

13. It makes no logical sense for the Amalekite to bring David the crown unless he had some connection with David, especially if a reward were at issue, since the Israelite camp would have been much closer and quicker to reach.

14. David killed the Amalekite, the only witness who could explain why the Amalekite happened to be far from his normal habitat and why he chose to bring the crown from Israel to Judah.

15. If the Amalekite mistakenly brought the crown to David, why didn't David return it to Saul's family?

16. The argument that David had just finished extracting vengeance against the Amalekites, fighting and killing them as punishment for kidnapping his family, and, therefore, wouldn't have been involved in any shady dealings with them, is contradicted by the Book of Chronicles, which omits the entire kidnapping episode, as well as the taking of vengeance against the Amalekites, and simply says that David and his men fought against local bandits.

17. The argument that David had an alibi for the time of Saul's death because he was far away in Ziklag has no validity if he hired assassins to kill the king.

18. The two loyalty stories claiming that David spared Saul's life are in actuality variations of only one story.

19. In neither loyalty story do we have a credible or independent witness to David's charity towards Saul.

In summary, then, we can say that although we have no smoking gun (or blood-dripping sword) inexorably linking David to Saul's death, we do have a very strong circumstantial case against him. The most compelling evidence consists of Saul's crown being brought to David's court over a long distance by an individual who claims to have slain the king.

On the other hand, none of David's defenses seem valid, and the insincerities of the rebuttal evidence suggest guilty behavior. As to his chief defense, that he had twice spared Saul's life when he had the opportunity to take it, the only witnesses are his close friends. His alibi not only doesn't absolve him of guilt to the charge that he hired an Amalekite assassin, his claim of hostility towards the Amalekites falls apart on further examination. Finally, the claim that God wanted Saul dead doesn't mean that David didn't act as God's servant in the matter.

The case against David is strong and compelling. Still, at least under the American system of justice, the accused doesn't have to prove he's innocent. The prosecution must prove beyond a reasonable doubt that the defendant is guilty. A good lawyer might be able to squeeze out a "not guilty" verdict, but not without a lot of hard work and fancy word play. And we must remember that an acquittal doesn't mean the individual is innocent or that jurors thought the person innocent, only that the prosecution failed to meet a higher degree of proof than we usually use in our own day to day judgments about the behavior of others.

CHAPTER 7

Civil War

Now there was long war between the House of Saul
and the House of David: but David waxed stronger and stronger,
and the House of Saul waxed weaker and weaker. 2 SAM 3:1

The death of Saul and his son Jonathan, two of Israel's greatest heroes, had a devastating effect on the Israelite kingdom. Achish, the Philistine king of Gath, captured much of the western front and drove Israel's army east toward the Jordan. In the south, David, Achish's vassal, consolidated control over Judah and points south. A few years earlier, David married the daughter of the king of Geshur, an independent kingdom in the northern territories in the Golan Heights just east of the Sea of Galilee, which provided a modest pressure on Israel's northern frontier. And in the Transjordan, David had solid relations with the Ammonites and probably with the Moabites, two major aggressive enemies of the House of Saul.

2 Samuel 2:9 suggests that after Saul's death the kingdom of Israel consisted of the two and a half tribes in the Transjordan (Reuben, Gad, and half of Manasseh, collectively known as Gilead), Ephraim and Benjamin (the two central tribes north of Judah), Asher on the northwest coast, and a piece of the northern tip of Manasseh on the Israel side of the Jordan River (leaving the bulk of western Manasseh in Philistines hands). Not only did Israel lose major ground to enemies, war with David broke out over the issue of succession to Israel's throne.

According to 1 Sam 14:49, Saul had three sons, Jonathan, Ishui, and Melchishua. Later, in 1 Sam 31:2, describing the Philistine battle that claimed Saul's life, we are told that the Philistines killed Saul's sons, and

the bible lists their names as Jonathan, Abinadab, and Melchishua, substituting Abinadab for Ishui. These two passages imply that Saul actually
had four sons, Jonathan, Ishui, Melchishua, and Abinadab, but only three
of them died in the Philistine battle, leaving Ishui as Saul's heir.

Consistent with this interpretation, the Book of Samuel tells us that
a son of Saul named Ishbosheth claimed the kingship and that Saul's
cousin Abner, general of the Israelite army, brought Ishbosheth to Mahanaim to rule over Israel. Ishui and Ishbosheth appear to be the same person, and both names appear to be alterations of the name Eshbaal, the
latter being the name used for Saul's fourth son in Chronicles. The *baal*
element of the name corresponds to the name of one of the chief Canaanite deities, and the term means "Lord." At the time of the United Monarchy and earlier Israelites may have used *baal* as a title for Jahweh. The later
Deuteronomistic editors, however, associated that title with the Canaanite "baal" and often altered earlier biblical names with that element. One
of their ways of doing so was to substitute the Hebrew word *bosheth*,
meaning "shame" as a substitute for "baal." (See for example the name of
Jonathan's son, given as Mephibosheth in 2 Sam 4:4 and as Meribbaal in
1 Chr 8:34 and 1 Chr 9:40.)

The withdrawal of Abner and Eshbaal (i.e. Ishbosheth) to Maha-
naim reinforces the earlier biblical claim that the Philistines drove the
Israelite army east after Saul died. Mahanaim is located on the eastern
side of the Jordan River, in the Jordanian portion of the territory of
Manasseh, Israel's largest tribal territory. The war between David and
Eshbaal lasted about two years, ending with the assassinations of both
Abner and Eshbaal.

Although Chronicles lists all four sons of Saul (1 Chr 8:33), it completely omits any mention of the civil war or Eshbaal's claim to the throne.
This omission coincides with the Chronicles approach of eliminating
anything that cast doubt on David's legitimacy.

David, of course, did not accept Eshbaal's elevation to the throne. He
himself claimed the right of succession, relying on Samuel's anointing of
him as king over Israel and Samuel's denial of succession rights to Saul's

children. In addition, David had a somewhat tenuous legal claim to the
kingship based on his earlier betrothal to Saul's daughter Michal, although the marriage never took place and she had taken a different husband. Throughout the conflict David continued to press his legal claim to
Michal, and Eshbaal's reaction to the demand had an important effect on
the outcome of the conflict. We will discuss the matter shortly. Nevertheless, Abner and Eshbaal held out and resisted David's advances, especially
as it was believed that David had Saul murdered and perhaps had also
killed Saul's son Jonathan, the heir apparent.

THE BATTLE AT GIBEON

The first major confrontation between the House of Saul and the House
of David occurred at Gibeon, in a somewhat strange scene that puzzles
scholars. According to 2 Samuel 2, where the story appears, Abner brought
some troops to Gibeon, and Joab, by coincidence or otherwise (we aren't
told), also arrived there with some troops. Each group sat on opposite
sides of a large pool, a natural water formation.

Abner then suggested that there be some sort of martial games between the opposing sides. Each army fielded twelve men and the two
teams simultaneously managed to kill each other off. A large-scale battle
followed the deaths and we are summarily informed that David's army
defeated Abner's, and the Israelites fled. Asahel, brother of Joab and
Abishai, chased after Abner, but his intended victim kept urging Joab's
brother to cease and turn away:

> Turn thee aside from following me: wherefore should I smite thee to
> the ground? how then should I hold up my face to Joab thy brother?
> (2 Sam 2:21).

But Asahel wouldn't yield, and Abner had no recourse but to defend himself and slay the pursuing warrior. When Joab learned what
happened, he and Abishai chased after the Israelite general. The pursuit

continued until hunter and quarry found themselves close upon a Benjaminite army under Abner's command. Abner called out to his pursuers and urged an end to the fighting. Joab, recognizing his tactical disadvantage, withdrew.

The most important part of this story concerns the death of Asahel. The biblical author intended that the account of Abner taking Asahel's life establish an alibi for David with regard to Joab's subsequent execution of Abner in the middle of negotiations between the Israelite general and David. By making Abner responsible for the death of Joab's brother, David could be disassociated from Joab's rash, angry act of vengeance.

A major difficulty with that biblical argument arises from 1 Chr 27:7, which preserves part of an account of David's administrative arrangements after he became king of Israel. In that passage we learn:

> The fourth captain for the fourth month was *Asahel the brother of Joab*, and Zebadiah his son after him: and in his course were twenty and four thousand (emphasis added).

In other words, after David had become king, and after Joab slew Abner, David had appointed Asahel to supervise the fourth month of forced labor over the Israelites. It's unlikely that Asahel was a dead and buried corpse at the time of this appointment.

Since the Chronicler had omitted the entire civil war from his account of the rise of David, he had no problem pointing out that Asahel served as an official in David's administration. The editor of Samuel, anxious to defend David against charges that he put Joab up to the assassination, inserted a phony story about Abner killing Joab's brother, giving David's general an independent motive to slay David's chief enemy. The editor of Samuel then omitted the little trifle about Joab's deceased brother surviving his death to become a member of David's administrative team. This is one of several occasions where Joab gets blamed for committing crimes or other violent acts that benefit David.

Following the battle at Gibeon we learn that "there was long war between the House of Saul and the House of David: but David waxed stronger and stronger, and the House of Saul waxed weaker and weaker" (2 Sam 3:1).

After this we have no further account of military conflict between the two houses or between either house and the Philistines of Gath. The biblical author proceeds to rapidly wind up matters by relating the events that brought the war to an end and led to David being crowned king over all of Israel.

The ultimate collapse of the House of Saul occurred through two major events. First came the assassination of Abner, then the assassination of Eshbaal. At no time during this internecine strife do we have any indication that anyone drove the Philistines out of Israel's central and western territories.

THE MURDER OF ABNER

According to the biblical account, Eshbaal accused Abner of trying to replace him on the throne by sleeping with Saul's concubine (2 Sam 3:7). (The biblical account of David has several instances in which sleeping with the king's concubine constitute a claim to the throne. See, for example, the stories of Absalom and Adonijah discussed in later chapters. The first-century Jewish historian Josephus records an Egyptian account about a pharaoh going off to war and instructing his brother not to sleep with his concubines or wear the crown. The brother did sleep with the concubines and triggered a civil war. This suggests that in the ancient Near East, sleeping with a ruler's concubine was considered a legitimate claim to the throne.) Abner rejected the charges, pointing out that he was responsible for saving Eshbaal's life (2 Sam 3:8). The accusations riled Abner, who took this as a threat to his position in the court. Consequently, according to the biblical account, he determined that he should make a deal with David to deliver Israel to Eshbaal's rival (2 Sam3:12).

Although it appears that Abner did visit David's court, the idea that he did so to deliver Israel to David has little plausibility. Abner headed the military and was the power behind the throne. In order to turn Israel over to David he would have to either convince the elders of Israel to do so, even though Eshbaal was on the throne, or he would have to lead a military coup designed to surrender to David. If he had the power to do either, he had nothing to fear from Saul's son.

The true reason Abner went to meet with David appears to have been to settle the dispute over David's claim to Michal. The real purpose for David inviting Abner to the Judaean court seems to have been to set him up for assassination.

Immediately following Abner's encounter with Eshbaal over sleeping with Saul's concubine, 2 Sam 3:12 says he opened up a channel of communication with David, asking for an alliance. David, however, hesitated, saying that if Abner wanted to meet with him, he should first arrange to bring Michal to the meeting (2 Sam 3:13). David followed up the secret communication with a public demand on Eshbaal to return Michal to him, "which I espoused to me for an hundred foreskins of the Philistines" (2 Sam 3:14).

Eshbaal agreed to the demand and Michal was taken from her husband and sent to David (2 Sam 3:15). Abner began to talk to the various parties about making David king and following his negotiations with the elders of Israel and the Benjaminites, which allegedly resulted in an agreement to appoint David king, Abner went to David at Hebron for the purpose of sealing the agreement (2 Sam 3:20).

Consider the context for a moment. Eshbaal accused Abner of seeking the throne by sleeping with Saul's concubine, but agreed to send Saul's daughter to David without fear that Israel would interpret this as a claim to his throne. Further, we are asked to believe that Abner could talk to the elders of Israel and the leaders of Benjamin about making David king without Eshbaal becoming aware of his conduct or taking action to prevent this event from occurring. The entire scenario seems to make little logical sense. If Abner had all this power, what did he fear from Eshbaal, and what could David deliver to Abner to justify such a transfer of power?

The only reason for any such behavior by Abner would be fear that David would militarily overcome the Israelites, a real fear to be sure, but one that would not lead him to try to seize a doomed throne by sleeping with a king's concubine.

David had a good legal claim to Michal—he had paid Saul one hundred Philistine foreskins for her—but, given the implications of such a return, the only sensible scenario that would lead Eshbaal to give her back to his arch rival for control of the kingdom would have been one that incorporated a peace treaty between the two sides, the delivery of Michal to seal the deal.

After meeting with David, Abner announced that he would return to Israel to make arrangements for David to assume the throne (2 Sam 3:21). By coincidence, Joab just happened to be away from the court when Abner met with David. When Joab learned that his brother's killer (according to the Samuel account) had been allowed to leave freely, he became furious and said that Abner had only come to spy out David's situation and report back to Eshbaal (2 Sam 3:25).

Joab sent messengers after Abner to indicate that David wanted further discussions. When Abner returned, Joab took him aside and "smote him, there under the fifth rib" (2 Sam 3:37) and Abner died from the wound. When David learned what happened he publicly proclaimed his innocence and publicly cursed the House of Joab.

> Let it rest on the head of Joab, and on all his father's house; and let there not fail from the House of Joab one that hath an issue, or that is a leper, or that leaneth on a staff, or that falleth on the sword, or that lacketh bread (2 Sam 3:29).

He followed up the curse on Joab with a round of public mourning, demanding that Joab participate in the rituals (2 Sam 3:31). Finally, he buried Abner in Hebron (although no explanation is given for not returning the body to the House of Saul) (2 Sam 3:32). Still, despite all the calumny heaped upon Joab and the massive show of public mourning, David inflicted no punishment whatsoever. Joab retained his position as military commander, his power remained undiminished, and he continued to exercise considerable influence over David and David's court. (As Joab's literary role was to function as a scapegoat for many of David's alleged crimes, it's unlikely that the biblical editors would remove him from the scene.)

In summary, then, the pro-David editors of Samuel argued that David had no role in Abner's death because 1) Joab killed him out of revenge for his brother, and 2) Abner planned to make a deal with David to surrender Israel to Judah. To emphasize David's innocence the editors add, "For all the people and all Israel understood that day that it was not of the king to slay Abner the son of Ner" (2 Sam 3:37).

As noted above, the first argument is false. Abner didn't kill Joab's brother. The Samuel editor invented the story. This casts doubt on the credibility and integrity of the second argument, which is witnessed only by David and his closest advisors, not exactly the most trustworthy source.

Joab's execution of Abner, Israel's military commander and power behind the Israelite throne, eliminated one of the two chief stumbling blocks to David's efforts at taking over all of Israel. If it were true that all Israel knew that David was innocent of the murder, and had already authorized Abner to make a deal on their behalf, then it is likely that they would have delegated someone in Abner's place to continue the negotiations. Such was not the case. Eshbaal remained the last remaining barrier to David's elevation.

He, too, had to be eliminated by assassination.

THE MURDER OF ESHBAAL

In direct contrast to the earlier claim that all Israel knew that David was innocent in the murder of Abner, shortly thereafter we are told, "And when Saul's son heard that Abner was dead in Hebron, his hands were feeble, and all the Israelites were troubled" (2 Sam 4:1).

If David were innocent and the Israelites had authorized Abner to offer David the kingship, why were they all so troubled? As to Eshbaal, one can understand. He had no intention of voluntarily giving up the throne, and the loss of his general undermined his military defense. As to the rest of Israel, the elders could have simply moved forward to work out a deal. But they didn't put forth any proposal or send any emissaries. Obviously, they didn't quite trust David or believe him.

Although the Book of Samuel acknowledges that Eshbaal was assassinated, the account is problematic. The story begins with an introduction to the two assassins.

> And Saul's son had two men that were captains of bands: the name of the one was Baanah, and the name of the other Rechab, the sons of Rimmon a Beerothite, of the children of Benjamin: (for Beeroth also was reckoned to Benjamin: And the Beerothites fled to Gittaim, and were sojourners there until this day) (2 Sam 4:2–3).

We need to put this information in political context. The Beerothites were not Israelites. They were part of a four-city coalition, together with Gibeon, Kiriath-Jearim, and Chephirah, and tradition held that these territories were assigned to Benjamin as a subservient class, allegedly because of events that happened during the time of Joshua, when the inhabitants tricked Joshua into signing a peace treaty (Josh 9:22–27, 18:25–28, 2 Sam 4:2). Gibeon was the chief city in this coalition and according to the distribution of territories in the Book of Joshua, Gibeon together with Hebron, David's capitol, were assigned to the Aaronite priesthood (Josh 21:13, 17). One of the other city members, Kiriath-Jearim, housed the Ark of the Covenant while Saul was on the throne and upsetting the priests by failing to consult that holy icon. This suggests some political connections between David and some of the Gibeonite priests. In fact, the biblical editors tell us in 2 Sam 21:1 that the Gibeonites hated Saul over some earlier previously unmentioned dispute in which Saul killed several people in that city.

One more unusual fact in the assassins' résumé states that the Beerothites dwelled in Gittaim, a name meaning land of Gath, which is the Philistine city with which David had allied himself.

On the other hand, these two assassins were officers in Eshbaal's army, which suggests that they may have demonstrated some reasonable degree of loyalty to the House of Saul. If so, then why would they kill their king unless either they were paid off to do so or someone planted the idea that they would be rewarded for their act of regicide?

Therefore, as we study this account of Eshbaal's assassination, we must at the least become suspicious of a possible connection between David and the two assassins, as all the information implicit in their description points to either a secret support for King David over the House of Saul or bribery.

After introducing the people who will kill Eshbaal, the biblical editors insert a strange passage, which seems to disrupt the flow and which many scholars consider out of place:

> And Jonathan, Saul's son, had a son that was lame of his feet. He was five years old when the tidings came of Saul and Jonathan out of Jezreel, and his nurse took him up, and fled: and it came to pass, as she made haste to flee, that he fell, and became lame. And his name was Mephibosheth (2 Sam 4:4).

The passage states that after learning of Saul's death, the nurse of Jonathan's five-year-old son took the child up and fled and in her haste she dropped him, causing him to become lame in the leg. The immediate question is this: why does this passage appear here instead of in some more obvious context, such as the aftermath of Saul's death some two years earlier? And why does it appear just before the passage in which the two Beerothites kill Eshbaal? I'd like to suggest here that the passage is not a clumsy intrusion, but a reworked account of what happened in Eshbaal's palace during the assassination.

According to the story, the two Beerothites found Eshbaal asleep, smote him in the traditional fifth rib location, and chopped off his head, which they brought to David at Hebron (2 Sam 4:6–8). Now clearly the Beerothites were taking action designed to make David king. Killing Saul's son would not have been sufficient, though. Jonathan also had a son, and he would have been the direct heir after Eshbaal's death. If David were to be king, Mephibosheth would also have to be killed.

I suggest, therefore, that the two assassins also tried to kill Jonathan's son, and either wounded him in the attempt, or the child's nurse dropped him when she fled from the Beerothites, rather than fleeing with him after Saul's death. The editors, terribly worried about allegations that David murdered Saul and perhaps Jonathan too, would have feared that any attempt to kill Jonathan's son would make David look like a sponsor of this assassination attempt. Consequently, they rewrote the passage to change the time frame of the nurse's flight in order to cover up the attack on Mephibosheth. We will look at this child's fate in a later chapter, in connection with the Gibeonites.

Arriving at David's court, the two assassins said, "Behold the head of Ishbosheth the son of Saul thine enemy, which sought thy life; and the LORD hath avenged my lord the king this day of Saul, and of his seed" (2 Sam 4:8). As with the Amalekite, David immediately executed the two witnesses to the rival sovereign's death before they could make any further statements.

Eshbaal's head was tossed into the same sepulcher that housed Abner (2 Sam 4:12). As with Abner, we are given no explanation as to why the king would keep the remains in Hebron instead of returning them to the House of Saul.

While David's hand appears more isolated in the death of Eshbaal than it does with regard to Saul and Abner, the circumstances are certainly suspicious. The killers have connections to the territory of Gath, belong to a coalition of cities that have a strong hatred of Saul, and, more importantly, appear to have a close relationship to the religious priesthood that supported David.

On the other hand, it is not unlikely that people having an enmity towards the House of Saul and an affinity towards David might take the opportunity to act independently and strike down Saul's son when they had the chance. Still, when they brought Eshbaal's head to David, they didn't announce their opposition to the House of Saul as the reason. Instead they declared the act to be the Lord's vengeance, a religious motivation, suggesting at the least that if David wasn't directly responsible then his Shilohite allies may have had a hand in the outcome.

The murder of Eshbaal turned the tide in David's favor. The Israelite tribes sent representatives to Hebron to ask David to become king. Whether this was an act of enthusiastic support or surrender to the inevitable is difficult to say. But at least the Israelites might think at the time that some degree of peace might prevail. David had a close relationship with the Philistines that took over part of central Israel and a good relationship with many of Israel's enemies. If peace was Israel's primary concern, however, they made a strategic mistake in allying themselves with their new king.

CHAPTER 8

Kill the Lame and the Blind: The Taking of Jerusalem

And David said on that day, Whosoever getteth up to the gutter, and smiteth the Jebusites, and the lame and the blind, that are hated of David's soul, he shall be chief and captain. 2 SAM 5:8

*U*pon becoming king over Israel and Judah, David moved his capitol from Hebron to Jerusalem. Both Samuel and Chronicles briefly describe the military capture of that city from the Jebusites, a non-Israelite people usually included in the bible among a list of Canaanite nations. Some questions may be raised as to whether David actually conquered the city, simply inherited it through his kingship, or more likely bought the territory from a Jebusite who owned the land. Another question of interest concerns the sudden appearance of a previously unmentioned political faction. Its leaders were Zadok, who David appointed as one of two chief priests (the other being the Shilohite Abiathar), and Nathan, an influential prophet in David's court who played a key role in making Solomon the successor to David. Zadok's heirs became the dominant line of priests in Judah's history, giving shape to many Jewish traditions.

The Capture of Jerusalem

The story of David's taking of Jerusalem appears in 2 Sam 5:6–10. A sanitized version appears in 1 Chr 11:4–9. Both accounts are short. Here is the version from 2 Samuel.

> And the king and his men went to Jerusalem unto the Jebusites, the inhabitants of the land: which spake unto David, saying, Except thou take away the blind and the lame, thou shalt not come in hither: thinking, David cannot come in hither. Nevertheless David took the strong hold of Zion: the same is the city of David. And David said on that day, *Whosoever getteth up to the gutter, and smiteth the Jebusites, and the lame and the blind, that are hated of David's soul, he shall be chief and captain. Wherefore they said, The blind and the lame shall not come into the house.* So David dwelt in the fort, and called it the city of David. And David built round about from Millo and inward. And David went on, and grew great, and the LORD God of hosts was with him (emphasis added).

The horrific reference to David hating the blind and the lame and wanting them dead so shocked the editors of Samuel that they attempted to soften the impact by inserting immediately thereafter the phrase "Wherefore they said, The blind and the lame shall not come into the house." The meaning of this verse is that the blind and lame (and other physically injured individuals) could not enter into the Temple, and this territory was to become the home of the Temple. Therefore, in order to sanctify the city for the future temple, the blind and lame had to be removed.

Here is the Chronicles account of the same incident. You can see how closely this modified version follows the Samuel version.

> And David and all Israel went to Jerusalem, which is Jebus; where the Jebusites were, the inhabitants of the land. And the inhabitants of Jebus said to David, Thou shalt not come hither. Nevertheless David took the castle of Zion, which is the city of David. And David said, Whosoever smiteth the Jebusites first shall be chief and captain. So Joab the son of Zeruiah went first up, and was chief. And David dwelt in the castle; therefore they called it the city of David. And he built the city round about, even from

Millo round about: and Joab repaired the rest of the city. So David waxed greater and greater: for the LORD of hosts was with him.

The Chronicler, ever watchful over David's image, went further than the Samuel editor and struck out all the offensive references to the lame and blind. He also added some additional information. Where the Samuel account promises the chieftainship over the army to whoever gets into the city first, the Chronicler tells us that the person who earned that honor was Joab.

To this day biblical scholars continue to struggle over some way to interpret this account in a manner that does less dishonor to David's reputation, but despite a variety of tentative explanations, none has garnered any widespread acceptance.

Problems with the Conquest Story

The history and archaeology of Jerusalem, when coupled with various biblical passages, raises a number of questions as to whether David actually took possession of Jerusalem in military fashion. Implicit in this idea is that the attack described in the bible may originally have been on some city other than Jerusalem, and that one of the early editors substituted the name of Jerusalem for the city originally conquered.

Our inquiry begins with the area now identified as the City of David. That site, according to archaeologists familiar with the Jerusalem materials, has been inhabited since about 3500 BCE, and, if the biblical account can be trusted, until the time of David Israelites did not live there. The area itself consumed about twelve acres of space, and at about the time of David it expanded to about fifteen acres. Its population at the time is unlikely to have been more than about a thousand people, something on the order of about one to two hundred families. (For the archaeological history of Jerusalem see the summary in the Anchor Bible Dictionary, s.v. "Jerusalem".)

The earliest evidence for the name "Jerusalem" comes from about 1900 BCE, in some Egyptian texts that mention a city named "Rusalimmum." In the fourteenth century BCE, a series of tablets written in the Akkadian language (a widely used Semitic language at the time) and sent to Pharaoh Akhenaten, records a letter from the besieged king of "Urusalim" requesting the Egyptian king's help. Prior to the time of David, that is the full epigraphic record. None of these texts specifically describe where this city is located, other than in Canaan, and it is still speculation that these names refer to the biblical city of Jerusalem. However, after the time of David, Assyrian texts in the eighth century BCE also use the name "Ursalimmu" or variants of that name to refer specifically to biblical Jerusalem, suggesting that at least the fourteenth-century Egyptian texts probably refer to the same city.

As most biblical scholars acknowledge, this strongly indicates that the name Jerusalem goes back to at least the fourteenth century BCE. But, for some reason, the bible on several occasions says the name of the city in the time of David and earlier was Jebus or Jebusi (see, for example, 1 Chr 11:4), which gave its name to the Jebusites, one of the names in a litany of Canaanite peoples mentioned several times in the early portions of the bible. However, there is no extra-biblical record for a city named Jebus, and no extra-biblical record identifying the Jebusites.

It is only because the bible equates Jebus with Jerusalem that we describe pre-Israelite Jerusalem as a Jebusite city. But we don't know that this is the case, and we have no extra-biblical evidence that Jebus and Jerusalem were actually the same city. Many scholars argue that they are not. If the city captured by David was Jebus, then the account above may originally have been about Jebus rather than Jerusalem.

A second difficulty with the Jerusalem conquest account is ambiguity in the story itself. Although the story says that David went "to Jerusalem unto the Jebusites," it then says that the place he captured was known as "the strong hold of Zion," not Jebus or Jerusalem. It is only later that Zion becomes equated with Jerusalem. In fact, over time, the location and association of Zion with respect to Jerusalem has shifted about. Biblical scholars do not know the origin of the name Zion and that name appears in the bible for the first time in this account. So, it is possible that the Jebusite city conquered by David was Zion and not Jerusalem. When David moved into Jerusalem and named the city that then existed as the City of David, the biblical editors may have shifted the name of the fortress at Zion to the City of David.

Some other biblical passages present further difficulties with the idea of a military conquest of Jerusalem. Consider the two following verses, both of which describe a portion of the story concerning Israel's entry into Canaan after the Exodus but which were each written long after the event.

> And the children of Benjamin did not drive out the Jebusites that inhab-ited Jerusalem; but the Jebusites dwell with the children of Benjamin in Jerusalem unto this day (Judg 1:21).
> As for the Jebusites the inhabitants of Jerusalem, the children of Judah could not drive them out: but the Jebusites dwell with the children of Ju-dah at Jerusalem unto this day (Josh 15:63).

Obviously the author of each passage wrote what was believed to be an accurate description of Jerusalem in the author's time. The phrase "unto this day" clearly indicates that the author is writing long after the events under discussion. We just don't know when "unto this day" occurred. Still, the two verses in context suggest a relative time frame. Jerusalem stands along the Judah-Benjamin border, just within the Benjaminite boundar-ies. Both verses contemplate an inability to capture Jerusalem and depict Jebusites living in the city peacefully with their neighbors, Benjamin or Judah. These passages suggest the following scenario:

In the time of Saul and David, the area of Jerusalem now known as the City of David, was a small walled city that peacefully housed Jebus-ites, Benjaminites, and Judahites all at the same time. It was on top of a high hill and difficult to reach. When David became king, he recognized the strategic value of placing his administrative center in this fortified lo-cation. As the city was of mixed population, many of whom were his subjects, if not all of them, he would not have faced any military resis-tance to his entrance therein.

Moreover, a city with that small of a population would probably have had no more than a dozen or two trained soldiers to defend it even if it wanted to resist. Such a miniscule force could not defend itself against several hundred well-trained soldiers under David's command. If there were a military challenge, surrender was the only feasible option.

Still, the two passages that talk about the Israelites and Jebusites living together in Jerusalem were written long after David came to power, perhaps a century or two later, and show that the earlier tradition was that no military conquest of Jerusalem occurred.

Another possible interpretation suggested by these two passages is that Jerusalem had a combined Jebusite and Benjaminite population during Saul's reign, and when David became king over Israel he expelled the Benjaminites and took their property for himself and his court. (We'll explore the relationship between David and the Benjaminites more closely in chapter 12.)

As a last note on this point, we will learn in chapter 13 that David actually purchased a substantial piece of property in Jerusalem from a Jebusite king or merchant in that city, which seems inconsistent with the claim that David's army forced its way into the city, killed off the Jebusites, and seized the territory for its own purposes.

The Mysterious Jerusalem Party

After David made Jerusalem his capitol, two men appeared on the scene who exercised extraordinary influence over David. The first was Zadok, whom David appointed as co-chief priest of Israel alongside of Abiathar, and the other was Nathan, a prophet who had no fear of David, guided him in political and religious affairs, and played a key role in making Solomon the successor to David. This Nathan is almost certainly the title character of the Book of Nathan the Prophet, cited in Chronicles as a source of information about the reigns of David and Solomon. Whether this Nathan actually wrote the book or someone else wrote it long after we have no way of knowing because we have no extant copy of the work.

The appointment of Zadok as a second chief priest seems particularly shocking. At no time during the prior accounts of David's history does this man appear. The loyal priest at David's side was Abiathar. Yet, out of the blue, David appointed Zadok a chief priest, Abiathar's equal.

There have been many theories about Zadok's identity. One popular school of thought holds that he was the chief priest of Jerusalem, and when David made that city his capitol he elevated Zadok to that high position. This argument rests on 1) the fact that he doesn't appear until after Jerusalem becomes David's capitol and 2) the similarity of his name to some earlier figures in the bible who have the same name and may be connected to Jerusalem. Let's look at the second argument first.

According to the Book of Joshua, the king of Jerusalem in the time of Joshua had the name Adoni-zedek, meaning Lord Zedek (Josh 10:1). The names Zedek and Zadok are identically written in vowelless Hebrew. In addition, the Book of Genesis tells of a meeting between Abraham and Melchizedek (meaning "King Zedek"), priest-king of Salem who worshipped El Elyon, a variant on the name of the Israelite god (Gen 14:18). Abraham agreed to pay him a tithe.

Salem may be a shortened form of Jerusalem. Psalms 76:2, for example, equates Salem with Zion as the residence of the biblical god. Many scholars believe that the name Jerusalem means "Foundation of Salem," Salem being a Canaanite deity. If this is the case, then the only two prior mentions of Jerusalem identify it with a ruler named Zadok/Zedek, and at least one of them is a priest-king worshipping the Hebrew god.

Putting the evidence in context, Zadok, appears on the scene only after Jerusalem becomes David's capitol, and the only two earlier mentions of Jerusalem's rulers (assuming Salem and Jerusalem are the same) both refer to men named Zadok, one of whom is a priest who worships the same god as Israel. For many, this is too much of a coincidence.

On the other hand, Abiathar served David loyally as chief priest. Jerusalem was a small economically poor city that had little to offer except that it was on an out-of-the-way hill. If David took it forcibly, he's not likely to appoint its religious leaders to be the chief religious spokesman for David's own kingdom, and if he took it peacefully, what incentive has he to give such a valuable position to someone who did nothing to help him achieve his kingship? And, in either case, why would he appoint a Jebusite priest to tell Israelites how to practice their religion?

There is a more logical explanation for Zadok's sudden appearance. Chronicles traces Zadok's roots to Aaron's son Eleazar and Abiathar's roots to Aaron's other son Ithamar. The priesthood in Israel, according to the biblical history, descended from the Levite tribe through Moses and Aaron, but the Aaronites were given the more important supervisory roles. Eleazar, as the older of the Aaron's two sons, inherited his father's primary position, giving the Eleazarite branch of the family primacy in the priesthood. Ithamar's family also had an important role, but a lesser one, supervising the lesser Levite clans.

Yet, the Shiloh priesthood that dominated Israel in the time of Saul traced its descent to Ithamar. The Ithamarite priest Samuel backed David against Saul. The Eleazarites were a rival priesthood. Hebron, where David first served as king over Judah, was allegedly assigned to the Aaronites as a city of refuge (while the Calebites were given all the suburbs and surrounding areas) during the Canaanite conquest. Shiloh, where the Ithamarites held sway, was not an Aaronite city.

The earlier division of authority between Eleazarites and Ithamarites was a biblical fiction written to reflect later reality, when the Eleazarites controlled the priesthood and ruled over their rival Aaronite factions. So, Shiloh became the religious center of Israel under a line of priests that claimed descent from Ithamar. Hebron, the Aaronite city, became the center of a separate line of priests who served as chief priests in Judah and claimed descent from Eleazar.

Zadok, then, would have been the chief priest of Judah, operating out of Hebron. Since David first served as king in Hebron, Zadok would have been his kingdoms' chief priest. However, when David became king over both nations, the Shilohites who backed him and came from the north, insisted that they be granted equal power with the Hebronite priests. David, in order to strike a balance, moved his capitol to the Judah-Israel border at Jerusalem and appointed a chief priest from each of the two kingdoms.

The biblical editors, having carefully attempted to conceal all reference to David's earlier independent kingship, made it appear that Zadok first emerged when David elevated him in Jerusalem and made him Abiathar's equal. In fact, it was Abiathar who was elevated to make him the equal of Zadok. That David had to balance Ithamarites and Eleazarites in his capitol can be seen from the fact that there were eight Ithamarite clans and sixteen Eleazarite clans serving in David's court (1 Chr 24:4). Rivalry between the two factions would have been inevitable.

As to Nathan, we have less to work with. He was a prophet, not a priest. Although he was a man of God, he didn't preside over religious rituals and procedures as the priests did. He, too, probably joined with David in Hebron. The existence of a Book of Nathan the Prophet suggests that he had a great reputation for wisdom in his time and that may be what brought him into David's court. The biblical accounts of Nathan's role emphasize his cleverness.

CHAPTER 9

Consolidation

Now Joab was over all the host of Israel: and Benaiah the son
of Jehoiada was over the Cherethites and over the Pelethites:
And Adoram was over the tribute [i.e., forced labor]:
and Jehoshaphat the son of Ahilud was recorder:
And Sheva was scribe: and Zadok and Abiathar were the priests:
And Ira also the Jairite was a chief ruler about David. 2 SAM 20:23–26

*I*srael wanted two basic services from its king, justice in the court and military defense. This Saul provided and, with the exception of his opposition to the corrupt Shiloh priesthood, there is little evidence that his ambition extended much beyond fulfilling those basic needs. David, on the other hand, sought to live the grand profligate life of a typical Near Eastern tyrant-fancy house, large public works programs with forced labor, heavy taxation, and an expansionist military policy. His lust for power so overwhelmed his concern for justice that his failure to provide fair judgment eventually led rebellious subjects, under the leadership of his son Absalom, to temporarily drive him from the throne and chase him out of Jerusalem.

OBSTACLES TO DAVID'S AMBITION

David's elevation to the kingship over Israel did not automatically endow him with the powers necessary to achieve his goals. The nation, even under Saul, remained highly decentralized. It was a relatively large territory, stretching from the Syrian border in the north to the Egyptian border in the south and occupying large swatches of land on both sides of the Jordan, with diffused centers of power. Clans and priests filled local power vacuums in the different regions, and they weren't prepared to easily surrender control.

1 Chronicles 21:5 indicates that Israel had well over a two to one advantage in military manpower over Judah. Since David could not rely on local authorities to provide the military forces necessary to divert the local resources to Jerusalem he was at a distinct military disadvantage in these early days.

The Benjaminites, on Judah's border, served as an ongoing source of anti-David animosity and as a constant irritant to the king. Their strategic location also created a military buffer between Jerusalem and the northern Israelite territories. On at least one occasion a Benjaminite leader named Sheba led a major military revolt that came close to overthrowing David's government. The biblical editors place this event late in David's reign, but I will argue from evidence in subsequent chapters that this occurred not long after David became king.

The elevation of the Judahite Zadok and the Shilohite Abiathar to the positions of chief priest also created problems for David. Giving Zadok equal power with Abiathar diluted the authority of Shiloh, undercutting the tacit understanding that in return for Shiloh's support David would take religious direction from the Shilohite camp. This created a situation of extreme political volatility within the Jerusalem court with two rival political-religious camps competing for power in the capitol.

Additionally, the betrayal of Saul by the Shilohites enabled rival priesthoods who remained loyal to Saul to become much more influential among the Israelites than they had been when Shiloh reigned supreme. This created a rival third religious force in the Israelite countryside and outside of the power center in the capitol.

Another factor undercutting David's authority was the presence of the Ark of the Covenant in the Benjaminite sphere of influence. This was Israel's holiest relic and a constant reminder that David was not to be an absolute ruler but merely a servant of God. The Ark provided a rallying point for those who challenged the legitimacy of David's reign and expanded monarchy.

DAVID'S RESPONSE

David took several steps to consolidate and expand his power, mostly through the use of brute force. In addition to his own personal army from his outlaw days and the Judahite army, he also created an elite military unit known as the Thirty, consisting of Israel's most famous and popular warriors, and placed Abishai at its head. He also hired two foreign mercenary armies, the Cherethites and Pelethites, to serve as royal bodyguards, defend Jerusalem, and supplement his military authority. He could count on, and did receive, military backup from the Philistine king at Gath. If the Israelites got too far out of line, David could even take advantage of his close friendships with the kings of Israel's various enemies and allow them to raid his adversaries.

Political Steps

As David's numerous sons matured he made them chiefs over the country, the equivalent of regional governors (2 Samuel 8:18). This practice would have enabled David to set up an alternative administrative structure to that which existed within the tribal territories, complete with its own bureaucracies.

Other tactics included placing Jonathan's son under house arrest and executing any potential rivals from the House of Saul. To raise funds for public works and military adventures, he confiscated property and instituted a system of forced labor. (2 Sam 20:23–26 indicates that a minister over forced labor played a key role in David's administration.) His military successes provided him with additional resources that enabled him to impose his will on the people.

Military Steps

The bible credits David with establishing a far-reaching empire, extending from the borders of Egypt to the Euphrates River, the western boundary of Mesopotamia. To the east of the Euphrates we find Assyria in the north and Babylonia in the south, the two territories approximately equivalent to modern Iraq. The bible, however, is our only source for claims that David successfully defeated his many foreign enemies and attained sovereignty over them. We lack any contemporaneous evidence from those neighbors, or even subsequent evidence, that such claims are true.

We have good precedent in the archaeological record to consider one-sided accounts of victory to be unreliable. The most famous is the account of Egyptian Pharaoh Ramesses II describing his victory over the Hittites at Kadesh. Luckily, we found the Hittite records of the same event, and at best Ramesses II had a stalemate, and the more likely proposition is that he suffered a defeat.

Some also see a substantial inconsistency between the biblical account of Egyptian Pharaoh Shishak's raid on Jerusalem and the Egyptian records depicted on a wall of the temple of Amen-Re at Karnak. The biblical account simply says that Shishak came against Jerusalem and Rehoboam, the king and Solomon's successor, and paid him off, after which the pharaoh departed (1 Ki 14:25–26, 2 Chr 12:1–9). The Egyptian records show a wide military campaign that destroyed 150 cities in Judah and Israel but omits Jerusalem from the itinerary.

Religious Steps

One of David's most successful reforms was to centralize religious authority in Jerusalem, requiring the Israelites to come to David's capitol several times a year to discharge their religious obligations. (Although the great Temple of Solomon had yet to be built, it is most likely that the pre-existing Jebusite population had previously erected either a temple or sacred altar in David's capitol that he could easily utilize for the purpose of religious centralization.)

The Book of Samuel tells us little about David's accomplishments with regard to religious practices, but Chronicles credits him with substantial contributions. Although 1 Chr 21:6 tells us that no count of the Levites (priests) took place, shortly thereafter we are told that there were 38,000 Levites over the age of thirty (1 Chr 23:3).

The Chronicler depicts a vast army of priests engaged in a host of activities, many of which were dedicated to the future building of the great Temple. According to 1 Chr 23, David delegated twenty-four thousand priests to prepare for building the Temple, and another eight thousand were appointed judges and officers in Israel. Another four thousand were assigned the task of praising the Lord with instruments and another four thousand were to serve as porters. The account goes on to describe the ways in which the Levites were subdivided and some of the rituals to be performed, along with a number of musical practices.

To what extent the Chronicler accurately portrays David's religious organization is hard to say, especially since such detail is missing from the earlier Book of Samuel. It is not unlikely that to a large degree the account reflects more closely what took place in the time of Judah's return from exile in the early fifth century BCE. Nevertheless, it seems clear that priestly affairs greatly dominated early biblical life and the priesthoods contained substantial numbers of people. That would explain why the Shilohites could continue to be such a strong religious and military opponent to Saul, and why David would have needed to bring the priesthoods under his control by appointing both Zadok and Abiathar as chief priests.

Perhaps the most important propagandistic victory, at least according to the bible, is that David brought the Ark of the Covenant to Jerusalem, making his capitol the seat of God. There is, however, some reason to suspect that David never managed to bring the Ark to Jerusalem, and that it remained for Solomon to complete the task. We will discuss this issue later in chapter 14.

CHRONOLOGICAL ISSUES

The bible presents the history of David's reign in pseudo-chronological order. According to 2 Samuel, David's earliest deeds in narrative order were the building up of Jerusalem and fortifying its walled defense (2 Sam 5:9); the building of a grand palace to serve as his home (2 Sam 5:11); defeating the Philistines in the territory of Benjamin, which presumably cleared a path for bringing the Ark to Jerusalem (2 Sam 5:17–25); bringing the Ark to Jerusalem (2 Sam 6); planning for a great temple to serve as a house for the Lord (2 Sam 7); the defeat of Israel's enemies and expansion of David's empire beyond the Israelite boundaries (2 Sam 8); and the redemption of his promise to Jonathan to do kindness to Jonathan's family (2 Sam 9). All of these events just listed occurred, according to the flow of the biblical narrative, prior to the infamous incident with Bathsheba, a chronology that we will challenge in later chapters.

Many scholars have recognized that various phrases and passages in David's history seem to be out of place or inconsistent with the surrounding text. Even the casual reader can find some chronological inconsistencies.

For example, 2 Sam 7:1 says, "And it came to pass, when the king sat in his house, and the LORD had given him rest round about from all his enemies..." Then, only a few verses later, David contends with wars breaking out on several fronts. And in another instance, 2 Sam 9:1 says, "And David said, Is there yet any that is left of the House of Saul, that I may show him kindness for Jonathan's sake?" The next several verses indicate that only one son of Jonathan still lived but later we learn that several other members of the House of Saul were still alive (2 Sam 21).

Scholars familiar with this problem have suggested that the biblical editors set forth David's story in topical order rather than chronological order. That is, the editors selected a series of stories that related to a particular theme and placed them together, and then gathered another set of stories related to a specific theme, and placed them together, and so on. This, of necessity, resulted in chronological overlap, with some passages seeming out of place in respect to other passages.

This may be the case. However, I suspect that the editors were motivated more by covering up some of David's repellant deeds by 1) placing the more positive material up front and 2) chopping up some of the more negative accounts and redistributing the pieces in an unconnected and non-chronological order. In some of the next few chapters we will look at David's deeds as king and attempt to impose some chronological order on the events surrounding his life. We will examine the biblical claims and then look more closely at what is the more likely account of what occurred.

CHAPTER 10

The Murder of Uriah

Wherefore hast thou despised the commandment of the LORD,
to do evil in his sight? thou hast killed Uriah the Hittite
with the sword, and hast taken his wife to be thy wife, and hast slain
him with the sword of the children of Ammon. Now therefore
the sword shall never depart from thine house; because thou hast
despised me, and hast taken the wife of Uriah the Hittite
to be thy wife. 2 SAM. 12:9–10

$\mathcal{T}$he infamous story of David and Bathsheba presents David as not only a morally corrupt and wicked man but as a failed king who needs to take guidance from a man of God. Not only did David carry on an illicit affair with the wife of one his most devoted and pious soldiers while her husband Uriah was away fighting the Ammonite enemy, he arranged to have her husband killed in combat in order to cover up his own role in getting Bathsheba pregnant. So notorious was the incident that even his own allies could not defend him.

So strongly did the charges resonate among the people of Israel and Judah in later years that the biblical obituary of King Abijam, Solomon's grandson who died about sixty years after David, included the following note.

> David did that which was right in the eyes of the LORD, and turned not aside from any thing that he commanded him all the days of his life, *save only in the matter of Uriah the Hittite* (1 Ki 15:5, emphasis added).

While the Deuteronomist editors retained the story of David and Bathsheba for reasons I set forth later, despite the negative impact on

David's image, the Chronicler, always concerned with protecting David's reputation as a righteous servant of God, omitted the entire scandal from his account of David's reign, acknowledging only that David had a wife named Bathsheba and that she bore him children, one of whom was Solomon.

Later in the story, we are told that God punished David's wrongdoing not only by taking the life of the child that was born out of this sinful union, but also by inflicting much violence upon the people that David loved. As one biblical author put it, in words attributed to Nathan the Prophet,

> Wherefore hast thou despised the commandment of the LORD, to do evil in his sight? thou hast killed Uriah the Hittite with the sword, and hast taken his wife to be thy wife, and hast slain him with the sword of the children of Ammon. Now therefore the sword shall never depart from thine house; because thou hast despised me, and hast taken the wife of Uriah the Hittite to be thy wife. Thus saith the LORD, *Behold, I will raise up evil against thee out of thine own house, and I will take thy wives before thine eyes, and give them unto thy neighbour, and he shall lie with thy wives in the sight of this sun.* For thou didst it secretly: but I will do this thing before all Israel, and before the sun. And David said unto Nathan, I have sinned against the LORD (2 Sam 12:9–13, emphasis added).

The biblical editors of the story of David and Bathsheba framed the tawdry tale with a series of military actions that highlight David's failure to lead his troops in a battle against the Ammonites. This, too, depicted David's failings as a king.

The king had to perform two main functions, provide for justice and lead the nation in war. The Bathsheba incident emphasized his lack of justice and his presence in Jerusalem instead of at the battlefield emphasized a failing in his role as military leader. In fact, after the entire Bathsheba affair had been exposed, Joab sent an angry message to David saying that if the king didn't drag himself out to the Ammonite front, Joab would capture the Ammonite capitol and name the city after himself.

The opening frame of the Bathsheba story begins with the death of Nahash, king of the Ammonites and, according to our analysis in earlier chapters, the father-in-law of David and grandfather of Joab and Abishai. Upon learning of the king's death David says, "I will show kindness unto Hanun the son of Nahash, as his father showed kindness unto me" (2 Sam 10:2). The statement clearly implies that David and Nahash had a friendly relationship until this point and that Ammon had yet to be subjugated to David's rule.

David sent a delegation to pay honor to Nahash's successor, but the Ammonite court complained that David's delegation was actually sent to spy out the territory in preparation for an attack (2 Sam 10:3). So the new Ammonite king humiliated the ambassadors, shaving the beards off one side of their face and cutting their clothing up the middle to the buttocks (2 Sam 10:4).

This, of course, offended David, and when the Ammonite king learned how angry the Israelite king was, he took protective steps (2 Sam 10:6). Although 2 Sam 8 previously reported that David defeated all the surrounding peoples, including the Ammonites and the principal Syrian kingdoms of Rehob and Zobah, this later episode shows an independent Ammon hiring as protectors the very same Syrian kingdoms supposedly defeated by David, casting serious doubt on the reliability of biblical accounts concerning David's military exploits.

In response, David sent Joab to lead the Israelite army against the recalcitrant monarch, but for some unexplained reason, David remained behind in Jerusalem. As noted above, this action constituted a serious breach of protocol. Not surprisingly, this faux pas led to the king's undoing.

One night, David strolled across his roof and looked down, where he saw Bathsheba bathing herself. She was the wife of Uriah the Hittite, one of the heroes of Israel, a member of David's elite fighting force known as the Thirty, who went with Joab to fight against Ammon. Given to lust, David sent messengers to bring her to him and he lay with her. Afterwards, she advised him that she had become pregnant.

This generated the seed of a scandal. Her husband had been away fighting and questions would be asked about the timing of her pregnancy. If people learned that the king had done this while the husband fought against Israel's enemies, it could lead to a major embarrassment, perhaps a loss of the kingship itself.

To prevent the affair from being discovered, David sent for Uriah under the pretense that he wanted an update on the fighting. He had hoped that when Uriah arrived in Jerusalem he would go home to his wife and sleep with her, thus creating the impression that Uriah was indeed the father. But the plan went awry.

After getting the battle report, David told Uriah to go home and freshen up. Uriah left the palace but didn't return home. Instead, he remained in the door of the king's house where all the servants were.

David summoned Uriah back in and asked why he didn't go back to the house. Uriah replied:

> The Ark, and Israel, and Judah, abide in tents; and my lord Joab, and the servants of my lord, are encamped in the open fields; shall I then go into mine house, to eat and to drink, and to lie with my wife? as thou livest, and as thy soul liveth, I will not do this thing (2 Sam 11:11).

Talk about rubbing salt in the wounds. The contrast between Uriah's loyalty to Israel and David's behavior couldn't be starker. Next, David tried to get Uriah drunk, hoping to weaken his will. Though the soldier had become intoxicated he still chose to sleep among David's servants.

Uriah's high moral turn set David on edge and he conceived a final scheme to do away with Uriah and marry Bathsheba so that he could claim to have fathered the child after the marriage took place. The king gave Uriah a letter to give to Joab. The missive contained instructions for disposing of the messenger. "Set ye Uriah in the forefront of the hottest battle, and retire ye from him, that he may be smitten, and die" (2 Sam 11:15).

When Joab saw the Ammonites send a fighting force outside the gates of the city, he sent Uriah to fight among the most effective of the Ammonite soldiers. As instructed, Uriah was left without support and an Ammonite soldier ran him through with a sword. ("[Thou] hast slain him with the sword of the children of Ammon" [2 Sam 12:9].)

Following a period of mourning for Uriah, David sent for Bathsheba and married her (2 Sam 11:27).

David thought he had solved the problem—he could now become the legitimate father—but once again his plan went wrong. Nathan the Prophet came before David and asked the king to render judgment on a disturbing case:

> There were two men in one city; the one rich, and the other poor. The rich man had exceeding many flocks and herds: But the poor man had nothing, save one little ewe lamb, which he had bought and nourished up: and it grew up together with him, and with his children; it did eat of his own meat, and drank of his own cup, and lay in his bosom, and was unto him as a daughter. And there came a traveller unto the rich man, and he spared to take of his own flock and of his own herd, to dress for the wayfaring man that was come unto him; but took the poor man's lamb, and dressed it for the man that was come to him (2 Sam 12:1–4).

When David heard this tragic tale he angrily declared to Nathan,

> As the LORD liveth, *the man that hath done this thing shall surely die*: And he shall restore the lamb fourfold, because he did this thing, and because he had no pity (2 Sam 12:5–6, emphasis added).

Nathan then replied, "Thou art the man" (2 Sam 12:7). Then Nathan furiously denounced David's sin, one which David himself had just said deserved a death penalty. David acknowledged his wrongdoing but Nathan announced that the Lord had spared the king's life and that as punishment God would take the life of the child now carried by Bathsheba (2 Sam 12:14).

Unfortunately, the text doesn't tell us if this conversation between David and Nathan took place in the open before the King's Court, where such judgments would normally be rendered, or in secret. However, the almost universal acceptance of this story by both David's enemies and friends, as well as the later biblical editors, suggests that Nathan's confrontation occurred in public. Although the Chronicler omits this story, he does cite as one of his sources for the history of the United Monarchy a Book of Nathan the Prophet. It may be that book which perpetuated the charge against David.

There is another incident in this story that casts further aspersions on David's honesty and sincerity. After the birth of the child by Bathsheba the baby became ill, as prophesied by Nathan. During the illness, David acted as if he were thoroughly aggrieved at the turn of events:

> David therefore besought God for the child; and David fasted, and went in, and lay all night upon the earth. And the elders of his house arose, and went to him, to raise him up from the earth: but he would not, neither did he eat bread with them (2 Sam 12:16–17).

On the seventh day the child died. Astonishingly, David's grief immediately dissipated. He got up, washed and anointed himself, changed his clothes, went to pray, and then sat down to eat. The servants were shocked by David's behavior. They expected him to mourn the child's death and asked why he didn't. David replied,

> While the child was yet alive, I fasted and wept: for I said, Who can tell whether God will be gracious to me, that the child may live? But now he is dead, wherefore should I fast? can I bring him back again? I shall go to him, but he shall not return to me (2 Sam 12:22–23).

David's explanation seems rather heartless and hypocritical. This is a king who is portrayed in later biblical chapters as one who always loves his children so much that he hesitates to take action against them even when they embarrass him or threaten to kill him. Here he seems indifferent to the child's death, his earlier actions merely ceremonial displays.

Soon thereafter David impregnated Bathsheba again and she gave birth to Solomon. (Nathan renamed him Jedediah.)

This episode in David's life is the most troubling for his theological defenders. They toss about bizarre explanations like confetti. "Bathsheba and Uriah," some say, "weren't yet married," thus explaining away the adultery that flies in the face of the text and which ignores the obvious need for a cover-up. Another strange argument is that "Uriah ignored a royal command to go back to his house," a claim that allegedly justifies David having him put to death.

Modern writers, often less concerned with the theological implications, try to portray the king as a human with frailties, just like other people, but who managed to overcome them to become a favorite of God and a religious and pious man. Such explanations tend to focus on the adultery—"everyone does it"—and overlook the fact that David had a fellow human being murdered merely to avoid embarrassment and humiliation for his wrongful behavior.

In ancient times as well as now, murder was a horrible crime and looked upon with great disgust. While the later theologians and modern writers try to humanize David's wicked and cruel behavior, the early biblical authors knew better. David committed a horrible sin; everyone knew it and they told us what he did and how he behaved. They did not excuse him. They did not justify it. They accepted that he was wrong and flawed, and not to be emulated in that regard.

While the story of David and Uriah stands on its own as a moral tale of dangerous corruption, it also has important political dimensions with regard to Israel's history.

The biblical account not only emphasized the extraordinary moral failure of even a beloved king devoted to God, but also showed how necessary it was for a man of God (i.e., Nathan) to serve as the king's guide. This is a throwback to the earlier arguments between Samuel and Saul.

When Saul rejected Samuel, the Shilohite priesthood threw its lot in with David, the understanding being that when David became king he was to adhere to the word of the Lord as annunciated through the men of God. The Bathsheba incident showed a king trying to transcend moral law as an absolute ruler, but Nathan's trap made it clear how important it was for the king to remain humble before the Lord and the men of God. The Bathsheba incident was a cautionary warning in the ongoing struggle for power between priests and kings. It remained within the Deuteronomist tradition of the Book of Samuel precisely because it emphasized that obedience to God's law is the first duty of every king.

Nevertheless, this was only the first of several thematic stories about David's failure to deliver justice and perform his kingly duties. Immediately following the Bathsheba episode the bible turns to the events leading up to the partially successful revolt by David's son Absalom, another series of stories that demonstrate David's failure to administer justice. We take up those matters in the next chapter.

CHAPTER 11

Absalom's Rebellion: No Justice, No Peace!

And Absalom said unto him, See, thy matters are good and right;
but there is no man deputed of the king to hear thee. Absalom said
moreover, Oh that I were made judge in the land, that every man
which hath any suit or cause might come unto me,
and I would do him justice! And it was so, that when any man
came nigh to him to do him obeisance, he put forth his hand,
and took him, and kissed him. And on this manner did Absalom
to all Israel that came to the king for judgment: so Absalom stole
the hearts of the men of Israel. 2 SAM 15:3–6

*D*avid's third son, Absalom, launched a military rebellion against his father that temporarily removed the king from the throne of Judah and Israel. The long, dramatic arc that details several incidents in the life of Absalom begins immediately after the Bathsheba affair and continues the biblical assault on David's character and moral failings as ruler of the kingdom. While the Bathsheba incident focused on David's personal moral corruption (and to a lesser extent his failure to fulfill the monarch's obligation of leading his troops into battle), the Absalom saga upped the ante by showing David's larger failure as king—his unwillingness to provide justice for his people, either on a personal level with his children or on a public level as the reigning monarch.

In these episodes, David appears as a foundering parent when it comes to dealing with the terrible wrongdoings of his children. Theologians and modern commentators twist these incidents in order to show what a loving and deeply emotionally father David was, and claim that his inability to face up to his responsibilities provides an example of David's humanity and illustrates the bible's concern with the human condition.

These views are questionable. The editors of 2 Samuel, as we shall see, did not view David's emotional reactions as a warm reflection of his basic humanity, but rather as evidence of how emotional weakness interferes with the ability to administer justice. They considered his lack of moral action a distinct failing that needed to be remedied. The Chronicler, continually concerned with whitewashing David's reputation, omitted the Absalom episodes from his own recitation of the king's career.

Before looking at this portion of David's history, let me first remind you of my previously stated opinion that the biblical account of Absalom incorporates within it several small incidents that together with other material outside the Absalom arc belong to a separate unrelated story about a Benjaminite revolution that happened much earlier in time, probably in the first years of David's reign over a combined Judah and Israel. For the sake of simplicity and continuity I will recount the events in the order presented by 2 Samuel and note some of the difficulties to be discussed at greater length in subsequent chapters.

THE RAPE OF TAMAR

The opening episode in the Absalom saga involves serious wrongdoing by Amnon, David's eldest son and heir-presumptive to the throne. Amnon had fallen in love with his half-sister, the beautiful Tamar, who was also a full sister to Absalom. Obsessed with having her sexually, Amnon and a friend concocted a scheme to get her into his chambers so that he could forcibly take her (2 Sam 13:5).

As part of the plan he feigned illness. When David came to see what the matter was Amnon asked his father to send in Tamar to make him some little cakes (2 Sam 13:6). David complied and Tamar came to her half-brother's chamber to prepare the meal (2 Sam 13:7). As she approached,

He took hold of her, and said unto her, Come lie with me, my sister. And she answered him, Nay, my brother, *do not force me; for no such thing ought to be done in Israel*: do not thou this folly. And I, whither shall I cause my shame to go? and as for thee, thou shalt be as one of the fools in Israel. Now therefore, I pray thee, speak unto the king; for he will not withhold me from thee (2 Sam 13:11–13, emphasis added).

Although Tamar reminded her half-brother that David would give her to him as a wife if he asked, Amnon continued to force himself upon her and raped her. When he completed the deed his love instantly turned to hate and he ordered her out of his chambers. This left Tamar even more distraught and ashamed.

And she said unto him, There is no cause: this evil in sending me away is greater than the other that thou didst unto me. But he would not hearken unto her (2 Sam 13:16).

He then ordered his servants to remove her and to bolt the door (2 Sam 13:17). She suffered greatly from what Amnon did and she took to placing ashes on her head and tearing her robe, a special garment that had signified that she was a virgin (2 Sam 13:19). Absalom found her in tears and asked what had happened, and if Amnon had mistreated her (2 Sam 13:20). When she told him what had occurred he advised her to remain quiet because Amnon was her brother, but he despised his half-brother for what he done (2 Sam 13:22). When David heard what had occurred he became upset but took no action (2 Sam 13:21). Absalom held his tongue but plotted revenge.

This is one of those incidents that commentators talk about when they praise David as a warm, loving father who hesitated to punish his children. What kind of love, though, would allow his daughter's rapist to go unpunished? As Tamar complained, "For no such thing ought to be done in Israel." To truly understand David's indecision, we have to place the story in both literary and political context.

On the literary level, the rape of Tamar appears immediately after the story of David's own sexual crimes, his adultery with Bathsheba and the murder of her husband. Now, his oldest son and presumptive heir to the throne has similarly abused his power and privilege. The act cries out for punishment, but David takes no action. He has failed to administer justice and has allowed a member of his own family to get away with rape. David will allow a rapist, an abuser of power, to succeed him on the throne.

The editorial juxtaposition of these two violent crimes, murder following adultery by David and rape by Amnon, seems to be deliberate. They share common themes—the ongoing corruption of kings with absolute power, and the danger of an unchecked authority. The biblical author almost certainly wants the reader to conclude what Lord Acton later put into words: "Power tends to corrupt and absolute power tends to corrupt absolutely." The remedy, from the biblical author's point of view is that the people must not grant the king absolute power but must instead insist that the monarch subject himself to God's authority as enunciated by the men of God.

The biblical author, however, ignores the political factors that underlie David's inaction. The king fails to render judgment not because of emotional weakness but because of political reality. Amnon is David's oldest son by his first wife, Ahinoam, and born in the Judaean capitol of Hebron. Earlier we observed that this Ahinoam was almost certainly the same as the Ahinoam married to Saul. The prophet Nathan appears to corroborate that fact when he confronted David after the Bathsheba incident and said to him,

> Thus saith the LORD God of Israel, I anointed thee king over Israel, and I delivered thee out of the hand of Saul; And I gave thee thy master's house, and thy master's wives into thy bosom (2 Sam 12:7–8, emphasis added).

Amnon represented Hebron's claim to the throne after David's death, and Hebron was David's power base. Additionally, if we are correct in concluding that Ahinoam was Saul's wife, this would have given Amnon a potential claim to the Benjaminite throne also, thus uniting the houses of Judah and Israel through his father and mother.

Absalom also came from Hebron, but his mother, Maacah, was the daughter of the king of Geshur, a strong Syrian enclave to Israel's north

(2 Sam 3:3). The marriage between David and the daughter of a significant non-Israelite king may have had implications of royal succession for
the child of such a union. This threatened not only to undermine the
potential of a Judah-Benjamin union through Amnon but, more importantly, Absalom's Canaanite family connections could undermine the authority of the Judahite and Israelite priesthoods. Punishing Amnon could
have serious political consequences.

If David showed favoritism towards Absalom, he could undermine
Amnon's claim to the throne, anger his political and religious base, and
divide Judah from Israel. If he showed favoritism towards Amnon, he
might destroy his alliance with the Syrians and weaken his northern perimeter. Avoiding a decision altogether seemed like the smart political
move. It wasn't deep love of Amnon that generated inaction, but politics.

Nevertheless, a king's job is to administer justice and the failure to
punish serious wrongdoing undermines confidence in the king. If he
won't do justice within his personal family, how can he be expected to
do justice within his political family, the people of Judah and Israel?
Surely, from the biblical perspective, this was a case in which David
should have sought guidance from God rather than make his own independent judgment.

ABSALOM'S REVENGE

Absalom nursed his hatred for two years and plotted out revenge (2 Sam
13:23). He had a farm in a place called Baal-Hazor, which, according to
the biblical account, was near Ephraim. Ephraim begins at Benjamin's
northern border and occupies the central highlands north of Benjamin,
but the bible is unclear as to whether the city is by the Benjaminite border
or the northern border of Ephraim. Scholars suspect that Baal-Hazor
corresponds to a modern site known as Jebel el-Asur, somewhere between
Shiloh and Jerusalem, placing it near the Benjamin-Ephraim border.

When sheep-shearing season arrived, Absalom invited David and all
his sons to a festival but David declined (2 Sam 13:24). So Absalom asked

that at least Amnon be allowed to go (2 Sam 13:26). David, apparently suspicious of his son's motives, questioned why his son would want Amnon to come to the ceremony (2 Sam 13:26). Absalom persisted, however, and David relented, although the particulars of the conversation are omitted. The biblical account then confusingly says that Amnon and all of the king's sons departed to Baal-Hazor (2 Sam 13:27). As Absalom had only initially pressured David with regard to Amnon, we might suspect that the author adapted this story from an earlier source and omitted much of the dialogue between David and Absalom.

When the family arrived at Absalom's farm, the host told his servants to wait until Amnon became drunk and then kill him (2 Sam 13:28). Absalom's men followed his command and when the other sons saw Amnon put to death, they jumped on their mules and fled (2 Sam 13:29). Absalom, on the other hand, raced north to his grandfather's court in Geshur, where he remained for three years (2 Sam 13:37–38). Absalom's initial invitation to both David and all of his sons, coupled with the subsequent execution of Amnon, suggests that he originally planned to kill not only Amnon, but David and the king's other sons as well.

When David, the ever-weeping father, learned of Amnon's death he mourned for his son (2 Sam 13:37). But, as with the death of his first son by Bathsheba, he quickly got over it. "And the soul of King David longed to go forth unto Absalom: for he was comforted concerning Amnon, *seeing he was dead*" (2 Sam 13:39, emphasis added). Nevertheless, he kept Absalom at a distance, no doubt to avoid the appearance of political impropriety, and wouldn't bring Absalom back to Jerusalem. While Absalom understandably remained in exile, there is no evidence that David ever ordered or acted to punish Absalom in any meaningful fashion.

Joab, however, observed David's demeanor and thought it best that David and Absalom be reunited, so he conceived a plan to reconcile David with his distant son (2 Sam 14:1). He arranged for a woman to bring a fake claim to David for his judgment (2 Sam 14:2–3). David summoned her before him and she told a sad tale of family woe.

I am indeed a widow woman, and mine husband is dead. And thy hand-maid had two sons, and they two strove together in the field, and there was none to part them, but the one smote the other, and slew him. And, behold, the whole family is risen against thine handmaid, and they said, Deliver him that smote his brother, that we may kill him, for the life of his brother whom he slew; and we will destroy the heir also: and so they shall quench my coal which is left, and shall not leave to my husband neither name nor remainder upon the earth (2 Sam 14:5–7)

David ruled that the surviving son should remain free from harm in order to preserve the family name and that he would take action against wrongdoers (2 Sam 14:10–11). The woman thanked him, and then said,

Wherefore then hast thou thought such a thing against the people of God? for the king doth speak this thing as one which is faulty, in that the king doth not fetch home again his banished (2 Sam 14:13).

After further discussion, David asked her if Joab had suggested she come forth with this tale and she replied in the affirmative (2 Sam 14:19). The king yielded to Joab's wish and directed his general to bring Absalom back to Jerusalem, but directed that there be no face-to-face meeting between the two (2 Sam 14:24). Absalom arrived in David's capitol but remained separate from his father. David's decision allowed a murderer to go free, both figuratively in the case before the court and literally with regard to Absalom.

The biblical author then interjects an out-of-context passage about all of Israel recognizing Absalom as a man of great beauty, with not a blemish from head to foot, with a very full head of hair (2 Sam 14:25). He also adds that he had three sons and a daughter (2 Sam 14:27). This passage clearly foreshadows Absalom's claim to the kingship, as the description of his beauty recalls similar language about Saul and David (1 Sam 9:2, 1 Sam 16:12).

Consistent with this interpretation, it now appears that Absalom has, in fact, become the heir-presumptive to David's throne. Although he is

David's third child in chronological order (2 Sam 3:3), the first child, Amnon, is dead, and the second child goes completely unmentioned in the bible after the birth notice, suggesting that the second child may have died at a very young age.

Parallels with the Bathsheba Story

Not only does the Absalom-Amnon feud come close on the heels of the Bathsheba story, the two accounts share a number of similarities. In both stories David's failure to do justice leads to the death of one of his children—in the Bathsheba case to her first child and in the Amnon case to David's first child. In both instances David mourns over the child's loss and then quickly gets over it because the child is dead. And, in both stories, David is undone by the presentation of a false case involving implications of murder that require his judgment. However, there are significant differences between these two trials. In the Bathsheba account, a man of God initiates the case and David condemns the murderer, proposing a just solution that leads to his own condemnation and God's forgiveness. In the Amnon incident, the case is initiated by the pragmatic general concerned only with political implications, and David absolves the murderer and offers him protection, an act that should be seen as an immoral judgment, the consequence of which will lead to his subsequent removal from the throne and to reinforce the idea that the king should consult with God before making important decisions.

Another aspect of the Amnon story may also parallel the Bathsheba incident but the evidence is ambiguous. In the Bathsheba incident, David sent Uriah to the battlefield, for the secret purpose of having him killed. In the Amnon incident, David's haggling over whether Amnon should go to Absalom's farm suggests that David knew what Absalom planned to do but that he allowed his son to go unwittingly to his death.

ABSALOM SEIZES THE THRONE

Absalom remained in Jerusalem for two years without seeing David's face and became angry that his father ignored him (2 Sam 14:28). So he sent for Joab in order to arrange a meeting, but Joab wouldn't respond (2 Sam 14:29). He sent a second message to Joab and again he wouldn't respond. Absalom decided he needed to get Joab's attention and ordered his servants to burn down the general's barley field (2 Sam 14:30). Joab paid attention. He met with Absalom and received the following message to deliver to the king.

> Wherefore am I come from Geshur? it had been good for me to have been there still: now therefore let me see the king's face; and if there be any iniquity in me, let him kill me (2 Sam 14:32).

In fact, despite his offer to David, Absalom faced no risk of execution. His relationship to the king of Geshur and his closeness to the throne insured his safety. Joab brought the son's words to the father, and David sent for Absalom and the king kissed him (2 Sam 14:33).

Immediately upon this peaceful reconciliation "Absalom prepared him chariots and horses, and fifty men to run before him" (2 Sam 15:1). Absalom's action here corresponds exactly to that of the later actions of Adonijah, who did so in order to proclaim himself king after David's death (1 Ki 1:5). Absalom's action, therefore, should be seen as the first stage in his plan to seize the throne from David and become the new king. (The earlier passage about Absalom's great beauty, which had been interjected in a manner disruptive to the narrative, probably belonged originally with this section and the biblical editors may have moved it to diminish the legitimacy of Absalom's claim to the throne.) After gathering his chariots and runners,

> Absalom rose up early, and stood beside the way of the gate: and it was so, that when any man that had a controversy came to the king for judgment, then Absalom called unto him, and said, Of what city art thou? And he

said, Thy servant is of one of the tribes of Israel. And Absalom said unto
him, See, thy matters are good and right; but there is no man deputed of
the king to hear thee. Absalom said moreover, *Oh that I were made judge in
the land, that every man which hath any suit or cause might come unto me,
and I would do him justice!* And it was so, that when any man came nigh to
him to do him obeisance, he put forth his hand, and took him, and kissed
him. And on this manner did Absalom to all Israel that came to the king
for judgment: so Absalom stole the hearts of the men of Israel (2 Sam
15:2–6, emphasis added).

Implicit in Absalom's complaint is that David had a widespread reputation for failure to administer justice within the kingdom. The role of
"judge" belongs to the king and Absalom's publicly expressed desire to be
a judge should be understood as an effort to stake out a claim to the
throne and find backers for his efforts. Absalom exploited David's apparent weakness to build up a large and loyal following of his own. "And the
conspiracy was strong; for the people increased continually with Absalom" (2 Sam 15:12).

After reaching a critical mass in popular support, Absalom approached David and asked for permission to go to Hebron and make his
vows (2 Sam 15:7). He explained that he made a promise to God that if
the Lord brought him back to Jerusalem, he would go to Hebron and
thank him. This closely echoes the very strategy used by David when he
failed to come to Saul's table for dinner. David, too, alleged a need to go to
his hometown in Judah for religious reasons, and when he left he posi-
tioned himself in opposition against Saul. Absalom had similar goals.

Nevertheless, David gave his son permission to go and Absalom immediately sent spies throughout Israel, telling them to wait for a specified signal
and then declare, "Absalom reigneth in Hebron" (2 Sam 15:10). He then
proceeded to Hebron with two hundred chosen men, although these com-
panions apparently knew nothing of Absalom's conspiracy (2 Sam 15:11).

He also secured the support of an important figure in David's administration, Ahithophel, who served as a chief counselor to David (2 Sam
16:15). The narrative says of this advisor, "And the counsel of Ahithophel,
which he counseled in those days, was *as if a man had inquired at the oracle*

of God: so was all the counsel of Ahithophel" (2 Sam 16:23, emphasis added). Ahithophel, although not specifically described as a prophet or a man of God, appears to have been thought of as someone with such credentials. For all practical purposes, Ahithophel should be recognized as the religious authority who will anoint Absalom king of Hebron just as Samuel did for David

Word reached David of Absalom's mounting support, and the king ordered an immediate evacuation of Jerusalem, leaving behind only ten concubines to keep the house (2 Sam 15:16). Absalom's troops moved in afterwards and captured control of the city. One of his first acts, suggested by Ahithophel (2 Sam 16:21), was to publicly sleep with these ten concubines, the wives of David, thus fulfilling Nathan's earlier prophesy, to wit,

> Thus saith the LORD, Behold, I will raise up evil against thee out of thine own house, and I will take thy wives before thine eyes, and give them unto thy neighbour, and he shall lie with thy wives in the sight of this sun. For thou didst it secretly: but I will do this thing before all Israel, and before the sun (2 Sam 12:9–12).

Sleeping with the king's concubines should be understood as an assertion of authority by the claimant to the throne. David slept with Saul's concubines to signify his succession to Saul's throne; Absalom slept with David's concubines to signify his succession to David's throne. And later, a request by Adonijah, a rival to Solomon for the throne, to have one of David's concubines given to him as a wife is recognized by Solomon as claim to kingship (1 Ki 2:22).

The Flight from Jerusalem

As David departed from Jerusalem, the royal bodyguards, the Cherethites and Pelethites, joined him, along with six hundred Philistine soldiers from the city of Gath who came to his assistance (2 Sam 15:18). The size of this evacuating army suggests how strong and widespread Absalom's support was from the Judahite kingdom that initially backed David.

As David's mercenary guards and Philistine support troops pulled out, David offered the leader of the Philistine unit, Ittai, the right to withdraw from the coming conflict as this wasn't his fight and that he should return home. But Ittai responded,

> As the LORD liveth, and as my lord the king liveth, surely in what place my lord the king shall be, whether in death or life, even there also will thy servant be (2 Sam 15:21).

David's instruction and Ittai's response suggests a friendly and close relationship between David and Philistine Gath, one that does not show the Philistines as subservient to David, as the biblical editors would otherwise want us to believe. The Philistines at this time apparently enjoyed good relations with the man who once served as chief bodyguard to the Philistine king that tried to destroy Israel.

Also joining the flight from Jerusalem were Zadok and Abiathar and the Jerusalem priests, who allegedly brought the Ark of the Covenant with them (2 Sam 15:24). David, however, directed Abiathar and Zadok to take the priests back to the city and act as spies on his behalf, sending information to David though their sons (2 Sam 15:27–28). So the priests returned to Jerusalem.

Along the way out David learned that Ahithophel had joined with Absalom, and it deeply disturbed him (2 Sam 15:31). Then he caught up with a man named Hushai, who held the royal title of King's Friend, a position that usually went to a clever counselor (2 Sam 15:37). Hushai offered to remain with David, but the fleeing king told him to go back and feign loyalty to Absalom so that he could counter Ahithophel's advice with weaker alternatives (2 Sam 15:34). This Hushai agreed to do (2 Sam 15:37).

Continuing along, he came upon a man named Ziba, who brought with him two asses laden with food and drink for David's assemblage (2 Sam 16:1). Ziba had been a servant in the House of Saul and came to David's court earlier, before the Bathsheba incident (2 Sam 9). In that earlier story, David had inquired if there was anyone left in the House of

Saul to whom he could show kindness. Word came that there still lived a son of Jonathan named Mephibosheth, and David brought Jonathan's son to Jerusalem. Ziba continued to administer Mephibosheth's property while his master remained in David's court. We will examine this story in more detail in Chapter 12. For now, bear in mind that Mephibosheth was supposed to be the last living member of the House of Saul.

David asked Ziba where Mephibosheth was and Ziba replied,

> Behold, he abideth at Jerusalem: for he said, Today shall the House of Israel restore me the kingdom of my father (2 Sam 16:3).

As a reward for Ziba's loyalty, David gave him all of Mephibosheth's property (2 Sam 16:4).

This passage about Mephibosheth's boast is oddly out of place and incoherent in political context. It places the Saulide heir in Jerusalem and he sees the revolt as one that would place him on the throne of Israel. But the revolution in effect at the time was about making Absalom king, not the last of the living Saulides, and Absalom had just captured Jerusalem. We will return to this point later in chapter 12, when we make sense out of what Mephibosheth had to say.

Next along the way came a man described in the biblical account as "a man of the family of the House of Saul, whose name was Shimei, the son of Gera" (2 Sam 16:5). This, too, is a strange claim in that Mephibosheth was supposed to be the last of the House of Saul. Again, we will return to this point in chapter 12. In any event, Shimei approached David and his entourage and hurled stones at them and cursed the king:

> Come out, come out, thou bloody man, and thou man of Belial: The LORD hath returned upon thee all the blood of the House of Saul, in whose stead thou hast reigned; and the LORD hath delivered the kingdom into the hand of Absalom thy son: and, behold, thou art taken in thy mischief, because thou art a bloody man (2 Sam 16:7–8).

Abishai, Joab's brother, took offense and wanted to kill this "dead dog" (2 Sam 16:9). David said to leave the man alone, that God probably put the words in the man's mouth, and that he had a lot worse to deal with now that his own son had revolted against him (2 Sam 16:11). Politically, David did not want to incite the Benjaminites and northerners against him and have them join up with Absalom. Taking Shimei's life might have encouraged just such a result. As usual, when it was necessary for David to show compassion against his enemies, the biblical editors place the words of anger in Abishai's mouth and the words of compassion come from David.

The king and his forces moved on, coming to the agreed-upon location where they would await messages from the sons of Zadok and Abiathar. In the meantime, Absalom's counselors met to discuss plans, Hushai having convinced them that he would be a loyal member of Absalom's inner circle (2 Sam 17:5).

The Battle for Control

At Absalom's war room, Ahithophel counseled Absalom to immediately assemble an army of twelve thousand soldiers and chase after David while he was still tired and disorganized and before he could rally the people of Israel to his side (2 Sam 17:1). The council agreed that this made sense, but then Hushai spoke up and offered a different strategy (2 Sam 17:8).

David and his troops, he suggested, were seasoned fighters who would strike back "like a bear robbed of his cubs," and that David and his troops would be well hidden and a large slaughter would occur. The people of Israel, he argued would think that Absalom had gone down to defeat and would rally to the king. Instead, Hushai suggested that Absalom take the time to gather a large army from all over Israel and march after him. And if he retreats to a city for protection, he advised, we'll simply tear the walls down and grab him (2 Sam 17:9–13).

Absalom's counselors agreed that this was the better plan, not recognizing that Hushai's plan gave David time to recover his strength and escape (2 Sam 17:14). When Ahithophel learned that his advice had been rejected, he committed suicide, obviously believing that David would now defeat Absalom and punish the traitors (2 Sam 17:23). Hushai, in the meantime, went to Zadok and told him what had occurred (2 Sam 17:15). He told the priest to send a messenger to David, and tell him what the two sides proposed (2 Sam 17:16). He told the messenger to urge David to break camp and flee (2 Sam 17:16). Strangely, when the messenger arrived, he delivered only Ahithophel's plan, rather than the two opposing plans as he had been directed to do (2 Sam 17:21).

David and his forces immediately departed, allegedly crossing over the Jordan to the area of Mahanaim (2 Sam 17:24). This is a strange location for David to go to. It was the center of resistance to David when Eshbaal was king, and when David arrived there he was greeted and assisted by two men closely affiliated with the House of Saul, and a son of Nahash the former Ammonite king (2 Sam 17:27). This makes little logical sense. Saul's allies wouldn't be expected to aid David, and if the Ammonites had been subjected to forced labor after David defeated Nahash's successor, as the biblical account indicates, we shouldn't expect the Ammonites to give comfort to David. This is one of those matters that we will have to discuss in more detail later.

David divided his troops into three divisions, one led by Joab, another by Abishai, and a third by Ittai of Gath (2 Sam 18:2). The textual evidence doesn't indicate any long delay in joining battle, suggesting that Absalom's court had adopted Ahithophel's advice of a quick strike rather than Hushai's advice of delaying until a larger army could be assembled. (If Ahithophel's plan in fact had been adopted, the story of his suicide may have been an editorial cover-up for his execution by David when the king returned to Jerusalem.)

The biblical account tells us that the battle occurred in a place called the "Woods of Ephraim" or the "Forest of Ephraim" (2 Sam 18:6). This is the only mention of such a place in the bible and the name is inconsistent with the location of the battle. Ephraim is on the western side of the Jordan; David and his troops are supposedly on the east side of the Jordan. A "Forest of Ephraim" should be located in Ephraim, not on the other side of the Jordan where the battle allegedly took place. This suggests that there may be something wrong with the biblical description of the battle site, a matter we will take up in more detail later.

The battle went badly for Absalom's army. The biblical author claims that the Israelites lost more men to the dense foliage of the forest than they did to the swords of David's army (2 Sam 18:8). David's army had Absalom's in retreat (2 Sam 18:17).

The Death of Absalom

As David's army prepared for the final mop-up, the king's fatherly impulses returned:

> And the king commanded Joab and Abishai and Ittai, saying, Deal gently for my sake with the young man, even with Absalom. *And all the people heard when the king gave all the captains charge concerning Absalom* (2 Sam 18:5, emphasis added).

Once again, Joab will conveniently kill an enemy of David and the biblical author will absolve David from blame by having him publicly proclaim that he didn't want such a result.

Shortly thereafter, a troop from David's army saw Absalom and chased after him. Absalom tried to escape but the woods were dense and as he rode away on his mule his head (or more likely his hair) got caught in the branches of a tree and he hanged suspended from the ground (2 Sam 18:9). The soldiers brought this news to Joab who asked why they didn't kill him and claim the reward he offered (2 Sam 18:11). In response, the soldiers reminded Joab of David's instruction not to harm his son (2 Sam 18:12).

Furious, Joab grabbed three darts (or sticks) and hurled them at Absalom's living body while he dangled in the air (2 Sam 18:14). Ten of Joab's soldiers then closed in on Absalom and struck him dead (2 Sam 18:15). They buried him in a pit and filled it with stones (2 Sam 18:17). The remaining Israelites fled. The next and final step was to break the news to David.

When David learned what happened to his son, he wept.

And the king was much moved, and went up to the chamber over the gate, and wept: and as he went, thus he said, O my son Absalom, my son, my son Absalom! would God I had died for thee, O Absalom, my son, my son! (2 Sam 18:33).

David's public expression of grief had a desultory effect on the troops.

And the victory that day was turned into mourning unto all the people: for the people heard say that day how the king was grieved for his son. And the people gat them by stealth that day into the city, as people being ashamed steal away when they flee in battle. But the king covered his face, and the king cried with a loud voice, O my son Absalom, O Absalom, my son, my son! (2 Sam 19:2–4).

This angered Joab and he read David the riot act.

Thou hast shamed this day the faces of all thy servants, which this day have saved thy life, and the lives of thy sons and of thy daughters, and the lives of thy wives, and the lives of thy concubines; In that thou lovest thine enemies, and hatest thy friends. For thou hast declared this day, that thou regardest neither princes nor servants: for this day I perceive, that if Absalom had lived, and all we had died this day, then it had pleased thee well. Now therefore arise, go forth, and speak comfortably unto thy servants: for I swear by the LORD, if thou go not forth, there will not tarry one with thee this night: and that will be worse unto thee than all the evil that befell thee from thy youth until now (2 Sam 19:5–7).

Joab's threat to abandon David and leave him in ruin had the desired effect. David no longer wished that it were he himself that died instead of Absalom and took his position at the gate of the city to exercise command (2 Sam 19:8).

Absalom's death caused the Israelites to reconsider their options and send messengers to David, asking him to resume his role as king (2 Sam 19:9–10, 16). David then sent a complaint to Zadok and Abiathar (2 Sam 19:11). What he wanted to know was why Judah, "my bones and my flesh" were the last to invite him back to his house (2 Sam 19:12). The message also instructed the priests to advise Amasa, the Judahite general, that he would replace Joab in the new administration (2 Sam 19:9–13). David's concern about Judah's hesitancy to act reflects how deeply estranged his own power base had become.

It's also interesting to note here that Amasa appears to be David's stepson through the king's marriage to Abigail, Amasa's mother. Abigail had previously been married to Nabal at Hebron, the wealthy farmer who died shortly after David threatened to forcibly take his property. Amasa might have been heir to Nabal's influential position in Hebron if David hadn't married his mother, and he might have borne a grudge against the king.

In any event, Judah sent back welcoming words and Israel and Judah raced to the Jordan to see who could get there first and win over David's affection. Shimei arrived at the same time as the Judahite delegation (2 Sam 19:16). It was Shimei who had stoned David's troops and cursed the king as he fled Jerusalem. This time, Shimei appeared with an army of one thousand Benjaminites to provide an escort.

Shimei bowed down before David and asked forgiveness, which David granted (2 Sam 19:19–20). But Abishai again proclaimed that the man should be put to death (2 Sam 19:21). David, recognizing that Shimei had a large army behind him, did not want to risk further fighting and rebuked Abishai, once again reverting to the literary pattern (2 Sam 19:22).

Also arriving at the scene were Ziba, the servant of the House of Saul who brought David provisions during his flight (2 Sam 19:17), and Mephibosheth, Jonathan's son, who claimed that Ziba tricked him and left without him (2 Sam 19:26). (Mephibosheth was lame and could not easily get about.) David granted clemency to Jonathan's son and returned to him a half share of all that he given away to Ziba (2 Sam 19:29).

As David's procession made its way back towards Jerusalem, a dispute broke out over the composition of the escort (2 Sam 19:41). The Israelites claimed that Judah took possession of David and cut Israel short, and Israel complained that it had ten parts in the king and that the guard should be adjusted (2 Sam 19:43). The wrangling continued to escalate. At issue was not just the matter of who would be in the escort, but how relations between the two sides would be handled. Each claimed to be entitled to more favor than the other. As the words became more belligerent, a political breach opened up between the two kingdoms and a Benjaminite named Sheba called Israel to arms against David (2 Sam 20:1). We will look at Sheba's revolt more closely in the next chapter. The king decried the state of affairs. "Now shall Sheba the son of Bichri do us more harm than did Absalom" (2 Sam 20:6).

THE DEUTERONOMIST'S PURPOSE

At this point, one might ask why the pro-David Deuteronomist would have included such strong moral assaults on David's character instead of following the Chronicler's strategy of editing out the negative images of David. The answer has to do with political agendas.

The problem facing the Deuteronomist was that David committed many immoral and corrupt acts, was widely perceived by his critics as lacking in kingly virtue, and was indeed temporarily thrown off the throne by his son Absalom because of his failure to provide justice. The history, passed on mostly through various priestly and northern Israel writings, would have been well known to the educated classes of the Deuteronomist's time and couldn't easily be covered up. The concern of the earlier priesthood and the Deuteronomist was that the king be subservient to God, that the king was not an absolute power in his own right but one beholden to the men of God for leadership and guidance.

The priestly classes then used David's failings as a theological lesson. Even a king as good and pious as David, a man whose heart was with God, they argued, would become corrupted by power and wrongly influenced by family emotions. The only solution to such a problem, the priesthood contended, was for a king to submit to the men of God for advice and to hear the word of God before making judgments.

The Chronicler, on the other hand, writing long after Israel disappeared and the Davidic dynasty had ended, had the advantage of David's almost complete rehabilitation by this time. The center of anti-Davidic propaganda had been eliminated three to four hundred years earlier with the Assyrian conquest and destruction of Israel. The defensive writings of the Deuteronomist succeeded in rehabilitating much of David's reputation because no strong anti-David political center existed to counter the Deuteronomist.

The Chronicler, however, did not share the same view as the Deuteronomist with regard to the relation between the priesthood and the king.

For the Chronicler, the salvation of Judah through a future Davidic heir was the primary theological concern, and all negative depictions of David had to be buried or hidden. To a large extent, one should see the Chronicler's goal as replacing 1 and 2 Sam with his own sanitized history that expanded upon David's central role in defining Jewish religion.

CHAPTER 12

Sheba's Rebellion: No Part in David!

We have no part in David, neither have we inheritance
in the son of Jesse: every man to his tents, O Israel. So every man
of Israel went up from after David, and followed Sheba the son
of Bichri: but the men of Judah clave unto their king,
from Jordan even to Jerusalem. 2 SAM 20:1–2

(Note: In this chapter we revisit David's flight to Mahanaim and Sheba's revolt. It will be argued below that David's journey was not a flight from Absalom but a march to Mahanaim to accept the surrender of Israel after the deaths of Abner and King Eshbaal. In addition, it will be argued that Sheba's revolt did not happen after Absalom's revolt but earlier, right after Israel surrendered to David.)

With the death of Absalom, David sought to reestablish his control over the kingdom. He had the support of his own loyal forces and the Philistines of Gath. Opposed were the armies of Judah and Israel. Absalom's revolt originated in Judah and, despite the claim of a countrywide revolt, the uprising seemed to confine itself mostly to the south, centered in Hebron.

Israel in the north did not appear to have a strong role in Absalom's challenge, a conclusion supported by the fact that Hebron's rebel army didn't wait for the northern tribes to join the chase after the fugitive king. Although the north clearly harbored a strong prejudice against David because of his usurpation of the Saulide throne, the Israelite leaders appeared to hold back until they could see how well David fared against his son.

With Absalom's defeat, Israel sent the first encouraging words to David, reiterating its support for David and sending out an escort to take him back to Jerusalem (2 Sam 19:43). Judah, on the other hand, seems to have held out to the last minute, apparently trying to negotiate a settlement with David to protect their interests.

Angered by his kinsmen's failure to respond even after Israel had already invited him back, David asked Zadok and Abiathar to make inquiry as to why his own flesh and blood had yet to call for his return, but he also told the priests to tell the people of Judah that if they accepted him as king, he would replace Joab as head of the army with Amasa, Absalom's general (2 Sam 19:11–13). This appeared to be the clincher, breaking the monopolistic hold of the Jerusalem court over the kingdom and giving Judah a strong voice in what would follow when David returned (2 Sam 19:14).

Judah then sent out its own escort to meet David and the two kingdoms raced to see who would be first to welcome David back (2 Sam 19:15–16). Both arrived at Gilgal, on the west side of the Jordan, and waited for David to come across. At about the same time, Ziba, the servant of Saul who had provided food to David on his flight from Jerusalem and received Mephibosheth's estate as a reward, arrived with a large retinue of sons and servants and splashed his way through the Jordan to directly greet and kowtow before David on the other side, no doubt determined to hold on to his profits (2 Sam 19:17).

That an Israelite army had to race across the countryside to beat Judah to Mahanaim seems rather odd. Mahanaim was in Israel and had been an important Israelite stronghold. An Israelite army would already have been in the vicinity of the city before Judah even set out. The presence of the Benjaminites Barzillai and Machir at Machir, who greeted David when he arrived there, reinforces the idea that an Israelite army would already have been present with David.

Nevertheless, on the route back, an argument broke out between Israel and Judah over the composition of the escort to Jerusalem, each side claiming priority over David (2 Sam 19:41–43). Eventually, the Israelites charged that David favored Judah even though Israel was the first to welcome him back. Israel, its leaders argued, had ten parts in David while Judah had only one, and that relationship should be reflected in the escort. Obviously, the debate over how to form the escort was merely a symptom of the larger dispute over how David would rule his realm vis-à-vis Israel and Judah. As the dispute escalated out of control, a Benjaminite leader named Sheba son of Bichri blew on his trumpet and declared:

> We have no part in David, neither have we inheritance in the son of Jesse: every man to his tents, O Israel. So every man of Israel went up from after David, and followed Sheba the son of Bichri: but the men of Judah clave unto their king, from Jordan even to Jerusalem (2 Sam 20:1–2).

David returned to Jerusalem, locked away the ten concubines that Absalom had slept with, and then ordered Amasa to assemble the army of Judah within three days and put down Sheba's revolt, fearing that "Sheba the son of Bichri do us more harm than did Absalom" (2 Sam 20:6).

Despite the looming threat, Amasa failed to act quickly enough for David's purposes and the king summoned Abishai, telling him to organize the king's personal forces and set out after the Benjaminite troublemaker (2 Sam 20:6). Abishai immediately organized the Cherethites, Pelethites, Joab's personal guard, and the elite fighting force known as the Thirty, and set out in pursuit (2 Sam 20:7).

Sheba, in the meantime, tried to rally Israel to his side but without much apparent success. His efforts brought him to the far northern territory of Dan, where he and his band sought shelter in the walled city of Abel of Beth-Maacah (2 Sam 20:14).

Amasa, obviously concerned that David was unhappy with the delay in chasing Sheba, moved to catch up with Abishai's troops and caught up with them at the city of Gibeon, where the demoted Joab pretended to remain friendly and approached him for a hug of greeting (2 Sam 20:8–9). Hidden within his garments was a knife and when Joab came up to Amasa, he took his rival's beard in his hand and leaned over as if to give him a kiss of friendship (2 Sam 20:9). As Amasa also leaned over Joab stuck the blade below his rival's fifth rib and killed him (2 Sam 20:10).

The Judaean troops under Amasa's command must have been in shock, their leader now dead and the basis of Judaean support for David destroyed. The Judaean troops stood mute as Joab and Abishai moved out after Sheba, but Joab left one of his men behind to rally them to David's side (2 Sam 20:11). As the troops saw Amasa's bowels spilled along the ground, Joab's man called out: "He that favoureth Joab, and he that is for David, let him go after Joab" (2 Sam 20:11).

Amasa's troops still stared in astonishment at their leader's corpse, so Joab's man grabbed the body, dragged it off the road, and placed a cloth over it (2 Sam 20:12). The dismayed soldiers took this as a final warning from Joab and rode after him (2 Sam 20:13).

David's army laid siege to Abel of Beth-Maacah and began to batter down the walls when a wise woman from the city came to the parapet and asked to speak to Joab (2 Sam 20:16). When the general came to the wall she said:

> They were wont to speak in old time, saying, They shall surely ask counsel at Abel: and so they ended the matter. I am one of them that are peaceable and faithful in Israel: thou seekest to destroy a city and a mother in Israel: why wilt thou swallow up the inheritance of the LORD? (2 Sam 20:18–19).

Joab replied that they meant the city no harm but that they were chasing the scoundrel Sheba, who had dared to raise his hand against King David (2 Sam 20:21). The woman replied that the fugitive's head would be tossed over the wall, and it was (2 Sam 20:21–22). Joab retreated and returned to Jerusalem (2 Sam 20:22).

CHRONOLOGICAL PROBLEMS

In the last chapter I alluded to some problems with certain events within the Absalom arc that seemed out of order or lacking in credibility. In this chapter we will take a closer look at such matters, but first we must also look at some other incidents that shed further light on the chronological issues as well as the nature of David's reign. One concerns the arrival of Jonathan's son in Jerusalem. Another deals with a famine and the demand of the Gibeonites that Saul's children be executed as a sacrifice to eliminate the plague. This latter incident appears in 2 Samuel after Absalom's death, but, as will be obvious when we examine it, the episode belongs to a much earlier period in David's reign than Absalom's uprising.

In addition, there is another problematic story concerning the conducting of a census in Israel that, according to the biblical sequence, occurred near the end of David's life. We will look at that incident in the next chapter and will relocate the time frame to David's early years.

KINDNESS FOR JONATHAN'S SAKE

The lynch pin for our chronological reconstruction concerns the events surrounding the arrival of Jonathan's son in Jerusalem. In 2 Sam 9:1, which in the biblical sequence of events occurs early in David's reign and before the story of Bathsheba, David asks,

> Is there yet any that is left of the House of Saul, that I may show him kindness for Jonathan's sake? (2 Sam 9:1).

The allusion is to David's promise to Saul's son Jonathan, who secretly aided David in his escape from Saul's house and later in escaping Saul's troops. The biblical editors want us to believe that David is motivated in this request by his respect for Jonathan, but, as will be obvious, a more Machiavellian framework underlies David's concern.

In response to his query, the king learned that there existed a servant of Saul named Ziba and David had him brought to the Court (2 Sam 9:2). This was the Ziba that provided David with food on his flight from Jerusalem and who raced across the Jordan to greet David after the defeat of Absalom. When Ziba arrived David reiterated his question, to which the servant responded, "Jonathan hath yet a son, which is lame on his feet" (2 Sam 9:3). As you may recall, this is the child that was dropped when the nurse rescued him from the assassins that killed Eshbaal. His name was given at that time as Mephibosheth.

The identification of the child as lame serves the purpose, from the biblical author's point of view, of a disqualifying feature for an eventual elevation to kingship, theologically eliminating a potential Saulide rival for David's throne. Note, for example, the various descriptions of Saul, David, and Absalom as beautiful, and Absalom as without blemish.

David next inquired as to where he could find this child. Ziba informed him that the child was in the house of Machir, the son of Ammiel in Lodebar (2 Sam 9:4). This is the same name given to one of the three men who greeted David when he crossed the Jordan over to Mahanaim. Machir, therefore, lived in Mahanaim, the stronghold of Eshbaal during his reign as Saul's successor, and Saul's grandson had been placed in his care after the murder of Eshbaal. This tells us that Machir played an important role in Saulide circles.

The king sent for Mephibosheth and the child was delivered to Jerusalem. When he came before David, he fell on his face and did reverence. David said to him,

> *Fear not*: for I will surely show thee kindness for *Jonathan thy father's sake*, and will restore thee all the land of *Saul thy father*; and thou shalt eat bread at my table continually (2 Sam 9:7, emphasis added).

(Note here some confusion over the identity of the child's father, referring to both Jonathan and Saul as his father within the same verse. See the discussion below about Mephibosheth's identity.)

David's efforts to calm the child reflect the political reality. The Benjaminites in general, and the Saulides in particular, believed David to have been an assassin who murdered Saul, Eshbaal, and Abner, and who wanted to eliminate any threat of a Benjaminite resistance or of a Saulide claim to the throne. The child had every reason to be fearful that David would want him dead, too, and would use any means necessary to achieve his goal.

But David is smarter than that. Bringing the child to his court gives him a political hostage. The child is the last Saulide of the line and a revolt against David could lead to the termination of Saul's house without any hope of an heir. The Israelites, in order to protect the child and preserve Saul's line, would not risk a revolt while the child was in David's hands. On the other hand, killing the child could trigger a massive outrage leading to a breakup of the kingdom. What the bible depicts as an act of kindness actually represents the taking of a political hostage and keeping him under house arrest. That this is the case can be seen from David's next instruction to Ziba.

> I have given unto thy master's son all that pertained to Saul and to all his house. Thou therefore, and thy sons, and thy servants, shall till the land for him, and thou shalt bring in the fruits, that thy master's son may have food to eat: *but Mephibosheth thy master's son shall eat bread always at my table* (2 Sam 9:10–11, emphasis added).

Surely, if David's motivations were kindness rather than political considerations, the better act of charity would be to allow Mephibosheth to go back to his estate and be with his own people.

One other observation should be made. The entire story of how David asked after the existence of a member of the House of Saul sounds forced and artificial. David almost certainly had detailed and up-to-date information on everyone and anyone from the House of Saul. They were the enemy and there was no way that he would not know what was going on. Indeed, if an heir to Saul existed it would have been well known and widespread throughout Israel. At the very least, David would have had spies keeping him informed. Nor would the Benjaminites or Israelites casually let Saul's heir go to Jerusalem unless there was a threat of force behind the demand. The leaders of Benjamin and many Israelites believed David was a bloody murderer with regard to the House of Saul. Recall the curse uttered by Shimei from the House of Saul:

> Come out, come out, thou bloody man, and thou man of Belial: The LORD hath returned upon thee all the blood of the House of Saul, in whose stead thou hast reigned (2 Sam 16:7–8).

All in all, it is quite obvious that whether Mephibosheth was the son of Saul or the son of Jonathan, he was a political hostage under house arrest.

As we review the additional chronological evidence, keep in mind that the arrival of Mephibosheth in Jerusalem occurs after the House of Saul appears to be otherwise extinguished.

WHOSE SON IS MEPHIBOSHETH?

This biblical account of Mephibosheth's arrival in Jerusalem confusingly identifies the child as the son of both Jonathan and Saul, Later on there is additional confusion as to who the father was. After the Absalom revolt when
David queries Mephibosheth about where he was during the rebellion, he is
identified solely as the son of Saul (2 Sam 19:24). And still later, in the famine
incident to be discussed below, the text indicates that there are two Mephibosheths, one the son of Saul and one the son of Jonathan (2 Sam 21:7–8).

Further complicating the issue is that the Chronicler identifies Jonathan's son as Meribbaal and says that Meribbaal was the father of Micah
(1 Chr 8:34). Assuming that Mephibosheth's name was originally Mephibaal (as Ishbosheth's name was Eshbaal), many scholars have suggested that either Meribbaal or Mephibaal is a corruption of the other. Still,
this leaves two Mephibosheths walking around, one the son of Saul and
one the son of Jonathan, and 2 Samuel contradicts itself as to which one
was in David's court.

If it was the son of Jonathan that David summoned to Jerusalem,
where than was the son of Saul? For that answer we must now look at the
famine incident.

THE FAMINE SACRIFICE OF SAUL'S SONS

At some unidentified time during the reign of David, a famine struck Israel and lasted for at least three years (2 Sam 21:1). According to the account, David inquired after the cause of the famine and the Lord replied
(presumably through the counsel of Zadok or Abiathar), "It is for Saul,
and for his bloody house, because he slew the Gibeonites" (2 Sam 21:1).
This claim is problematic because there is no evidence anywhere in the
bible other than this passage that Saul took any such action.

When the Lord told David that the famine occurred because of Saul's
actions against Gibeon, he sent for the Gibeonites to see if he could make
amends and lift the curse (2 Sam 21:2). The Gibeonites responded that

they didn't want any gold or silver from the House of Saul or the deaths of any innocent Israelites (2 Sam 21:4). All they wanted was that David give them seven of Saul's sons to be hanged on a high hill in Saul's town of Gibeah (possibly a confused reference to Gibeon, both names stemming from a Hebrew word meaning hill) (2 Sam 21:5–6).

How convenient for David. Here he is worried about the House of Saul posing a threat to his reign and Benjaminite rebels seeking to dethrone him, and the peaceful servants of a city under Aaronite control (theoretically aligned with David's priests, Zadok and Abiathar) say that the king can end a three-year-old famine by exterminating members of Saul's household. David lost no time in agreeing to the terms and the king rounded them up for delivery.

Although we had been told much earlier in 2 Sam 9 that Mephibosheth was the last remaining member of Saul's household, David manages to round up seven more sons or descendants of the deceased king's family in addition to Mephibosheth.

Two of the sons belonged to Rizpah, Saul's concubine (and the woman over whom Abner and Eshbaal had a falling out), and one of them was named Mephibosheth (2 Sam 21:8). This would be the second Mephibosheth described as Saul's son rather than Jonathan's son. The text conspicuously notes the similarity of names by saying that David spared Jonathan's Mephibosheth but turned over Saul's Mephibosheth for execution.

In addition, it turns out that there were five additional sons raised by Michal, Saul's daughter who had been betrothed to David, and these sons belonged to a man named Adriel the son of Barzillai the Meholathite (2 Sam 21:8). All seven sons were turned over to the Gibeonites who hanged them in the first days of the barley harvest (2 Sam 21:9).

This story presents a number of important problems for our consideration. First, on a chronological level, when David brought Jonathan's son to Jerusalem, he was supposed to be the last remaining member of the House of Saul. How likely would it be that in addition to not knowing about Mephibosheth at the time he inquired after any survivors from the House of Saul, he would also not know about two sons by Saul's

concubine and five sons by one of Saul's daughters? In fact the existence
of these sons appears to have been of such wide common knowledge that
even the Gibeonites knew about them.

For this reason, as many scholars have concluded, this famine story
must have preceded the summoning of Mephibosheth to Jerusalem. As
the famine story also indicates, David also knew about Jonathan's son at
the time he turned over the other sons for execution. No wonder the child
was frightened when he arrived in David's court.

We also have another significant fact to accommodate in the famine
story. Five sons of Saul belonged to the son of Barzillai the Meholathite.
When David fled to Mahanaim one of the three men who greeted him on
the Jordanian side of the river was "Barzillai the Gileadite of Rogelim" (2
Sam 17:27). The two Barzillai's seem to be one and the same person.

The description "Meholathite" applied to one of them refers to the
town of Abel-Meholah in the Transjordan. The descriptive term "Gileadite"
refers to the name Gilead, a biblical term often used to describe most of
the Transjordan region. So Gilead would encompass Abel-Meholah.
"Rogelim" refers to an unknown location but has the meaning of "cloth-
workers" so it might be more a description of what Barzillai did for a living (i.e., runs a fabric manufacturing operation) rather than where he
comes from. The overlapping of names strongly suggests that the two
Barzillais are one and the same. This, of course, raises the question of how
likely would it be for Barzillai to happily provide aid and comfort to David after the king had his five grandchildren executed?

We will have more to say about Gibeon and the three-year famine in
the next chapter.

THE GREETING AT MAHANAIM

When David arrived at Mahanaim in the course of his flight from Jerusalem, three men greeted him warmly: Shobi the son of Nahash; Machir
the son of Ammiel; and Barzillai the Gileadite. This is a most strange assemblage in the biblical context.

After the murder of Eshbaal at Mahanaim, Jonathan's son was placed in the custody of Machir the son of Ammiel. Machir would have been a trusted ally of the House of Saul and unlikely to happily provide aid and comfort to David in the midst of a revolution that has chased him off the throne and which the Israelites were cautiously observing for signs of the outcome.

Similarly with Barzillai, whose five grandsons by Saul's daughter had been given to the Gibeonites for execution. He too would have been unlikely to provide aid and comfort to David. He would have been deeply resentful towards David and hopeful that Absalom's revolution would succeed.

The third person present was Shobi, the son of Nahash the Ammonite king. David and Nahash had close relations, and if Nahash was still on the throne, we could reasonably expect him to receive aid from the Ammonites. But, according to the biblical sequence of events, Nahash had died several years earlier and Hanun, his son and successor, went to war with David at the time of the Bathsheba incident. David defeated the Ammonites and subjected them to forced labor. If David were in flight from Absalom the Ammonites would be thrilled and would be more likely to attack David as he came to Mahanaim than aid him.

So there is something seemingly very wrong with the picture presented regarding David's greeting at Mahanaim. It seems out of chronological context. If David is being greeted in friendly fashion by 1) the guardian of Mephibosheth, 2) the grandfather of five of Saul's children, and 3) the friendly Ammonite son of Nahash, we must be talking about a time before Jonathan's son came to Jerusalem, before Saul's grandchildren were executed, and before Nahash died.

All this suggests that David's presence at Mahanaim occurred long before Absalom's revolt and prior to the incident with Bathsheba, and had nothing to do with his flight from Jerusalem. The biblical editors have inserted and integrated a separate, unrelated incident into the Absalom narrative and deliberately combined the two events in a misleading fashion.

But if David didn't go to Mahanaim in his flight from Absalom, where would he have gone? He had limited military options. Judah supported Absalom, so David couldn't head south. He couldn't necessarily expect a warm welcome in the north, either among the northern Israelite tribes or in Geshur, where Absalom's father ruled. The central portion of Israel was either under Ephramite control, which would have been in opposition to David, or under Philistine control as a result of the defeat of Saul.

To the east, Mahanaim should have been thought of as an anti-David stronghold where he could find little comfort. But, to the west, and perhaps in the center, were the Philistines, and David had good relations with them, so good in fact that the Philistines of Gath provided one third of his military support when he fled from Jerusalem. If David would head anywhere it would have been towards his Philistine allies.

This raises a secondary question. Where was the Forest of Ephraim, the battle site between David's and Absalom's forces?

The Forest of Ephraim, if the name can be trusted, should be somewhere in the territory of Ephraim, which stretches across central Israel from the west side of the Jordan River to the Philistine centers of influence in western Canaan. This incident is the only place in the bible where this particular forest is mentioned. Only because the bible implies that the battle happened east of the Jordan River do scholars speculate that it lay in Jordan. Still, even for many scholars this is a troubling conclusion because there doesn't seem to be any logical reason for there to be a Forest of Ephraim on the east side of the river. A location on the western side of Ephraim, by the Philistine border, would make sense and be consistent with a flight towards the Philistines, if David actually headed west instead of east.

Another strategic difficulty with the Forest of Ephraim being east of the Jordan River has to do with geographical problems. On the west side of the river, across from where David supposedly camped, was the cult site of Gilgal. We know from the Book of Joshua that this portion of the Jordan River was extremely difficult to cross. Joshua relied on an act of God to divide the waters so that the Israelites could cross over into the Promised Land.

If Absalom tried to cross over the Jordan at that location in order to confront David, he would have been at an extraordinary disadvantage. David's archers and slingers would easily have wiped out a large portion of the attacking army before it could even get to the other side, sort of the proverbial shooting fish in a barrel. Yet the battle reports in the bible say nothing about the loss of soldiers crossing the waters. We are only told that the dense forest killed more of Absalom's soldiers than did David's army. This makes it highly unlikely that the two sides fought on the east side of the river.

Mephibosheth's Boast

In the course of David's escape from Jerusalem, when he met Ziba and asked where Mephibosheth was, Ziba replied that Jonathan's son stayed behind and declared, "Today shall the House of Israel restore me the kingdom of my father" (2 Sam 16:3).

Even if Ziba made up this quote from Mephibosheth, it makes no sense in political context. First, the current revolution was for the purpose of putting Absalom on the throne, and came from Judah, not Israel. Anyone in Jerusalem's court at the time understood this, and if Mephibosheth, now an adult at the time of Absalom's revolt, were there, he would have known that. The quote makes more sense if it follows after Sheba's revolt, which is Benjaminite.

Second, it's not clear that Mephibosheth was in Jerusalem at the time of Sheba's revolt. There are some ambiguities. Right after Shimei met David at the Jordan and gave his apologies, the text switches to an anecdote about Mephibosheth meeting with David in Jerusalem:

> And *Mephibosheth the son of Saul* came down to meet the king, and had neither dressed his feet, nor trimmed his beard, nor washed his clothes, from the day the king departed until the day he came again in peace. *And it came to pass, when he was come to Jerusalem to meet the king,* that the king said unto him, Wherefore wentest not thou with me, Mephibosheth? And he answered, My lord, O king, my servant deceived me: for thy servant said, I will saddle me an ass, that I may ride thereon, and go to the king; because thy servant is lame (2 Sam 19:24–26, emphasis added).

Although the opening sentence implies that Mephibosheth came to meet the king at the Jordan, the next sentence more clearly implies that the meeting took place in the future at Jerusalem and that the boy had come to

Jerusalem for the meeting. Additionally, the passage describes him as the son of Saul, not Jonathan, another ambiguity in the text. If this were Saul's Mephibosheth, then the incident would have to have occurred prior to the sacrifice of Saul's sons to the Gibeonites. The confusion here may be due to the fact that the biblical author has integrated two different stories about two different Mephibosheths as if they were one and the same person.

A RECONSTRUCTION
OF THE MAHANAIM STORY

We have now discussed several inconsistencies with regard to David's flight to Mahanaim in the midst of Absalom's revolt. I will now attempt to reconcile some of these contradictions and ambiguities. At the heart of the solution is the recognition that David went to Mahanaim as part of the negotiations to assume control over Israel after Eshbaal's murder and not as a fugitive from Jerusalem.

Mahanaim was the Israelite capitol after Saul's death. As part of the negotiation with Abner, David secured physical possession over Michal, while Eshbaal was alive. Joab then murdered Abner, after which two traitors who sought to get a reward from David assassinated Eshbaal. They would also have attempted to kill Mephibosheth, Jonathan's son, but they failed when the nurse escaped with the child and brought him to Machir for safekeeping.

David, in the superior military position and backed by the Philistines, opened up negotiations with Israel over the terms for his becoming their king. He put together a large military force of Judahites and Philistines and set out to Mahanaim to begin discussion of terms for what was essentially an Israelite surrender. On the way he encountered Shimei, head of a large Benjaminite force, who cursed David for what he had done to the House of Saul. David, not looking to worsen matters before negotiations, ignored the insults and proceeded on to Mahanaim where he met with the elders of Israel. For additional support,

David arranged for his friend Nahash to send an Ammonite brigade under the control of his son Shobi.

At Mahanaim, David insisted that Machir bring Jonathan's Mephibosheth to him, and he demanded that Saul's other sons be brought to him including Saul's Mephibosheth and the five grandchildren of Barzillai. We should add that Barzillai's family, by virtue of his son's marriage to one of Saul's daughters, was a potential challenger to David's throne. It's interesting to note, therefore, that in the biblical account David also wanted Barzillai to accompany him to Israel and remain at his table, much as he did with Jonathan's son (2 Sam 19:33). Barzillai, claiming that his great age made him an undesirable guest (he was eighty years old), declined the invitation but offered to send one of his own sons along instead (2 Sam 19:37). This gave David hostages not only from the House of Saul but also from the House of Barzillai, leaving another potential rival in check.

A treaty was concluded and David marched out of Mahanaim with a joint escort of Israelites and Judahites, Shimei leading the Israelite escort. But as the biblical account records, a feud broke out between the Israelites and the Judahites over political divisions and the dispute caused Sheba to try to rally Israel against David. During this short-lived revolt, one of Saul's hostage family, possibly Mephibosheth the son of Jonathan, but more likely Mephibosheth the son of Saul, uttered the remark, "To day shall the House of Israel restore me the kingdom of my father" (2 Sam 16:3).

David returned to Jerusalem and Joab put down Sheba's revolt. At first, David kept all of Saul's family and Barzillai's family in Jerusalem and treated them with the respect due royal hostages, but soon thereafter a famine broke out. After three years, David used the famine as an excuse to execute most of Saul's children on a trumped-up proclamation about Saul's sins against Gibeon being responsible for the plague.

Many years later, reacting to David's tyrannical rule, Judah, under Absalom's leadership, rebelled and David had to flee his capitol city, but he headed west to join his Philistine allies and secure their military backing to put down the revolt. The decisive battle took place in the Forest of

Ephraim somewhere in the territory of Ephraim in central Israel. In order to induce Judah to end the rebellion he offered to replace Joab with Amasa. But once David secured his throne, Joab murdered Amasa and resumed his position as head of the army.

The biblical editors, anxious to cover up David's close relationship to the Philistines and the continued Saulide opposition to his assumption of the Israelite throne after Eshbaal's death, conflated many of the events leading to Sheba's revolt with the story of Absalom. Other portions of David's relationship with the Saulides were distributed throughout the bible in non-chronological and unconnected fashion. We consider some of those other portions next.

CHAPTER 13

The Devil Made Him Do It!

And Satan stood up against Israel,
and provoked David to number Israel. 1 CHR 21:1

*T*he separate authors of 2 Sam 24 and 1 Chr 21 both agree that in the last years of David's reign, 1) he committed a great "trespass to Israel" by numbering the people, 2) God punished Israel terribly during the counting, 3) David admitted to being the sinner responsible for the count, and 4) when God gave David a choice between risking his own life or that of thousands of Israelites in order to bring the punishment to an end David chose personal safety instead of national safety, and over seventy thousand people were struck dead by pestilence before the Lord stayed his angel's sword.

Scholars don't pay much attention to this story other than to try to extricate the king from any moral failings, but it raises some very difficult questions, many of which have yet to be satisfactorily answered. Why did David choose to sin by counting the Israelites? In what manner did Israel suffer during the count? Why did David choose personal safety instead of protecting the nation from devastation? And what sin by David or Israel could have justified the deaths of over seventy thousand people? (Even if we acknowledge that seventy thousand represents a huge bloated figure, as are the census figures recorded in the story, and the correct number should probably be a few hundred to a few thousand, the nature of the act is still horrifying.)

The story attributes the massive death total to a sudden pestilence that lasted at most three days and makes God the author of the destruction (2 Sam 21:13–15). Assuming for the sake of argument that during David's reign there was a period of plague leading many people to die, why did David become so publicly connected to the deadly results that even the pro-David apologist who authored Chronicles could not omit the connection as he did for other immoral acts by David? Why wouldn't the authors simply say that Israel suffered a period of plague or famine because Israel failed to follow God's word and the Lord sent a punishment (as was the claim in the Gibeon story)? Instead, both stories portray David's actions as the initiating cause.

As we read the two accounts, we find that the authors of both stories tried to spin the tale in a manner designed to protect David's reputation. When the two versions of the story are read together, a number of clues emerge as to the actual political events that lay behind the census story. In Appendix B I have reproduced the two accounts in side-by-side fashion, and highlighted key passages. You may want to read through them before continuing, or at least follow along with it as we examine the two reports.

There is a good deal more to this story than appears on the surface and one needn't dig too deeply to find some answers. The search begins with an understanding of what it means to conduct a census and why Israel considered it sinful.

Theologically, the Israelites thought of themselves as servants of God and their produce was God's produce, and if God wanted them to prosper economically and increase their population he would choose to do so. Conducting a count of the population and taking inventory would be an insult to God because the Lord had already determined how large he wanted the population to be and how much he wanted them to produce. Counting the number of people could be seen as questioning God's wisdom.

Politically, however, the purpose of a census was to tax the people, confiscate their property, and increase the wealth of the kingdom. As there was only a limited amount of wealth among the people and the vast majority were relatively poor, taxes on the poor would deprive the large priesthood of what little due they could receive from the people at large, and taxes on the rich not only reduced the amount available for the priests but fomented institutional resentment among the wealthy classes.

To a large part, taxation constituted a form of slavery, a bitter reminder of the days in Egypt when the people worked for the king instead of God. In addition, David also had enemies within Israel, especially among those who lost power and influence when the monarchy shifted from Benjamin to Judah. The Israelites never fully accepted him as their leader and several revolts broke out during his reign. For this reason he needed a non-Israelite mercenary army to keep himself in power.

TWO VERSIONS OF THE CENSUS STORY

The biblical account of David's census appears in both 2 Sam 24 and 1 Chr 21. When you compare the two stories you see that they obviously shared a common text, right down to the use of parallel phrasings and the sequence of events. Yet, despite the evidence of a common source text, the two accounts display some interesting discrepancies. This is also one of those rare instances where David comes off less heroic in the Chronicles account than he does in the Samuel version. That distinction suggests that the Chronicles account might be more faithful to the original textual source than the Samuel version.

In that regard, one of the key characters in this story is Gad the Seer, and Chronicles cites the Book of Gad the Seer as one of its sources for the history of King David (1 Chr 29:29). Gad also made an earlier appearance in our account when we discussed David's outlaw days in Moab.

The very first appearance in the bible of the title "seer" occurs in 1 Sam 9:9 and it tells us, "for he that is now called a Prophet was beforetime called a Seer." This means that the term "Seer" had ceased to be a common term at the time of the writing of Samuel and suggests that the Book of Gad the Seer had been written earlier than the Book of Samuel. This Book of Gad very likely served as the literary source for at least the census episode. Unfortunately, we have not yet found a copy of the Book of Gad the Seer and can't use it to resolve any questions.

The two biblical stories begin with similar announcements but with important and subtle differences. According to the Samuel account:

And again the anger of the LORD was kindled against Israel, and he moved David against them to say, Go, number Israel and Judah (2 Sam 24:1, emphasis added).

Notice here that it is God himself who puts this dangerous notion in David's head and that it is for the purpose of punishing Israel. But it does not describe what sin Israel committed or how taking a census would constitute a punishment. In other words, David may have done wrong, but he did so as an instrument of God to punish his subjects for their failure to follow some undisclosed religious obligations. However, compare Samuel's explanation for David's actions with the one given in Chronicles:

And Satan stood up against Israel, and provoked David to number Israel (1 Chr 21:1, emphasis added).

You can't find a more contradictory alternative to "God made me do it" than "the devil made me do it," but that is what we have here. Chronicles removes God as the active cause of David's actions and emphasizes the extreme evil of David's actions by attributing them to an evil spirit. We should note here that this is the first time in the biblical text that we find a reference to Satan, and outside of the story of Job, the name appears only three more times, in connection with events in the Persian period (fifth to fourth century BCE), suggesting that the blaming of Satan is an editorial touch from that time frame. Since both Samuel and Gad the Seer were probably written before the Persian period neither would have been the source of the reference to Satan and the use of that name suggests a possible alteration of the original source document.

So far, then, from the very outset, Samuel says Israel committed some sort of wrong and God wanted it punished by a census. Chronicles, however, simply says that David committed this evil act because Satan influenced him to do wrong and makes no reference to Israel having angered God.

MISSING BENJAMINITES

Having been provoked to do evil, David naturally asked Joab to execute the command. But Joab balked. Even he, who unhesitatingly murdered anyone who got in his way or David's, reacted hostilely to the king's request. As Chronicles puts it:

> And Joab answered, The LORD make his people an hundred times so many more as they be: but, my lord the king, are they not all my lord's servants? why then doth my lord require this thing? *why will he be a cause of trespass to Israel?* (1 Chr 21:3, emphasis added).

The Book of Samuel has a slightly different variation on Joab's complaint, but it expresses essentially the same point.

> And Joab said unto the king, Now the LORD thy God add unto the people, how many soever they be, an hundredfold, and that the eyes of my lord the king may see it: *but why doth my lord the king delight in this thing?* (2 Sam 24:3, emphasis added).

In Chronicles, Joab advises us that taking a census is a horrible crime against Israel, and in Samuel, we learn that David took great pleasure in committing this heinous act. One would think that a man after God's heart would be a little less joyful at committing evil, but then one would also expect such a person to resist Satan's temptations and not murder his mistress's husband.

The Samuel version of Joab's complaint also implies that God wouldn't have wanted the census conducted, which implicitly contradicts the introductory passage in Samuel that says God put the idea of a census in David's head. Nevertheless, both stories tell us that David prevailed and Joab reluctantly carried out the order.

Samuel says that the task took almost 9 months and 20 days and that Joab counted in Israel about "eight hundred thousand soldiers able to draw the sword, and those of Judah were five hundred thousand (2 Sam 24:8–9). Chronicles gives a somewhat different set of figures but of a similar order. Joab reported, "*they of Israel were a thousand*

thousand and an hundred thousand men [i.e., 1,100,000] that drew sword: and Judah *was* four hundred threescore and ten thousand men [i.e., 470,000] that drew sword" (1 Chr 21:5).

The total number of soldiers in the joint kingdom was 1,300,000 according to Samuel and 1,570,000 according to Chronicles. We should probably assume that those "able to draw the sword" probably meant the entire adult male population. How accurate these numbers are we cannot know, but in the time of David, the true numbers would probably be about 10 percent of the given figures, about 150,000 people total between the two kingdoms, perhaps even less.

After Joab gave his report, Chronicles adds a very strange claim that is omitted in Samuel. "But Levi and Benjamin counted he not among them: for the king's word was abominable to Joab" (1 Chr 21:6).

The Levites were the priestly class in Israel, so it's understandable that even Joab might hesitate to commit such an outrageous religious sin against the priests, but why did he not count Benjamin, the home of David's chief rivals throughout his rise to the throne? What was so abominable to Joab that he would number all the other tribes, but not Benjamin? Two answers seem most likely. Either Benjamin had been so greatly reduced in size by David, either through war or massacre, that the published numbers would be too embarrassing to note, or Benjamin continued in active resistance to David's usurpation of the Israelite throne and Joab couldn't get a count.

A Smiting of Israel

Immediately following this notice about a lack of a Benjaminite count comes another interesting discrepancy. Samuel tells us:

> And David's heart smote him after that he had numbered the people. And David said unto the LORD, I have sinned greatly in that I have done: and now, I beseech thee, O LORD, take away the iniquity of thy servant; for I have done very foolishly (2 Sam 24:10, emphasis added).

But Chronicles has this report.

And God was displeased with this thing; therefore he smote Israel. And David said unto God, I have sinned greatly, because I have done this thing: but now, I beseech thee, do away the iniquity of thy servant; for I have done very foolishly (1 Chr 21:7–8, emphasis added).

In both accounts, David recognizes that he is a sinner and asks forgiveness. But whereas Samuel says that David asked for forgiveness because his heart felt bad that he had committed this terrible act (even though he allegedly carried it out at God's will), Chronicles advises us that he did so only after God "smote" Israel. Although Chronicles doesn't tell us in what manner God struck down the people, the term usually indicates that a large number of deaths occurred.

Three observations should be made here. First, while Samuel says that God initiated the census to punish Israel, Chronicles says that God was displeased with the conducting of a census and punished Israel because of the census. Second, the connection between the census and a large number of deaths in the aftermath suggests active military resistance to David's "sinful" census. Third, although Samuel says that David became remorseful because he realized that the census was a terrible and that he should take blame so that Israel wouldn't be punished, Chronicles says that David repented only after a large number of deaths occurred.

To reconcile these two accounts, we need to recall the purpose of the census. It was a taxation and confiscation program by the king. The soldiers didn't merely count the number of people; they would have seized property and assets to take back to the royal court. Such actions would almost certainly have been met with resistance. Centralized taxation went against the lifestyle of the decentralized north.

If resistance occurred, then that would explain the lack of a count for Benjamin and the Levites. Benjamin, the center of anti-David resentment, would have led the resistance movement, and the northern Levites of the priesthood must have supported the rebellion, as they had a strong incentive to keep wealth out of royal hands. Many of the northern priests, especially the Mosaic branch as opposed to the dominant Aaronite branch, would also have remained loyal to Saul's house during his feud with the Aaronite Samuel and remained in opposition to the Aaronite priests surrounding David in Jerusalem.

From the Samuel perspective, taking property from the Israelites was the punishment for their wrongdoing, whatever that wrongdoing was. Most likely it was a failure to meet David's call for voluntary financial contributions to underwrite his building programs and dangerous expansionist foreign policy. The failure to support David would have been considered a sin against God according to David's priests, and the forcible taking of property would be the punishment.

In Chronicles, the punishment of Israel during the count would have been the result of Joab's countermeasures against the rebels. From the Chronicler's viewpoint, resistance to David's rule was a sin against God. The striking down of the rebels would have been God's punishment.

An Offer of Penance

Following David's confession of sin, Gad the Seer came to the king with an offer from God. The Lord had given David three choices for absolution:

> And the LORD spake unto Gad, David's seer, saying, Go and tell David, saying, Thus saith the LORD, I offer thee three things: choose thee one of them, that I may do it unto thee. So Gad came to David, and said unto him, Thus saith the LORD, Choose thee Either three years' famine; or three months to be destroyed before thy foes, while that the sword of thine enemies overtaketh thee; or else three days the sword of the LORD, even the pestilence, in the land, and the angel of the LORD destroying throughout all the coasts of Israel. Now therefore advise thyself what word I shall bring again to him that sent me (1 Chr 21:9–12).

I should note here that in the Samuel version of this prophesy there is a slight problem. The KJV translation gives the number of years of proposed famine as "seven" while the NRSV translation has "three" as in the Chronicles passage cited above. A footnote to the NRSV passage (at 2 Sam 24:13) indicates that the KJV translation stems from a Greek version of 1 Chr 21:12, which has "seven" years. "Three" then is what the Hebrew version of the text has and "seven" comes in from a Greek translation of the Hebrew text. A question that could be raised is whether the Greek translation reflects an earlier version of the Hebrew text or a copying error or a deliberate distortion.

The Hebrew arrangement of three years, three months, and three days sounds like the more poetically logical arrangement. The Greek version suggests a possible effort to break any possible link between this three-year famine connected to David's census and the three-year famine in the Gibeonite incident that led to the execution of Saul's sons.

In any event, David had to make a choice. Obviously the lengthy famine seemed the least acceptable option for both the king and for Israel. The other two choices involved either a period of three months being chased by enemies or three days of plague. The two accounts portray David as trying to diplomatically explain why it is better to punish the people than the king and both use approximately the same words in providing the excuse.

According to Chronicles, "David said unto Gad, I am in a great strait: let us fall now into the hand of the LORD; for his mercies are great: and let me not fall into the hand of man" (1 Chr 21:13). In other words, David said something to the effect of, "Being chased by enemies month after month is no fun and besides I might get caught, so let's do that other thing, you know, with the pestilence, which only lasts a couple of days." One would think that if David could trust the people to God's mercy, he could similarly trust himself to the same mercy and spare his subjects the holy wrath.

David's choice, as given in both versions, reflects a fundamental failure of divinely ordained kingship. If the king is the anointed of God, then he should always place God's people above himself and trust to the Lord. The truth is that David had no choices. An uprising threatened his reign and, as suggested in a clue below, famine was already upon the land. The so-called pestilence, described as the sword of the Lord, actually constituted a short-lived conflict between David and the rebels, and as we shall see, they had been marching on Jerusalem.

BUYING A SANCTUARY

The pestilence, according to both accounts, led to seventy thousand deaths throughout the country, about 5 percent of the population according to the census (2 Sam 24:15, 1 Chr 21:14). Even if we adjust the figure downward to correspond with the likely population estimate, the proportion of the population killed would remain the same.

God's angel then stood over Jerusalem, sword poised to destroy David's capitol, when the Lord had a sudden change of heart (2 Sam 24:16). The angel removed himself to the threshing floors of Araunah the Jebusite, flaming sword still in hand. (2 Sam 24:16. 1 Chr 21:15 says the threshing floor belonged to Ornan the Jebusite. The name is a slight variation on the one in Samuel.) Contextually, the threshing floor appears to be located just outside of David's Jerusalem perimeter. That the action shifts to a threat against a granary suggests that a famine was abroad.

Both accounts say that David saw the angel of God that had struck down the people of Israel and stood poised to destroy Jerusalem (2 Sam 24:16–17). At this point David tells God that the sin was his and not the people's and that they shouldn't be punished (2 Sam 24:17). He then asked of God, "Let thine hand, I pray thee, be against me, and against my father's house" (2 Sam 24:17).

This passage contradicts the introduction to the Samuel account, which stated that Israel, not David, made God angry and the Lord set out to punish Israel, not David. In any event, God agreed to end the slaughter if David would build an altar at the threshing floor of Araunah the Jebusite and make a large sacrifice (2 Sam 18:24). The bulk of the remaining story line concerns David's negotiations with Araunah for the threshing floor. The Jebusite wanted to give the land and the resources for a sacrifice to David, but David insisted on paying full price so that it would truly be a personal sacrifice for him. There are, however, a few inconsistencies in this portion of the story that bear some discussion.

A Chronological Problem

In both stories, the scene shifts to Araunah at the threshing floor, where he sees David coming. But Chronicles inserts a strange passage just before the Jebusite sees the Israelite king.

> And Ornan [i.e., Araunah] turned back, and saw the angel; and his four sons with him hid themselves. Now Ornan was threshing wheat (1 Chr 21:20).

The juxtaposition of hiding from the avenging angel and the claim that he was threshing wheat immediately thereafter seems inconsistent. If we substitute for the angel a rebel army invading David's Jerusalem in time of famine, then the passage makes more sense. The Jebusite had a lot of wheat and the people were hungry.

Samuel then adds a passage that is missing from Chronicles. "All these things did *Araunah, as a king, give unto the king*" (2 Sam 24:23, emphasis added). The verse acknowledges that Araunah was a Jebusite king functioning on the outskirts of David's Jerusalem, and even more likely, in Jerusalem.

In context, the Samuel passage also shows that David and Araunah had a friendly relationship. Given the biblical claim that David forcibly seized Jerusalem from the Jebusites and slaughtered the inhabitants, how likely is it that a Jebusite king would appear to be operating a granary just outside of David's walls? Not very, and this adds substance to our earlier argument that David's move to Jerusalem was peaceful and that the Jebusites continued to live there without difficulty. The Chronicler, recognizing that the presence of a Jebusite king at Jerusalem undermined David's authority as God's chosen ruler, omitted the detail of Araunah's title.

On the other hand, any strong Jebusite presence in Jerusalem, especially a royal presence, would have to have occurred very early in David's reign because in later years he was undisputedly the master of the city. The purchase of the threshing floor may, in fact, have been the event that symbolically transferred Jerusalem from Jebusite to Judahite control.

We come now to a pivotal point in the census story, one that appears in Chronicles but not in Samuel, and which enables us to draw some possible connections between this episode and the events surrounding the sacrifice of Saul's children at Gibeon.

> At that time when David saw that the LORD had answered him in the threshing floor of Ornan the Jebusite, then he sacrificed there. For the Tabernacle of the LORD, which Moses made in the wilderness, and the altar of the burnt offering, were at that season in the high place at Gibeon. But David could not go before it to inquire of God: for he was afraid because of the sword of the angel of the LORD (1 Chr 21:28–30).

If this census incident happened late in David's reign when religious worship was centered in Jerusalem under the leadership of Zadok and Abiathar, why would he want to go to Gibeon to make inquiry of the Lord? He should be able to do that in Jerusalem. Also, why did he need to make inquiry of the Lord when Gad the Seer had been right there with him to tell him what the Lord wanted?

Equally puzzling is why David feared to go to Gibeon because of the angel's sword. References to such things as "the angel's sword" should be understood metaphorically as a description of an armed religious group, just as the "smiting" of a people by God should be understood as a military attack by an army devoted to the Lord. That David feared to go to Gibeon strongly suggests that a large armed religious opposition to him existed in Gibeon.

The city of Gibeon was an Aaronite stronghold within the territory of Benjamin. As you will recall from the census conducted by Joab, no count was made of Benjamin or the Levites, suggesting that these two groups were in strong opposition to David's actions. When Samuel and Saul split, Gibeon would probably have remained loyal to Saul and become the religious center of the Saulide kingdom, replacing the Shilohites who sided with David.

Such an arrangement helps put many of the above events in chronological context. If a Jebusite king still had a strong presence in Jerusalem, then we are talking about an early point in David's reign, not long after his move to Jerusalem. If Gibeon is still the place to go to inquire of the Lord because the Tabernacle is there (and presumably the Ark also, which belongs in the Tabernacle), then again we are pointing to a time early in David's reign, before Jerusalem became the religious center of Israel.

The census would also have come early in David's reign as he sought to consolidate power around the country, take inventory of what he ruled over, and build up the treasury. The failure to conduct a count within Benjamin or among the Levites suggests an early period in David's reign, when there would still have been ongoing resistance within Benjamin and among a pro-Saul faction of northern priests.

After the census, we are told that David faced a choice of three years of famine (the same number of years of famine as alleged in the story of the Gibeonite famine sacrifice), three months of being chased by his enemies, or three days of pestilence (in the form of the sword of the Lord). I suggest that these weren't actual choices facing David but the ongoing reality. A famine existed (which may have started before David took control over Israel) and David faced armed opposition from within Benjamin, which used the famine as a basis for challenging David's role as God's chosen. The rebellion lasted for perhaps three months at the end of the census period, and ended in a short three-day battle near Jerusalem that resulted in the defeat of Benjamin and Gibeon.

As a condition of surrender, David demanded the execution of most of Saul's heirs and shifted the religious center to Jerusalem. The transfer of religious authority is signified by the establishment of an altar at Araunah's threshing floor. David publicly blamed Gibeon's opposition for the famine, calling it a punishment from God, and blamed Gibeon for the need to sacrifice Saul's children and end the opposition to God's will. Later biblical editors twisted the facts slightly to make it appear that Gibeon was responsible for the sacrifice of Saul's children because it requested such action rather than because it supported the Saulide resistance against David.

The census must have happened very early in David's reign, perhaps even before he moved his capitol to Jerusalem, and it may have triggered Sheba's rebellion. It probably also occurred before the Ark came to Jerusalem, if, in fact, the Ark ever came to Jerusalem while David was on the throne, a question that we explore in the next chapter.

CHAPTER 14

Bringing the Ark
to Jerusalem

And David was afraid of the Lord that day, and said, How shall
the Ark of the Lord come to me? So David would not remove the Ark
of the Lord unto him into the city of David: but David carried it aside
into the house of Obededom the Gittite. 2 SAM 6:9–10

One of the very first events ascribed to David after he became king was the building of a palace. "And Hiram king of Tyre sent messengers to David, and cedar trees, and carpenters, and masons: and they built David an house" (2 Sam 5:11). Almost immediately after David built his house the bible claims that he brought the Ark of the Covenant to Jerusalem (2 Sam 6). While the bible clearly states that David brought the Ark to Jerusalem amidst great ceremonies there are some odd claims in Chronicles that cast some doubt on whether David ever transported this holy icon to his capitol in his early years. In this chapter we will look at evidence that during David's reign the Ark had been kept at Gibeon, and that it wasn't removed from Gibeon until after Solomon became king.

Our first clue comes from the writings of the first century Jewish historian Josephus. He claims not only to have seen records pertaining to the kings of Tyre, but to have seen actual copies of the letters that were sent from Hiram to Solomon (*Ant.* 8.2.8, 55). According to Josephus' writings, Hiram was in the eleventh year of his reign when Solomon started building the Temple in his own fourth year (*Ant.* 8.3.1, 61).

If Josephus can be trusted, his evidence suggests that if Hiram sent supplies to David for the building of a palace the event must have happened sometime in the last seven years of David's reign, not in the beginning as presently recorded. This is significant in that it relates to a second chronological problem. When did the Ark of the Covenant come to Jerusalem? The biblical narrative says that David brought the Ark to Jerusalem after he built his house and that Hiram provided the supplies. This would suggest that if the Ark came to Jerusalem during David's reign it came in the last few years rather than shortly after the city's capture by David, as indicated in the bible.

Unfortunately, we don't know how reliable Josephus' claims about Hiram are, and it is hard to build up a strong thesis based on his arguments. Nevertheless, there are other reasons to think that if the Ark came to Jerusalem, it did so either at the end of David's reign or in the beginning of Solomon's reign.

THE ARK OF THE COVENANT

The Ark of the Covenant was Israel's holiest relic and it was believed to be the throne (and/or footstool) of God. According to instructions preserved in the Book of Exodus, which described the building and care of the Ark, this icon was to be kept in a moveable tent known as the Tabernacle, which Moses allegedly built pursuant to God's direct specifications (Ex 25:9). Presumably from the time of Moses, the Ark had been kept in the Tabernacle except in certain situations, usually involving war against Israel's enemies, when the Ark was brought out to aid the Israelites. The Ark represented the power of Israel's God, and whoever possessed it had considerable leverage over the people of Israel.

In the beginning of the Book of Samuel the Ark had been housed in Shiloh (1 Sam 3:3) but the Philistines captured it in battle and apparently destroyed Shiloh (1 Sam 4:10). When a series of divinely caused mishaps led the Philistines to return the Ark it initially came to rest in Bethshemesh (1 Sam 6:14). But because some of the Bethshemites looked inside the Ark the Lord struck them down and the Ark was moved to Kiriath-Jearim, where it supposedly remained for twenty years (1 Sam 7:1–2).

If David brought the Ark to Jerusalem in his last seven years, then the Ark must have been previously moved from Kiriath-Jearim to some other location because the twenty years in Kiriath-Jearim would have started before Saul came to the throne and would have ended well before David's last seven years. Again, however, that argument depends upon Josephus, whose credibility can't be confirmed in this regard.

The city of Kiriath-Jearim was a member of a four-city confederation that was headed by Gibeon (Josh 9:17). Kiriath-Jearim appears to have been a small and not physically well protected community. Gibeon had a reputation from earlier times as a royal city, suggesting that it was the largest of the four communities and probably protected by a wall (Josh 10:2).

Gibeon was one of the cities given to the Levites and there would have been a priestly cult there. Given its location in Benjamin one might suspect that the priests in that city remained loyal to Saul. In fact, 1 Chr 9:35–39 states that Gibeon was the ancestral city of King Saul. Given the importance of the Ark to Israel and the hostile surroundings it seems unlikely that it would be kept in the less well protected city of Kiriath-Jearim rather than in the larger more secure setting of Gibeon, especially given Gibeon's role as a major priestly enclave.

This suggests that the Ark may have been held in Gibeon rather than Kiriath-Jearim, or moved to Gibeon at a later time, perhaps under Saul's administration. Unfortunately, we don't actually know how long Saul ruled as that piece of information has been corrupted in textual transmission. The general consensus seems to be that he ruled twenty to thirty years.

Another possibility is that when the Shilohite Samuel threw in his lot with David, the Gibeonite priesthood, remaining loyal to Saul, forcibly removed the Ark from the hands of the Shilohites and kept it protected in Gibeon to reinforce Saul's authority.

The story of how the Ark came to the Gibeonite enclave of Kiriath-Jearim from the Levitical city of Bethshemesh following its return from the Philistines may dimly recall just such an early conflict between the Gibeonites and the Shilohites. According to the biblical account the Lord slaughtered over fifty thousand Bethshemites as a punishment for some of them looking inside the Ark. Immediately afterwards the Ark went to Kiriath-Jearim. Such a large number of deaths, although no doubt greatly exaggerated, suggests some sort of military conflict the upshot of which was that the Ark passed from Shilohite hands to Gibeonite control, and was placed in the city of Kiriath-Jearim or Gibeon.

The Ark was not moved about casually and only priests were supposed to carry it. Several stories indicate that just the accidental touching of the chest by the wrong person—someone not a member of the priesthood, for example—could lead to that person's death. Indeed, when David first tried to remove the Ark to Jerusalem, one of the handlers accidentally touched it and died, causing David to cry out, "How shall the ark of the LORD come to me?" (2 Sam 6:9). The Ark was then temporarily deposited in the house of Obededom, who, strangely, is described as a Gittite, i.e., a man of the Philistine city of Gath, who found favor with the Lord (2 Sam 6:10–11).

THE TABERNACLE IN GIBEON

Chronicles tells us that after the incident in which David sinned by conducting a census the Lord sent an angel to destroy Jerusalem and that the Tabernacle was located in Gibeon.

> For the Tabernacle of the LORD, which Moses made in the wilderness, and the altar of the burnt offering, were at that season in the high place at Gibeon. But David could not go before it to inquire of God: for he was afraid because of the sword of the angel of the LORD (1 Chr 21:28–30).

If the Ark was in Jerusalem why was the Tabernacle in the city of Gibeon, in Benjaminite territory? One only removed the Ark from the Tabernacle under limited ceremonial purposes and one didn't keep the Ark and the Tabernacle housed in different cities. The Tabernacle was the house for the Ark. Further, we have the strange observation in Chronicles that the Tabernacle was still in Gibeon at the time Solomon became king but that the Ark was in Jerusalem where David made a special tent for it.

> So Solomon, and all the congregation with him, went to the high place that *was* at Gibeon; for there was the tabernacle of the congregation of God, which Moses the servant of the LORD had made in the wilderness.

But the ark of God had David brought up from Kirjathjearim to *the place which* David had prepared for it: for he had pitched a tent for it at Jerusalem (2 Chr 1:3–4).

If David brought the Ark to Jerusalem why didn't he also bring the Tabernacle, the official tent in which the Ark was to be kept? Why was it necessary to provide a new tent for it in Jerusalem? This makes absolutely no sense. If David didn't bring the Tabernacle to Jerusalem then it seems highly unlikely that he brought the Ark there. The two belong together.

The verse about David fearing to go to Gibeon seems to implicitly acknowledge that the Ark was still there. It says David wanted to go there to inquire of the Lord. The only reason to go to Gibeon to make inquiry of the Lord was if the Ark was there. That was one of the functions of the Ark. As you may recall, one of the chief criticisms of Saul was that he didn't consult the Ark (1 Chr 13:3).

That there may have been a militant warrior-priest order in Gibeon to protect the ark is suggested by the textual claim that David feared to go from Jerusalem to Gibeon because of the angel's sword. The "sword of the angel" suggests a metaphor for religious armed resistance against David.

It might be argued that this discrepancy about the location of the Ark and the Tabernacle could be resolved if the census incident occurred very early in David's reign, perhaps while the Ark was still in Gibeon. That would be sufficient to resolve the matter if 2 Chr 1:3 didn't also tell us that shortly after Solomon became king the Tabernacle was still in Gibeon and that he made arrangements to bring it to Jerusalem to join up with the Ark. Again, the Ark would have been housed in the Tabernacle, which is clearly in Gibeon, and not in a special tent in Jerusalem.

Solomon became king in a palace coup and had the backing of David's army along with the Pelethite and Cherethite guards. He moved quickly to dispose of his enemies and banished Abiathar from Jerusalem, leaving Zadok as the chief priest. As noted in the passage quoted above, Solomon brought his entire congregation with him to Gibeon in order to conduct ceremonies at the Tabernacle. With the advantage of his military support and swift action in the face of the political chaos surrounding his succession, I suggest that Solomon quickly seized the Ark and took control of it away from the Gibeonites, placing it under the authority of the Zadokites.

Also in support of the argument that David did not bring the Ark to Jerusalem is that it was supposed to be under the special protection of the Shilohites in the north, or at least with northern priests. Bringing the Ark to Jerusalem, where the rival Zadokites would have partial control would have created a religious crisis and possible civil war within David's carefully balanced distribution of power. Not until Solomon expelled Abiathar and demoted the Shilohites would the king have risked such a dangerous strategy.

The biblical claim that David brought the Ark to Jerusalem probably belongs to a Solomonite apologia intended to deflect charges that he wrongfully seized the Ark from the Gibeonites. So his defenders claimed that he inherited it from the far more authoritative figure David, who, they claimed, had previously brought it to Jerusalem. As David and Solomon had served briefly as co-regents in David's last year or two Solomon's defenders would at least be technically correct when they said the Ark came to Jerusalem under David's reign and that Solomon inherited it. The defense just omits that it was Solomon and not David who brought it into Jerusalem.

CHAPTER 15

A Successful Coup

And he said, Thou [i.e., Bathsheba] knowest that the kingdom
was mine [i.e., Adonijah's], and that all Israel
set their faces on me, that I should reign. 1 KI 2:15

*U*nder normal circumstances, biblical and ancient Near Eastern traditions would lead us to believe that David's successor should be Adonijah,
David's fourth and oldest living son at the time of his death. Both the
Book of Kings and the Book of Chronicles, however, tell us that Solomon, David's tenth son, succeeded his father as King of Israel and that the
two monarchs shared a brief co-regency towards the end of David's life.
But the two biblical accounts contain radically different portraits of David's final years and of how Solomon came to the throne.

Given the importance of Solomon in the theological scheme, David's first heir and the builder of the Temple, one would expect that
the biblical authors would give us some background information
about him prior to his ascension to the throne. But this is not the case.
Other than the announcement of his birth as Bathsheba's second
child, we get no reports about his early life. Instead, he almost seems
to materialize out of thin air, as did his patrons, Nathan and Zadok,
when David captured Jerusalem.

Chronicles portrays David in his end days, now seventy years old,
as a vibrant, energetic king publicly and enthusiastically endorsing Solomon as his successor and devoting his time to organizing and planning for the building of the great Temple (1 Chr 22). The actual building would not begin until David passed away, but the Chronicles text

223

describes his elaborate stockpiling of riches and materials to be devoted to the task. When David died, Solomon smoothly assumed authority without any hint of trouble in the process (1 Chr 29:23).

The Book of Kings, on the other hand, depicts David as "old and stricken" and perhaps senile and easily manipulated, and Solomon's ascent anything but smooth and trouble free.

In the 1 Kings version, David lay cold and covered in bed (1 Ki 1:1). His advisors, concerned for his health, fetched an attractive virgin named Abishag to try and bring some warmth to him, but her efforts were in vain (1 Ki 1:2–4). A sickly king had diminished authority, his illness seen as a sign from God that the monarch's time had come to an end and that preparations for a successor should begin.

With David's failing health and the king's near demise, Adonijah, David's oldest living son, made preparations to succeed his father (1 Ki 1:5). Like Absalom before him, he gathered chariots, horsemen, and fifty runners to accompany him. At no time during his son's initial symbolic claims to the throne did David raise any objections. To secure his place, Adonijah consulted with Abiathar, the priest, and Joab, who agreed to back him, but the would-be monarch had opposition (1 Ki 1:7). Arrayed against him were "Zadok the priest, and Benaiah the son of Jehoiada, and Nathan the Prophet, and Shimei, and Rei, and the mighty men which belonged to David" (1 Ki 1:8).

In his final stages of succession, Adonijah arranged a coronation feast and invited all the king's sons, except for Solomon, and all the men of Judah, except for Nathan, Benaiah (who controlled the Pelethites and Cherethites), and the Thirty (1 Ki 1:9–10). Oddly, no claim is made here that Zadok had not been invited, but later on Nathan told David that Adonijah failed to invite Zadok. Also of interest, although we are specifically told that Adonijah invited the men of Judah, no similar invitation to the men of Israel is recorded.

Before we get into the intrigues and actions that led to Solomon's elevation, we should first pause to examine the political realities at this point in time.

Political Alignments

With Absalom's earlier revolt, we saw that a major breach existed between Judah, David's original home base, and the Jerusalem faction, including Nathan, Zadok, Abiathar, Joab, Benaiah, the Pelethites and the Cherethites, and the Thirty. In the negotiations to return David to the throne, the king agreed to replace Joab, who served as head of the army, with Amasa, a Judahite loyalist of Absalom. Once the two sides consummated the deal David returned to Jerusalem. Shortly thereafter, Joab murdered Amasa and once again became commanding general of the army.

To the north, Israel always remained a suspect and shaky member of the United Monarchy, strongly antagonistic towards Judah and deeply untrusting towards David. To hold some control over the northern kingdom, David kept Jonathan's son and grandson, Mephibosheth and Micah, under house arrest along with the son of Barzillai, a key backer of the House of Saul.

The bible tells us almost nothing about how Judah reacted to the assassination of Amasa or how Israel behaved while Saul's descendants were held in the Jerusalem court. In addition, we should assume that fierce rivalries existed between Zadok and Abiathar over control of the priesthood, as well as conflicts among the Jerusalem-centered priesthood under the joint control of Zadok and Abiathar, the alienated northern priests who followed Saul, and the alienated southern priests who backed Absalom.

No doubt a lot of political maneuvering went on, and alliances built on narrow interests may have formed and collapsed and reassembled from time to time. The divisions described in Adonijah's coronation plans give us some clear evidence and some ambiguous clues about how matters evolved in David's final years.

Adonijah, David's oldest living son, was a Hebronite from Judah and the expected natural successor. He even took preliminary steps to confirm this expectation. But obviously he was aware that strong opposition existed within the Jerusalem faction to the proper order of succession, and he took steps to isolate the opponents.

Joining the Hebronite heir were Joab and Abiathar. Although both previously belonged to the Jerusalem party, their participation in that faction stemmed more from deep loyalty to David rather than political support for the Jerusalem court.

Joab had a reputation as an ambitious and ruthless killer who would hesitate at nothing to keep himself in power. Few people would mourn his fall from grace, but he had retained power over a significant portion of David's military forces. On the other hand, Benaiah, who had control over the Pelethites and Cherethites and the Thirty, appears to have become more popular with the Jerusalem court than had Joab. With the imminent death of his chief patron Joab could foresee Benaiah taking over his post and himself being removed from the center of power, as was subsequently the case. His only hope was to leverage his weakening control over the army with some faction. Adonijah signed him on. Although Judah resented what Joab did to Amasa, if Joab could make Adonijah king he could be forgiven.

Abiathar, one of the two co-chief priests, also saw his power and Shilohite influence waning in the Jerusalem court. Nathan appeared to be the most influential religious person in David's court, and his protégé appeared to be Zadok, the other co-chief priest. Nathan seems to have had clear plans to centralize control over religion in Jerusalem, diminishing the Shilohite cult status and enhancing the Zadokites. In addition, Jerusalem wanted control over the Ark, which would weaken Shilohite influence over Israel's holiest relic, an important psychological source of Shilohite power. If the Ark hadn't already been brought to Jerusalem, the Jerusalem faction planned to bring it there. This did not bode well for Abiathar and he, too, needed to line up with another political team. Adonijah appeared willing to join with both Abiathar and Joab.

Whom Did Israel Support?

But where was Israel in all this maneuvering? An important clue appears in the list of people (cited above) who didn't join Adonijah's following. Among them was someone named Shimei and another named Rei (1 Ki 1:8). About the latter we know nothing. This is the only occasion where the name appears. But could this Shimei be Shimei the son of Gera who cursed David as a bloody murderer and who commanded a large Benjaminite army?

The identification is unclear. Usually, a name such as this would have a patronymic attached, such as "Shimei the son of Gera" or "Shimei the son of Elah." Up until this point in the story, Shimei the son of Gera is the only Shimei in the Davidic history. The reader's attention would naturally be drawn to the conclusion that this Shimei was indeed the Benjaminite commander who cursed David.

In support of this identification we should observe that later, when David advises Solomon about whom to treat well and whom to get rid of, the king tells Solomon, "And, behold, thou hast with thee Shimei the son of Gera, a Benjaminite of Bahurim, which cursed me with a grievous curse in the day when I went to Mahanaim" (1 Ki 2:8). Behold, indeed! This clearly says that Shimei is with Solomon, and David follows up this notice with a warning that Shimei should be put to death.

Absent other evidence, the likelihood is that this is the same Shimei. Perhaps the biblical editors were too embarrassed to have this enemy of David closely associated with David's chosen successor, fearing that it might undermine Solomon's credibility, and chose to create ambiguity by omitting Shimei's patronymic.

In the same chapter in which David advises Solomon on what to do with various people, he also says that Solomon should be good to the sons of Barzillai, another strong faction within the Israelite/Benjaminite camp (1 Ki 2:7). This unites two of the major Israelite factions behind David.

This evidence regarding Shimei and Barzillai's sons, while not conclusive and certainly subject to debate, does strongly suggest the likelihood that Israel came to terms with David and, at the very least, remained neutral in the showdown between Adonijah and Solomon. In that regard, it should be observed that while Shimei is described as not following Adonijah, nowhere does he take any positive action towards elevating Solomon.

In addition, we should also note that while Adonijah was born in Hebron in Judah, Solomon was born in Jerusalem, nominally in the territory of Benjamin, and came to power despite the opposition of Judah.

From the standpoint of an Israel-Judah rivalry, the Israelites probably would have been more comfortable with a king such as Solomon, who would have had some bias against his Judahite opponents, than a king such as Adonijah, who had deep roots in Judah and allied himself with the enemies of the House of Saul.

NATHAN UNDERMINES ADONIJAH'S CLAIM

Having set the events surrounding David's last years in political context, let's now see how Nathan manipulated events to make Solomon king.

When Nathan heard about Adonijah's planned celebration, he approached Bathsheba and asked if she had heard that Adonijah had declared himself king without David's knowledge. This situation could be dangerous, he told her, leading to her death and to Solomon's. Therefore, he advised her:

> Go and get thee in unto King David, and say unto him, Didst not thou, my lord, O king, swear unto thine handmaid, saying, Assuredly Solomon thy son shall reign after me, and he shall sit upon my throne? why then doth Adonijah reign? Behold, while thou yet talkest there with the king, I also will come in after thee, and confirm thy words (1 Ki 1:13–14).

In other words, she should tell David that he promised to make Solomon king and that Nathan would then come in after her and confirm to David that he made such a promise. Although not explicitly stated the assumption here is that no such promise was ever made, at least none that the biblical reader has been made aware of, and that David is too sickly to know better. Furthermore, Nathan is a man of God whom David closely trusts and relies upon for advice. If Nathan says that David made such a promise, he, David, would be hard-pressed to deny it.

Bathsheba followed Nathan's strategy and went to see David. The text reiterates that "the king was very old" (1 Ki 1:15). Upon entering David's chamber she delivers a speech that Nathan prepared for her and concludes by saying:

And thou, my lord, O king, the eyes of all Israel are upon thee, that thou shouldest tell them who shall sit on the throne of my lord the king after him. Otherwise it shall come to pass, when my lord the king shall sleep with his fathers, that I and my son Solomon shall be counted offenders (1 Ki 1:20–21).

At this point Nathan entered the room and asked if David had appointed Adonijah king, advising the monarch of his son's coronation feast and how Nathan and Zadok had been excluded from the guest list (1 Ki 1:24–27). Did you do this thing, Nathan asked ominously, and not tell me about it? (1 Ki 1:27). As David would have been expected to consult with the Lord about his successor, with Nathan and Zadok as his intermediaries, their exclusion from the banquet would appear to David as an affront to the God of Israel.

With Bathsheba telling the feeble David that Adonijah would put her and Solomon to death and Nathan apparently chastising him for not consulting the Lord (through Nathan) before making a decision on succession, and both telling him of an earlier promise to make Solomon the successor, David first said to Bathsheba:

Even as I sware unto thee by the LORD God of Israel, saying, Assuredly Solomon thy son shall reign after me, and he shall sit upon my throne in my stead; even so will I certainly do this day (1 Ki 1:30).

He then summoned Nathan, Zadok, and Benaiah, and instructed them to place Solomon on the king's mule and lead him to Gihon (1 Ki 1:32–33). There Zadok and Nathan were to anoint him king over Israel and to blow a trumpet and declare "God save king Solomon" (1 Ki 1:34). Then they were to bring him back and place him on David's throne, where he would rule in the king's stead. "For I have appointed him to be ruler over Israel and over Judah" (1 Ki 1:35).

Nathan and Zadok, accompanied by the Pelethites and the Cherethites, executed David's plan. The people seeing the procession and hearing the trumpet called out praise for King Solomon, as music and shouting followed him back to the palace (1 Ki 1:40). No doubt a good deal of the shouting and music came from Zadok's large priestly retinue and Benaiah's Pelethites and Cherethites.

The sound of trumpets and shouting reached Adonijah and Joab at the feast and raised concerns (1 Ki 1:41). Then, the son of Abiathar ran in and announced that David had made Solomon the king and filled them in on the details (1 Ki 1:43–48). Upon hearing the news, the guests all fled from the room and made their own way (1 Ki 1:49).

Adonijah, fearful of Solomon's reaction, raced to the altar in the Tabernacle, which was the holy House of God, and took hold of the altar's horns—apparently a means of claiming sanctuary—saying that he would not leave unless Solomon promised to spare his life (1 Ki 1:50). Solomon responded:

> If he will shew himself a worthy man, there shall not an hair of him fall to the earth: but if wickedness shall be found in him, he shall die (1 Ki 1:52).

With that, Solomon triumphed over Adonijah and eliminated his rival as a contestant for David's throne. The dispossessed heir appeared before the king and bowed to kiss him but Solomon dismissed him, telling him to go to his house.

David's Dying Advice to Solomon

As David perceived that the end was close he gave final guidance to his son. First came the religious advice:

> And keep the charge of the LORD thy God, to walk in his ways, to keep his statutes, and his commandments, and his judgments, and his testimonies, as it is written in the law of Moses, that thou mayest prosper in all that thou doest, and whithersoever thou turnest thyself: That the LORD may continue his word which he spake concerning me, saying, If thy children take heed to their way, to walk before me in truth with all their heart and with all their soul, there shall not fail thee (said he) a man on the throne of Israel (1 Ki 2:3–4).

Then came the practical advice. He told him how Joab killed Abner and Amasa and brought blood during peace, and that Solomon should use his wisdom and "let not his hoar head go down to the grave in peace" (1 Ki 2:6). On the other hand, he told him, "shew kindness to the sons of Barzillai, because they were kind to me" (1 Ki 2:7). And lastly, about Shimei the son of Gera, he said:

> And, behold, thou hast with thee Shimei the son of Gera, a Benjamite of Bahurim, which cursed me with a grievous curse in the day when I went to Mahanaim: but he came down to meet me at Jordan, and I sware to him by the LORD, saying, I will not put thee to death with the sword. Now therefore hold him not guiltless: for thou art a wise man, and knowest what thou oughtest to do unto him; but his hoar head bring thou down to the grave with blood (1 Ki 2:8–9).

Although the advice about Joab and Shimei has been placed in David's mouth, most scholars believe that pro-Solomon apologists inserted these instructions in order to exonerate him from guilt for his subsequent actions against these individuals.

Eliminating the Opposition

Solomon took no action against potential enemies while David was alive. How long the co-regency lasted we don't know, but many suspect that it lasted no more than three years, as Solomon began working on the great Temple in his fourth year and David would have been deceased when the building process began. With David's death, Solomon came into his own, but Adonijah may have tried one last time to turn things around.

According to the story, when David died Adonijah approached Bathsheba and asked her for a favor (1 Ki 2:14). He reminded her that he should have been king but for the intervention of God, and asked that he be allowed to take Abishag, the woman who ministered to David in his final days, for his wife (1 Ki 2:15–17). He told her that Solomon would not refuse a request from her and she agreed to do so (1 Ki 2:17–18).

Bathsheba approached Solomon and told her son she had a favor to ask (1 Ki 2:19). Solomon replied that there was nothing he would deny her (1 Ki 2:20). She them asked him to allow Adonijah to have Abishag

(1 Ki 2:21). When she presented this request Solomon understood it for what it was, an attempt to sleep with the king's (i.e., David's) concubine in order to establish a claim to the throne. He responded:

And why dost thou ask Abishag the Shunammite for Adonijah? ask for him the kingdom also; for he is mine elder brother; even for him, and for Abiathar the priest, and for Joab the son of Zeruiah. Then king Solomon sware by the LORD, saying, God do so to me, and more also, if Adonijah have not spoken this word against his own life (1 Ki 2:22–23).

(Note here Solomon's reference to Adonijah being the elder brother, and the implicit recognition of his stronger legal claim to the throne.)

The now sole monarch immediately dispatched Benaiah to execute Adonijah and the new commander of the military did so.(1 Ki 2:25). He also directed Benaiah to eliminate Joab, but Joab ran to the Tabernacle before he was caught and, like Adonijah before him, grabbed hold of the horns of the altar in order to claim sanctuary in the House of God (1 Ki 2:28).

Benaiah reported back to Solomon that Joab was in the Tabernacle of the Lord, but Solomon said, "fall upon him" (1 Ki 2:29). Benaiah returned to what was then the House of God and asked Joab to come out, but the fugitive refused, saying that he would die there (1 Ki 2:30). Benaiah returned to the king, concerned about bloodshed in this holy place, but Solomon said, "Do as he hath said" (1 Ki 2:31). So Benaiah entered the Tabernacle, the House of God, and Solomon's general struck Joab dead (1 Ki 2:34). The execution of Joab no doubt helped Solomon with the Israelites, as they held Joab directly responsible for the murder of Abner, Saul's general, and indirectly responsible for the deaths of Saul and Eshbaal. Solomon even mentions that Joab got David into trouble by killing Abner without David's knowledge (1 Ki 2:32).

As to Abiathar, the Shilohite priest who backed Adonijah over Solomon, the king granted him mercy, allegedly because he had previously carried the Ark and suffered with David in the fugitive days, but he also banished this Shilohite priest from the court with words of condemnation:

Get thee to Anathoth, unto thine own fields; for thou art worthy of death: but I will not at this time put thee to death, because thou barest the Ark of the Lord GOD before David my father, and because thou hast been afflicted in all wherein my father was afflicted (1 Ki 2:26).

With the expulsion of Abiathar, Zadok, formerly just the co-chief priest, now became the only chief priest, but the wheels of resentment were set in motion in Shiloh, and, as we shall see later, the Davidic dynasty paid a high price for Solomon's insult to the northern priesthood. Although the text says that Zadok was then put in Abiathar's room, a little later on, in 1 Ki 4, we find a list of administrative officials, with Abiathar still listed as a priest along with Zadok. The Shilohite may have still kept his official title, but Solomon almost certainly severely curtailed Abiathar's role to its most minimal functions.

Lastly, Solomon dealt with Shimei the son of Gera, who had cursed David when the king fled from Absalom. Although the text depicts David as having urged Solomon to execute Shimei as a punishment for cursing him, an excuse for such a bloody act was not easy to come by. Not only was Shimei an influential member of the House of Saul, possibly still in command of a large military force of Israelite loyalists; he may have, as argued earlier, remained neutral when Adonijah announced his intentions. It would be hard to justify his death under such circumstances, especially as David had previously publicly forgiven him.

So, Solomon did not put Shimei to death at that time. Instead, he ordered Shimei to build a house in Jerusalem and not to leave the city (1 Ki 2:36). If he ever passed over the Brook of Kidron, traditionally recognized as one of the chief boundaries of Jerusalem, he would be put to death (1 Ki 2:37). In effect, Solomon placed Shimei under house arrest, carefully circumscribing his range of activities. Shimei agreed to the terms and apparently swore an oath to the Lord to abide by those terms (1 Ki 2:38, 42).

Three years later, two of Shimei's servants fled to Achish, king of Gath (1 Ki 2:39). (This appears to be a different Achish than the one David served.) When Shimei heard the news he saddled up his ass and went after them, and brought them home (1 Ki 2:40).

When Solomon learned that Shimei left the city, he summoned the Benjaminite to the court and reminded him of the oath sworn to the Lord in which he promised not to leave the city under pain of death (1 Ki 2:43). Having sealed his own fate by violating an oath, Solomon had Shimei executed (1 Ki 2:46). The usurper of David's throne had now eliminated all his major opponents from positions of power.

It is interesting to note that the biblical text says that with the death of Shimei, the kingdom was established in the hand of Solomon (1 Ki 2:46). This suggests that Shimei still held a powerful position among a potentially rebellious Israel.

At this point, the bible proceeds to tell us of all the glories of Solomon's reign, another exercise in obfuscation of the truth.

CHAPTER 16

Collapse

And now whereas my father [i.e., Solomon] did lade you [i.e., Israel]
with a heavy yoke, I will add to your yoke: my father hath chastised
you with whips, but I will chastise you with scorpions. 1 KI 12:11

$\mathcal{D}$avid's dynasty lasted over four hundred years but his empire barely survived but one generation. (The bible describes David's kingdom as extending from the Egyptian border to the river Euphrates, i.e., to the western border of Assyria and Babylonia, corresponding approximately to the western border of modern Iraq [1 Ki 4:21].)

During Solomon's reign great swatches split off, particularly Syria to the far north and Edom to the southeast (1 Ki 11:14, 25). Also, Solomon transferred the title to twenty northern Israelite cities to the king of Tyre in order to help purchase Solomon's building supplies and hire Tyrian designers and craftsmen (1 Ki 9:11). In addition, the Philistines appear to have regained (or retained) control over the Mediterranean coast on Israel's western front (1 Ki 4:21).

Aside from the foreign losses, Solomon's harsh tyrannical rule triggered an Israelite revolt under the leadership of a local Benjaminite (or Ephraimite) hero named Jeroboam (1 Ki 11:26). Although the revolt failed and the rebel leader fled to Egypt for safety, when Solomon died Jeroboam returned to Israel, split the wealthier, more populated northern kingdom away from Judah, and became the first king of Israel after the collapse of the United Monarchy (1 Ki 11:40). Solomon's heir ruled over little more than the small impoverished Judahite shell that David governed during his outlaw days while Saul was on the throne.

Nevertheless, Solomon's vainglorious building of the great Temple, which he intended more as an exhibition of how wonderfully rich he was than as a display of any great respect for the God of Israel, planted the seed that nourished the mythic David legend that centuries later became the foundation stone of Jewish religion and early Christianity. It also served the politico-religious purpose of centralizing in Jerusalem the worship of Israel's God. But even that magnificent achievement was sullied under his son's rule when Shishak, pharaoh of Egypt, raided Jerusalem and removed all the gold and wealth stored in the great House of God, the contents later replaced by cheap replicas (1 Ki 14:25–28).

The biblical story of Solomon takes far less space than does the preceding account of David, but it exhibits many of the same tensions and divisions present in the Davidic histories, including pro-Solomon apologetics and anti-Solomon Shilohite charges of dereliction of duty to the Lord. Outside of the detailed accounts of the building of the Temple, most of the brief remainder is taken up with two basic themes. One shows Solomon as a wise and brilliant man whose devotion to God resulted in a showering of wealth upon the kingdom. The other portrays a cruel tyrant who persecuted Israel and rejected the God of Israel for the many pagan deities worshipped by his multitude of wives. The ultimate collapse of the United Monarchy following Solomon's death caused the Deuteronomist theologians much difficulty in integrating David's legacy with Solomon's folly.

CHANGES UNDER SOLOMON

Biblical chronology dates the start of Solomon's reign to about 1021 BCE but, as with David, scholars tend to move the date forward about fifty to sixty years.

A major change that distinguished Solomon's reign from David's was the emphasis on trade over militarism. However large the kingdom had been, and its true boundaries may have been far less extensive than the biblical claim, the biblical text, with but one minor exception in Chronicles, displays no record of Solomonic wars in foreign territories (2 Chr 8:3). The United Monarchy under David had apparently stretched as far as its military capabilities would allow.

Still, Solomon's trade advantage consisted of physical control over the major trade routes linking Egypt, Syria, Jordan, and the Arab states. The two most important were the Via Maris, which ran from Egypt to Damascus along the boundaries of Israel and Philistia, and the King's Highway, which went from Damascus down through Jordan into the Arabian states. In northern Israel several east-west routes linked these and other roadways.

Solomon leveraged these controls so that he could not only extract tariffs from passing caravans, but also buy goods from Egypt, such as linens and horses, and trade them to the Syrians and Hittites at large profits (1 Ki 10:29). In addition, he formed a strategic alliance with Hiram, the king of Tyre, whose expert sailors dominated sea-lanes in the Mediterranean. Solomon's alliance with Hiram developed out of the Israelite king's mammoth building programs, which poured huge amounts of wealth into Hiram's coffers in return for supplies and designers to implement the Israelite king's plans.

In furtherance of this alliance, Solomon built a fleet of ships at the eastern port to the Red Sea, providing for an eastern expansion of trade routes, and Hiram provided the sailors and experts necessary to run the trade missions (1 Ki 10:26–28). He also added ships to Hiram's fleet in the Mediterranean (1 Ki 9:26–28).

Another shift in Solomon's strategy from that of David's militarism was the use of marriage as a political and wealth-building tool. While David had a few wives, some of whom may have been of strategic importance, his son had over seven hundred wives and three hundred concubines (1 Ki 11:3). The most important of these would probably have been the daughter of the pharaoh, whom Solomon married and lodged in a palace specially built for her (1 Ki 9:24). This facility would surely have housed a large retinue of Egyptian servants and Egyptian priests. Recent excavations in the vicinity of Jerusalem have hinted at a possible large Egyptian structure of some sort that may date to this period.

The marriage of a pharaoh's daughter to a foreigner was a most unusual event in the ancient Near East and probably reflected the reality of Solomon's control over land (and perhaps Red Sea) trade routes from Egypt. The arrangement also guaranteed peace between the two nations, although a major dynastic change in Egypt during Solomon's reign appears to have led to a shifting of alliances that endangered Jerusalem and provided shelter to Solomon's enemies, including Jeroboam and perhaps the son of a king of Edom (1 Ki 11:14–17). As a dowry, the Egyptian pharaoh gave Solomon the city of Gezer, which he had earlier captured from the Canaanites and burned to the ground. Solomon allegedly rebuilt it at great expense, requiring the imposition of forced labor (1 Ki 9:15–17).

Solomon also married an Ammonite woman named Naamah (1 Ki 14:21). She is the only wife of his mentioned by name, attesting to her importance. She, too, must have been a king's daughter because she appears to have been the mother of Rehoboam, Solomon's heir to the throne. It's unlikely this honor would have gone to the son of a lesser background.

The hundreds of marriages attributed to Solomon would have been a vehicle for keeping many cities, towns, and villages under his control. The marriage to a powerful king would have been a great honor, and the pledge of loyalty by the smaller political entities would have been a form of dowry. The more prosperous communities would have added financial gifts as well.

Building Programs

The bible contends that Solomon engaged in many enormous building programs. In addition to the Temple and his own huge palace and the aforementioned works at Gezer, we are told of his rebuilding the walls around Jerusalem, and the rebuilding of Hazor, Megiddo, Beth-Horan, Baalath, Tadmor, and of building cities for store, cities for chariots, and cities for horsemen (1 Ki 10:15–19).

Solid archaeological evidence for this great extravagance is lacking. For a long time scholars have argued that finds of large scale structures at Megiddo and elsewhere appear to date to the time of Solomon (mid tenth century) and corroborate the biblical claims. No direct evidence specifically connects these structures to Solomon, though, and in recent years, Israel Finkelstein, a well-respected archaeologist who has extensively examined the sites in question, has developed a small but growing following for the view that these structures were erected perhaps a century later than Solomon's time and may have been part of the northern kingdom's building program after it split from Judah.

THE QUEEN OF SHEBA

Consistent with Solomon's control over trade routes, the bible relates a famous story about the visit of the Queen of Sheba to the Israelite court. Although the location of Sheba is in question, most scholars believe it to have been in Arabia while some others suspect Ethiopia. In any event, she arrived with a large tribute for the king and told him of his great reputation for wisdom, which she tested with "hard questions" (1 Ki 10:1), none of which have been preserved. The meeting went along quite well and mutual exchanges of compliments and gifts were plentiful.

Biblical scholars often cite this story as evidence of Solomon's great reputation for wisdom, but the fact of the matter is that Sheba headed a trade delegation seeking favors for her sponsors. In such an environment flattery flows like water and carries as much credibility as do the words of any obsequious court official.

THE BABY AND THE SWORD

Another famous biblical story about Solomon concerns his judgment in the dispute between two harlots who argued over who was the true mother of an infant child. Solomon offered to split the child in half with his sword and give one portion of the child to each of the women, causing the true mother to reject the offer in favor of allowing the living child to go to the rival claimant (1 Ki 3:24–27). The tactic worked and Solomon discovered the true mother's identity. Today, in recognition of that story, we call wise and clever decisions "Solomon-like."

We have no way to know if the story is true, such wisdom stories being a common folk motif in many cultures, but its importance in the biblical account is to credit Solomon with recognizing that David's shortcomings with the administration of justice led to a revolution that almost cost his father the throne. Solomon seems to have taken that concern to heart and attempted to rectify it in his own reign.

Nevertheless, Solomon engaged in many expensive building programs, far more so than did David, some for fortification purposes, some for administrative reasons, some for just simple luxury, and some for his many wives, and these building programs generated great friction and resentment within the Israelite populace. So, while he is almost always acclaimed as the wise man who built the glorious Temple to God, we have to balance such claims against shortcomings so obvious that one has to question how clever he truly was.

QUESTIONS ABOUT SOLOMON'S WISDOM

On the political level one of his greatest mistakes may have been to remove the Shilohites from the Jerusalem priesthood. Solomon did this, ostensibly, because Abiathar supported Adonijah's claim to the throne. But Adonijah was the lawful heir and, but for Nathan's timely intervention, should have been the legitimate king.

David knew that he had to balance the interests of the Shilohites against those of the Zadokites in order to hold the kingdom together. Solomon, in his arrogance, thought he could do without the Shilohites. So he punished Abiathar and his Shilohite following. This, in turn, forced the Shilohites, still an influential force in Israel, to seek new allies. They aligned themselves with Jeroboam in his eventually successful efforts to break Israel away from Judah, an event that we will discuss below.

Solomon's biggest political mistake, however, was the use of forced labor upon the Israelites. The king had strong control over the military forces in Israel. His elevation to the throne received the support of David's professionally trained foreign mercenaries (the Pelethites and the Cherethites) as well as the national army once commanded by Joab. Solomon united these forces under the leadership of Benaiah, another loyalist, and he no doubt kept the military well-rewarded for their support. He also kept his troops well-armed and supplied. This gave him a military advantage over the decentralized volunteers that made up the tribal muster. His military edge gave him the power to command forced labor and impose crushing tax burdens on the Israelites in order to finance his enormous expenditures. At the same time, he excused the Judahites from sharing similar responsibilities, bringing them into his military coalition.

In addition to the military power, the building of the Temple over seven years became a religious obligation of the Israelites, one heavily promoted by the priesthood, which made it a matter of deep personal sacrifice for the Israelites in order to help build the House of God.

This inflamed the already smoldering resentment of the north against the south. In order to diminish tribal opposition to his programs of forced labor, Solomon went as far as to revise the political boundaries associated with the ten tribes of the Israelite confederation. He re-divided their ten territories into twelve administrative districts (excluding Judah) and appointed local people of prominence to serve as the administrative heads (1 Ki 4:7–19). It was one of these local leaders, Jeroboam, who led the opposition against Solomon and eventually severed the relation between Israel and Judah.

The biblical editors tried hard to cover up this virtual enslavement of the northern tribes. In 1 Ki 5:15, for example, the bible says that Solomon had seventy thousand people to carry burdens and eighty thousand hewers, leaving the clear impression that the Israelites fulfilled this hard task. But several chapters later, in 1 Ki 9:22, after a substantial detour from the earlier claim, the editors apologetically add that Solomon didn't make bondsmen out of the Israelites, only out of the non-Israelites.

The Chronicler followed a similar pattern, apparently relying on either the Book of Kings or a common text as his source. 2 Chronicles 2:2 repeats the same figures as in Kings regarding the number of workers and their assignments: seventy thousand bearers and eighty thousand hewers, and, also after a detour, repeats the same figurers again in 1 Ki 2:17–18, but this time adds that only the foreigners did such work.

The truth, however, emerged in the later negotiations between Jeroboam and Solomon's son over the succession to the Israelite throne, and the forced labor imposed on the Israelites became the central issue in those discussions.

Politics aside, on the religious level we see not only the shallowness of Solomon's commitment to Israel's religion, the centerpiece of the nation's cultural life, but his total lack of respect for Israel's religious principles. After the Deuteronomist regales us with all of Solomon's glories, the narrative takes a sudden turn for the worse:

> But King Solomon loved many strange women, together with the daughter of pharaoh, women of the Moabites, Ammonites, Edomites, Zidonians, and Hittites; Of the nations concerning which the LORD said unto the children of Israel, Ye shall not go in to them, neither shall they come in unto you: for surely they will turn away your heart after their gods: Solomon clave unto these in love. And he had seven hundred wives, princesses, and three hundred concubines: and his wives turned away his heart. For it came to pass, when Solomon was old, that his wives turned away his heart after other gods: and his heart was not perfect with the LORD his God, as was the heart of David his father. For Solomon went after Ashtoreth the goddess of the Zidonians, and after Milcom the abomination of the Ammonites. And Solomon did evil in the sight of the LORD, and went not fully after the LORD, as did David his father. Then did Solomon build an high place for Chemosh, the abomination of Moab, in the hill that is before Jerusalem, and for Molech, the abomination of the children of Ammon. And likewise did he for all his strange wives, which burnt incense and sacrificed unto their gods (1 Ki 11:1–8).

There is not much worse that a king of Israel can do than to reject the nation's God and encourage the worship of foreign deities. That he built the great Temple only shows that he was ostentatious, not that he was religious, as his dalliances with other gods makes clear. Even the Temple, for all its glorious description, may not have been his most self-indulgent masterpiece. He spent only seven years building it, but thirteen years building his own home, almost twice as long on his own lodgings than on God's (1 Ki 6:37–7:1).

Solomon constructed his house from the cedars of Lebanon. David also built his house from the cedars of Lebanon, but apparently it was too small and spartan for Solomon's taste and a new house had to be erected. As with the Temple he preferred elaborate decoration:

> And King Solomon made two hundred targets of beaten gold: six hundred shekels of gold went to one target. And he made three hundred shields of beaten gold; three pounds of gold went to one shield: and the king put them in the house of the Forest of Lebanon. Moreover the king made a great throne of ivory, and overlaid it with the best gold. The throne had six steps, and the top of the throne was round behind: and there were stays on either side on the place of the seat, and two lions stood beside the stays. And twelve lions stood there on the one side and on the other upon the six steps: *there was not the like made in any kingdom.* And all King Solomon's drinking vessels were of gold, and all the vessels of the house of the Forest of Lebanon were of pure gold; none were of silver: it was nothing accounted of in the days of Solomon (1 Ki 10:16–21, emphasis added).

Nowhere in David's story do we find comparable descriptions of luxury. David took some privileges such as a nice home, but his tastes were rather pedestrian. He was more interested in the actual power itself rather than its trappings. The contrast is substantial and one can understand how forced labor in service to this profligate lifestyle might arouse resentment. But Solomon, for all his vaunted wisdom, appears to have been oblivious to it all. Eventually, Solomon's foolishness had a price.

ISRAEL BREAKS FROM JUDAH

The beginning of the end for David's empire dates to Jeroboam's initial rebellion against Solomon, but when in the course of Solomon's reign that occurred is difficult to determine. The full biblical account of Jeroboam's initial revolt and Israel's subsequent secession under his leadership appears as the last episode in the story of Solomon, but the arrangement is topical rather than chronological.

One clue as to the time frame comes from Jeroboam's flight to Egypt after the initial revolt failed. As Solomon had been married to a pharaoh's daughter, it is not likely that the same pharaoh would also provide shelter to her husband's chief rival. This suggests a change in administration in Egypt by the time Jeroboam arrived.

Coincidentally, the bible tells us that in the fifth year of Solomon's successor, an Egyptian pharaoh named Shishak invaded Jerusalem (1 Ki 14:25). Most experts in this period, relying on name similarity and some subsequent chronological correlations between the biblical king-lists and non-biblical ancient texts, identify this Egyptian as Sheshonk, the founder of a new dynasty who came to the throne at what would be the last few years of Solomon's forty-year reign.

Many Egyptologists would date the start of Sheshonk's reign to about 945 BCE and give him a reign of twenty-one years, while many biblical scholars would date the beginning of Solomon's reign to about 970–960 BCE. Since Sheshonk was on the throne during the fifth year of Solomon's successor, he would most likely have come to the throne sometime during Solomon's last sixteen years as king. Jeroboam's initial rebellion should be placed at some point after Sheshonk came to the throne. We can offer no more precise information at this time.

The bible identifies Jeroboam as an Ephrathite and a "mighty man of valour" (1 Ki 11:26–28). The term "Ephrathite" is somewhat ambiguous. It either refers to a place called Ephrath or is a miscopy of the word Ephraimite, which indicates a person from the territory of Ephraim. The bible seems to describe two different Ephraths, one in Judah near Bethlehem, David's hometown, and the other in Benjamin.

In any event, Solomon placed Jeroboam over the labor force from the House of Joseph, which should encompass the territories of both Ephraim and Manasseh, the large central heart of Israel (1 Ki 11:28). His assignment seems to have been to supervise this work force in the repairing of the Millo in Jerusalem, a large wall surrounding the city (1 Ki 11:27). One day, while outside of Jerusalem he met a Shilohite prophet named Ahijah, and when the two were alone:

> Ahijah caught the new garment that was on him, and rent it in twelve
> pieces: And he said to Jeroboam, Take thee ten pieces: for thus saith the

LORD, the God of Israel, Behold, I will rend the kingdom out of the hand of Solomon, and will give ten tribes to thee: (But he shall have one tribe for my servant David's sake, and for Jerusalem's sake, the city which I have chosen out of all the tribes of Israel:) Because that they have forsaken me, and have worshipped Ashtoreth the goddess of the Zidonians, Chemosh the god of the Moabites, and Milcom the god of the children of Ammon, and have not walked in my ways, to do that which is right in mine eyes, and to keep my statutes and my judgments, as did David his father. Howbeit I will not take the whole kingdom out of his hand: but I will make him prince all the days of his life for David my servant's sake, whom I chose, because he kept my commandments and my statutes: But I will take the kingdom out of his son's hand, and will give it unto thee, even ten tribes. And unto his son will I give one tribe, that David my servant may have a light always before me in Jerusalem, the city which I have chosen me to put my name there. And I will take thee, and thou shalt reign according to all that thy soul desireth, and shalt be king over Israel (1 Ki 11:30–37).

Those who do the arithmetic and remember that there were twelve tribal divisions should note that there is a missing tribe. Jeroboam will receive ten tribes and David's heirs but one tribe. There is no easy explanation for this, but most likely the missing tribe may be Simeon, which lay to the south of Judah and whose land apportionment came out of the territory assigned to Judah.

The above biblical passage shows that the Shilohite priesthood, banished by Solomon, allied itself with the northern kingdom against Solomon. Ahijah may even have anointed Jeroboam at the time of this prophecy. Although no specific rebellion on Jeroboam's part is described, in the biblical introduction to the Jeroboam story, we are told, "even he lifted up his hand against the king" (1 Ki 11:26). So some sort of conflict must have occurred. In reaction to either Ahijah's alliance or to Jeroboam's rebellion Solomon sought to have Jeroboam killed, but the new northern leader managed to escape to Egypt (1 Ki 11:40).

With Jeroboam's departure the story of Solomon comes to an end and the narrative shifts to the issue of succession. Solomon designated his son Rehoboam as his successor, but the northern kingdom was not ready to accept him as king (1 Ki 11:43). Talk of secession filled the air. To calm the waters, Rehoboam went to the northern city of Shechem, by Mount Ephraim, to meet with the Israelite leaders and discuss the transition (1 Ki 12:1). The Israelites, fed up with Solomon's tyranny and physical oppression of the people of Israel, summoned Jeroboam from Egypt to negotiate on their behalf. Jeroboam offered a compromise.

> Thy father made our yoke grievous: now therefore make thou the grievous service of thy father, and his heavy yoke which he put upon us, lighter, and we will serve thee (1 Ki 12:4).

The request seemed simple enough. Lighten our work loads and we will support you as king, but Solomon's heir was not so quick to accept a limitation on his authority and asked for three days to discuss matters with his own advisors. Rehoboam first consulted with the elders who had also advised Solomon in earlier years and asked for their advice. They told him:

> If thou wilt be a servant unto this people this day, and wilt serve them, and answer them, and speak good words to them, then they will be thy servants for ever (1 Ki 12:7).

The elders had essentially agreed to the northern offer and told Rehoboam to accept it, but this didn't satisfy him. So, he went to the younger crowd that he had grown up with, and who had acted as his personal advisors while his father was still on the throne. They took a harsher stand.

> Thus shalt thou speak unto this people that spake unto thee, saying, Thy father made our yoke heavy, but make thou it lighter unto us; thus shalt thou say unto them, My little finger shall be thicker than my father's loins. And now whereas my father did lade you with a heavy yoke, I will add to your yoke: my father hath chastised you with whips, but I will chastise you with scorpions (1 Ki 12:10–11).

This is what Rehoboam wanted to hear and that was the message he delivered to Jeroboam and his counselors. This obviously failed to assuage the resistance. The northerners reacted with the very same expression of discontent uttered by Sheba when he rebelled against David:

> What portion have we in David? neither have we inheritance in the son of Jesse: to your tents, O Israel: now see to thine own house, David (1 Ki 12:16).

The Israelites then withdrew and appointed Jeroboam king over Israel (1 Ki 12:20). Rehoboam initially sought to raise an army out of Judah to crush the rebellion, but wiser heads prevailed and he withheld his invasion. But Judah and Israel fought wars all of the days of Rehoboam and Jeroboam (1 Ki 14:30).

The Aftermath

Jeroboam used the time to solidify his forces. His chief concern had to do with the upcoming holiday sacrifices at the Jerusalem temple. He feared that if Israel went there to sacrifice the religious leaders there would be able to turn Israel's hearts back to Rehoboam (1 Ki 12:27). As a countermeasure Jeroboam announced several religious reforms. The most important involved the establishment of two new temples, one at the southern boundary of Israel in Bethel and the other at the northern boundary in Dan (1 Ki 12:29). In front of each temple Jeroboam placed a golden bull. He then announced:

> It is too much for you to go up to Jerusalem: behold thy gods, O Israel, which brought thee up out of the land of Egypt (1 Ki 12:28).

These events may have inspired later biblical authors to invent a story about Aaron sinfully building a golden calf during the Exodus and angering God. Despite the fact that Aaron built only a single statue, the author of the Aaron story put Jeroboam's very words in Aaron's mouth, including the reference to multiple gods *"These be thy gods*, O Israel, which brought thee up out of the land of Egypt" (Exodus 32:4, emphasis added).

Jeroboam also instituted other reforms, including the changing of the date for the sacrificial festival (1 Ki 12:33). But Jeroboam went further than even the Shilohites anticipated. In the tradition of Saul, Jeroboam downplayed the importance of the Shilohite priesthood and democratically allowed just about anyone who wanted to be a priest to become one.

> And he made an house of high places, and made priests of the lowest of the people, which were not of the sons of Levi (1 Ki 12:31).
>
> After this thing Jeroboam returned not from his evil way, but made again of the lowest of the people priests of the high places: whosoever would, he consecrated him, and he became one of the priests of the high places (1 Ki 13:33).

Naturally, this caused a split once again between the Shiloh priesthood and the king of Israel. The northern prophets and the later Deuteronomists depicted Jeroboam as the prototype of the sinful king and successfully destroyed the reputation of one of Israel's greatest liberators throughout all of history down to this time.

> And this thing became sin to the house of Jeroboam, so as to cut it off and to destroy it from the face of the earth (1 Ki 13:34).
>
> [King Baasha of Israel] did what was evil in the sight of the Lord and walked in the way of Jeroboam and in his sin which he made Israel to sin (1 Ki 15:34).
>
> [King Omri of Israel] walked in all the way of Jeroboam the son of Nebat, and in the sins that he made Israel to sin (1 Ki 16:26).
>
> And it came to pass, as if it had been a light thing for [King Ahab of Israel] to walk in the sins of Jeroboam the son of Nebat . . . (1 Ki 16:31).

Rehoboam ruled for eighteen years and Jeroboam for about twenty-two years. Jeroboam's son, Nadab, ruled for another two years, allegedly following in his father's path. Nadab's reign ended in assassination at the hands of a man named Baasha, who is described as the son of Ahijah of the House of Issachar (1 Ki 15:27). Baasha then seized the throne.

Given the enmity between Jeroboam's house and the Shilohite priesthood, one can't help but wonder if this Ahijah of the House of Issachar is not the very same Ahijah the Shilohite priest who initially allied him-self with Jeroboam. If so, this would suggest that the Shilohites encour-aged Baasha to seize control. That Shiloh had a hand in Baasha's plans finds some corroboration in 1 Ki 16:2, where the Lord says to Baasha (through a priest):

> Forasmuch as I exalted thee out of the dust, and made thee prince over my people Israel; and thou hast walked in the way of Jeroboam, and hast made my people Israel to sin, to provoke me to anger with their sins (1 Ki 16:2).

This description of Baasha, the murderer of Israel's king, as exalted by the Lord and made a prince over the people clearly implies that Baasha had priestly backing in his usurpation of the throne. Baasha ruled for about 24 years and was followed by Omri, the first king of Israel or Judah whose existence can be corroborated by extra-biblical records. A Moabite stele records the recapture of territory previously seized by Omri.

His son was Ahab, who had married the infamous Jezebel, a Phoeni-cian princess. The Omri-Ahab period appears to be one of great peace and prosperity for the northern kingdom, although there was a brief schism between Omri and another contender for Israel's throne in the earlier years of his reign. Although the Jehu dynasty replaced the Omri dynasty about forty years after Omri came to the throne, Omri's name appears to have become the synonym for ancient Israel in those times. Assyrian records from the time of Jehu and afterwards refer to the north-ern kingdom as the House of Omri.

The kingdom of Israel lasted until 722 BCE, when Assyria de-stroyed its last remnants and forcibly removed much of the local pop-ulation, dispersing it to other locations in the Assyrian empire. These Israelites were never heard from again, giving rise to the myth of ten lost tribes.

The Davidic dynasty in Judah outlasted Israel by about 150 years, enabling the Deuteronomist writers to have the final word on the his-tory of David and the subsequent disputes. The Deuteronomist de-fense of David successfully rehabilitated David's image, and a century or so later the Chronicler scrubbed clean whatever lingering doubts remained. By the good fortune of having outlasted Israel, Judah's spin doctors had the final words on David and greatly influenced the future history of the world, permanently changing the face of Israel's religion and planting the seeds that sprouted into rabbinical Judaism and Christianity.

CHAPTER 17

The Biblical David Versus the Historical David

*W*e have now reviewed the essential episodes in the biblical account of King David's life as recorded in the Books of Samuel and Chronicles (and briefly in 1 Ki). As we have seen, the accounts are occasionally duplicated, inconsistent, contradictory, altered, invented, redacted, or broken up and rearranged. It remains to recap what we have learned and put together as best we can the historical record of King David's life.

In what follows, I will set forth the story of David as known to or believed by the Israelites of David's time or shortly thereafter, and where appropriate I will contrast it with the biblical account and explain why there are differences. In the previous chapters, our analysis followed the story of David as it unfolded sequentially in the biblical accounts. The biblical editors, however, radically altered the original chronology, and in the reconstruction below I set forth the chronological order of events as they appear to have actually occurred.

THE YOUNG DAVID

The biblical account of David's youth, confused by contradictory claims within the narrative, relies mostly on fiction and distortion. The major events described are Samuel's visit to David's home to anoint the young lad as king of Israel and Saul's replacement, David's arrival at Saul's court because of musical talents, and the slaying of Goliath.

As argued in chapter 4, Samuel's anointment of David took place late in Saul's reign after David had already become a popular figure in Israel, and had been part of a plan to stage a coup against Saul and place David on the throne. The biblical editors transferred the event to an earlier time frame to enhance David's legitimacy as king and to isolate the priesthood from the later intrigues surrounding David's break from Saul.

The story of David and Goliath is pure fiction, based on an earlier legend about military confrontations between heroic members of King David's army and Philistine giants from the city of Gath. It was suggested in chapter 3 that this original legend was itself a distortion in which metaphors describing several Philistine military units as giants from Gath were confused with the underlying reality. The existence of this original story that contradicted the account of David's heroism so upset the author of Chronicles that he severely edited the account, leaving out certain details and altering the identity of Goliath by making him Goliath's brother.

This leaves us with the story of David coming to Saul's court as a youth with musical talents. We have no benchmarks against which to evaluate this portion of the story. The Davidic tradition closely associates David with music; Chronicles notes his attention to musical detail; Samuel includes several poems attributed to him; and the Psalms of David erroneously claim him as the author of the poems and prayers contained within. He also appears in the stories as a skilled user of clever words. It is not improbable that he was a musician and poet of some ability and, given his apparent charismatic character, I'm inclined to accept that David possessed such artistic skills.

I'm also prepared to accept that David may have come to Saul's court as a young boy and found favor there with Saul and Saul's children. He was the son of a well-heeled and influential family in nearby Bethlehem in Judah, and it is not unlikely that the son of such a family would have a position in the king's court. The biblical editors, however, embellished the story of David's arrival with an artificial account of Saul's mental anguish and the need for music to soothe his anguish.

THE BREAK BETWEEN DAVID AND SAUL

The biblical account portrays David as an effective warrior and military leader who quickly rises to a high position in the military structure. Along the way he became engaged to the king's daughter, and the two may have been married, although the biblical account implies that the marriage was not consummated. The story also depicts David as a close friend of Saul's son Jonathan, the heir apparent to Saul.

This much of the story we shouldn't doubt as it seems consistent both with the biblical account and my alternative scenarios. But the biblical editors overlaid this historical core with an important but fallacious claim that Saul had developed a paranoid fear that David's popularity would drive him to oust Saul from the throne or, at the least, deprive Saul's heirs from following in his royal footsteps.

The evidence, however, is that Saul remained a popular and beloved figure in Israel even after his death, and that David and Samuel did in fact plot against Saul and had planned a military coup to oust him. The biblical editors played fast and loose with the facts, rearranging incidents and yanking events out of context in order to obtain the desired impact.

That Saul remained highly popular and that the Israelites overwhelmingly preferred him to David can be seen from several factors. While Saul lived he appeared to be a model king, and after his death the people of Israel continued to resist David's elevation to the throne. Under Saul's leadership Israel remained decentralized, without any indications of attempts to centralize power within the royal family; we have not the least hint that he ran corrupt courts or lacked for justice; his military forces relied upon a voluntary muster that prevented him from imposing his rule over the nation against its will; he successfully fended off Israel's enemies; he launched no imperialistic land grabs in foreign territories; he didn't meddle in private affairs; he is not noted for grandiose lifestyles or public arrogance; nor is there any evidence that he sought to enhance his personal wealth at public expense. On this last point, the evidence suggests that he even used the family home as his royal court.

The biblical attack against Saul has two prongs. The first charges that the king failed to consult the Ark and follow the law of God. Since this charge reduces down to the claim that Saul rejected Samuel as the voice of God or the lawgiver of God, we can acknowledge that the charge is true and that the dispute is simply theological, representing different points of view among different religious factions within Israel. The second charge holds that Saul acted unjustly towards David because the king's paranoia led him to doubt David's loyalty. This charge is false. As the evidence in chapter 4 shows, David and Samuel plotted together to remove Saul from the throne through a military coup.

The plan called for an alliance among the military forces at Samuel's command through the Shiloh community, a large armed force raised by David's influential family in Judah, i.e., the volunteer army of Judah, and, perhaps, behind the scenes support from the Philistines. In furtherance of David's claim to the throne, Samuel planned to publicly anoint David king over Israel at a ceremony in David's home city of Bethlehem, establish a military foothold in Judah, and then march against Saul.

Wind of the intrigues breezed by Saul and he sought to place David under house arrest until he could get to the bottom of the rumors. But, before Saul could take custody of the would-be king, David, with the help of Jonathan, escaped Saul's clutches and fled to Samuel at Ramah, Samuel's home base, for protection.

Saul sent a military delegation to Ramah to demand that David be turned over to them, but Samuel's warrior priesthood refused to surrender the fugitive. After several threats from Saul's delegation, Saul himself confronted Samuel and delivered an ultimatum: David must return to Saul's house by the new moon or there would be an all-out military confrontation.

David wondered how much Saul actually knew about the plot between him and Samuel against the king and whether it might be safe to return to Saul's household. He conceived a plan to uncover Saul's intentions and duped his friend Jonathan into helping him find out. David told Jonathan that Saul wanted to kill him, presumably over his seemingly disloyal flight to Saul's enemy Samuel, and that he wanted to find out how angry Saul really was. Jonathan agreed to help.

When Saul asked about David's absence from the table, David told Jonathan to give the following explanation: David had been required by his family to attend a sacrifice in Bethlehem and Jonathan gave him permission to go. If Saul understood that David wanted to go to Bethlehem in order to be crowned king, he would become furious over David's actions; if he took it calmly, it meant that Saul was in the dark about David's true intentions. In the latter case, it would probably be safe for David to return to the palace and avoid a military confrontation.

While David went to meet with Jonathan, Samuel arranged for a military escort to whisk David away to Bethlehem if necessary. The soldiers were stationed at a sanctuary at Nob, which may have been under Philistine control at the time, and the escort may have included Philistine soldiers, a fact covered up in the bible by describing the escort metaphorically as the "sword of Goliath" (1 Sam. 21:9). The Philistines, of course, would have been happy to have an ally undermine Saul's strength and perhaps overthrow the Israelite king.

When Jonathan told Saul that David went to Bethlehem for a sacrifice, the king exploded in rage, making it very clear that he correctly believed that David plotted against him to take the kingship away from his family. He also accused both Jonathan and Jonathan's mother, Ahinoam, of joining with David in this act of betrayal. Later evidence showed that Jonathan did indeed aid David's efforts against Saul and other evidence suggested that Ahinoam had also allied herself with David.

The king's son, via a prearranged signal, warned David to flee. The would-be king raced to Nob, where he would catch his military escort. From there he hurried to Bethlehem to meet up with Samuel and be anointed by him as king over Israel.

Saul reacted as expected, with military force, and immediately wiped out the viper's nest at Nob. This show of force demoralized the opposition and weakened David's hand. Saul sent troops out after him but again David escaped Saul's grasp. David gathered his family and the remnant of his troops and took up a position behind Moabite lines, where he achieved a degree of temporary safety.

DAVID BECOMES KING OF JUDAH

David took swift action to counter Saul. He formed an alliance with the Moabite king and established a military base in Moab territory, from which he could strike over the border whenever he chose, actions that the Moabite king would heartily endorse and perhaps profit from. In addition, the biblical account shows that David had a close friendly relationship with Nahash, king of the Ammonites and Saul's bitterest enemy. A confusing genealogy in the bible suggests that David's chief military officers, the brothers Joab, Abishai, and Asahel, had blood ties to Nahash, thus implying that David might have had an Ammonite component in his army.

David's relationships with Moab and Ammon gave him some leverage against Saul, who could fight on only so many fronts at one time. From his Moabite base David consolidated his military force and then formed an alliance with the Philistines on the western front of Israel. Because the Philistines, Ammonites, and Moabites protected David, Saul abandoned his efforts to catch his disloyal protégé. This freed David to cross over into Judah and establish a territorial base for his kingdom on Israelite soil.

From this position, he used his military prowess to establish a terrorist-based extortion racket among the various towns and villages. In return for tribute from weakened villages, David agreed to leave the inhabitants unmolested.

While the biblical account of David's efforts at Keilah depicts him as rescuing the town from the Philistines, the evidence suggests that he himself was the attacker. As David had been a Philistine vassal, the bible may actually have been technically correct in describing the raiders of Keilah as Philistines. The editors just failed to disclose that David was the Philistine who launched the assault.

While David's extortion scheme enjoyed moderate success in smaller places such as Keilah, he met resistance from Hebron, one of the chief communities in Judah. The leader of the opposition was a man called Nabal, a Hebrew word meaning "fool" and almost certainly a name used by biblical editors to disguise the man's true identity. This Nabal appears to have been one of the wealthier men of Hebron and he was married to someone named Abigail. Again, confused and inconsistent genealogies show that this Abigail may have been the daughter of Nahash, the Ammonite king and an ally of David.

Abigail secretly declared her support for David, provided his army with provisions, and almost immediately thereafter her husband Nabal suddenly died, seemingly of an apparent heart attack, although poisoning appears to be the better explanation. Nabal's death freed Abigail to marry David and she did, making him heir to Nabal's fortune. His military backing established him as the dominant political force in this neck of the woods. At about the same time as his marriage to Abigail, he also appears to have married a woman named Ahinoam, who is very likely to have been the same Ahinoam, wife of Saul, whom the king denounced as that "perverse rebellious woman" (1 Sam. 20:30–31) who conspired with David.

With control of Hebron, perhaps the chief Judahite city in that day, David declared himself king of Judah, and the elders of Judah soon conceded his authority and accepted him as their ruler, causing a split between Judah and Israel. This took place about five years before Saul died, but the biblical editors went to great lengths to cover up the chronology. Evidence that David had become king of Judah while Saul still lived undermined the argument that David had remained loyal to Saul all through the years that Saul tried to hunt David down. Fortunately, the editors missed a few clues.

David continued his alliance with the Philistines, serving as a vassal to King Achish of Gath, and receiving Philistine protection against incursions by Saul. In return for David's strong demonstration of loyalty to the Philistines, Achish gave him a gift of the city of Ziklag, a rather substantial present that clearly indicates that David's actions had found favor in Philistine eyes. In the course of his reign as king of Judah, David extended his realm by conquering the various communities to his south, consolidating all of Judah under his administration as well as the southern portion of Israel known as Simeon.

While the Philistines recognized that David's conquests made him abhorrent to the people of Israel and those loyal to Saul, the biblical editors tried to bury the odious reputation under a mountain of obfuscation, claiming that David actually raided only the non-Israelite portions of Judah and

Simeon and covered himself by lying to the Philistines about whom he actually fought with. In either event, David expanded his Judahite realm.

During the period of David's reign in Hebron, the evidence suggests that Saul initiated peace talks with David seeking reconciliation between the two kingdoms. The meeting took place at Jeshimon, and Saul apparently offered David a right of succession to the Israelite throne if David would renounce his claim as king of Judah and bring his kingdom under Saul's rule. Saul, no doubt, worried about the strong alliance between David and the Philistines. The negotiations, however, failed to resolve differences and the discussions collapsed. Biblical editors transformed the diplomatic language used in these discussions to portray David as a man loyal to Israel who had the opportunity to take Saul's life but chose to spare him, while Saul continued to irrationally accuse David of disloyalty.

Several versions of this story seem to have circulated around Israel and Judah and biblical editors mistakenly thought they were separate incidents in which David's loyalty to Saul had been demonstrated. So they presented at least two alternative reports of David's behavior as if they were separate consecutive events.

About five years after David declared himself king of Judah at Hebron, King Achish of Gath planned an all-out offensive against Israel and David vowed Judah's support for the Philistines in the coming war. The Philistines, though, remained cautious about David's involvement in the battle and suspicious of his motives, wondering if he could enthusiastically fight against his own people. Even if we accept the biblical claim that David did not fight alongside the Philistines, the text clearly shows that David did nothing to help defend his homeland against an enemy invasion and that he betrayed his nation in the hope that the coming battle would so weaken Saul that the kingdom of Israel would fall into his hands.

THE MURDER OF SAUL

The Philistine assault on Israel was a major turning point in biblical history. Saul and Jonathan died during the course of the war and the

Philistines conquered much of the central Israelite kingdom up to almost the Jordan River. The Israelite army retreated across the Jordan to Mahanaim, where it established a new capitol.

Although the biblical account makes great efforts to isolate David from the cause of Saul's death, the underlying evidence strongly suggests that David hired an Amalekite hit squad to kill Saul and his sons. Even the apologetic defense of David in the bible concedes that shortly after Saul's death, the king's crown and bracelet wound up in David's hands. We have no evidence that David returned these items to Saul's family, and the textual evidence suggests that the Israelites held David responsible for Saul's death and believed him to be a murderer.

When the Philistines discovered Saul's corpse, they dragged it back to their home city and displayed it before the public. While David made no efforts to retrieve the body, the non-Israelite citizens of Jabesh-Gilead, in the Transjordan, remembered how Saul saved them from David's good friend, King Nahash of the Ammonites. A raiding party departed from the city and retrieved Saul's remains from the Philistines. The citizens of Jabesh-Gilead gave the deceased king a proper funeral.

The biblical editors try to cover up David's lack of concern for Saul's remains by portraying him as perhaps the only person in Canaan who had no idea of what happened to Saul. They even have him utter a funeral dirge that prays that his Philistine allies learn nothing of what happened to the deceased king.

Saul's death and Israel's loss to the Philistines triggered a civil war between Judah and the much-reduced in size kingdom of Israel. In Israel, Abner, Saul's uncle and general of the Israelite army, installed Saul's son Eshbaal as king over Israel, while David continued to aggressively pursue his claim to the same throne.

The bible tells us that the House of Saul and the House of David fought for about two years, and there is little reason to doubt this. The civil war demonstrates how strong a hold the House of Saul had on the loyalties of Israel and how little support David had amongst them. Otherwise, there would have been a loud clamor for the elevation of David to the throne. While David may have had a possible legal right to succeed Saul, due to his betrothal to the king's daughter, the belief among Israelites that he had Saul murdered undermined the legitimacy of any such claim. The biblical editors offer no more justification for David's claim to be king over Israel than the fact that Samuel designated him as Saul's successor. But Samuel, a bitter enemy of Saul, carried little weight among the Israelites.

During the course of the conflict, the Book of Samuel alleges that Abner killed Asahel, Joab's brother, and that Joab sought vengeance against Abner. This story, however, appears to be false, as the Book of Chronicles shows that Asahel survived well into David's subsequent reign over Israel and held down an administrative position. The false Samuel claim serves to provide cover for David and isolate him from charges of collusion in the murder of Abner by Joab. Without the Asahel vengeance story to fall back on, it becomes clear that David arranged for Abner's elimination, or at least so the Israelites appear to have believed.

Abner's death came about in the course of negotiations between Judah and Israel over the return of Michal, Saul's daughter and David's betrothed, to David. The biblical account alleges that Abner and Eshbaal had a falling out and that Abner sought to make a deal to bring David to the throne of Israel. As a sign of good faith, David asked that Abner personally bring Michal to his court. Astonishingly, Eshbaal, the Israelite king, agreed to this return. After Abner brought her to David and proceeded back towards Israel, Joab killed him, supposedly to avenge his brother's death.

The biblical editors depict David as heartbroken over Joab's deed and claiming complete innocence in the matter. He even denounced and cursed Joab for his actions. But the punishment for murder was not unduly severe as Joab remained as commander-in-chief of David's army. And for all of David's professed concern, he buried Abner in Hebron rather than return the martyred body to the people of Israel.

As portrayed, Eshbaal's agreement to allow Michal to return to David, strengthening David's claim to the throne of Israel, made no sense. The more logical explanation appears to be that David suggested a peace treaty between the two sides, with the return of Michal as a sign of good faith. More likely, the insistence that Abner personally bring Michal was a deliberate plan to lure him into a false sense of confidence and to arrange for his assassination.

Not surprisingly, shortly after Abner's death Eshbaal also fell to assassins, by two soldiers who allegedly belonged to his army. The assassins brought Eshbaal's head to David, allegedly in return for a reward, but David had them executed. Again, at the time of David it must have been common knowledge that after Eshbaal's death David had possession of the dead king's head, just as after the death of Saul David had the crown and bracelet of the deceased ruler. Once again, David chose not to return the remains to the House of Saul, reinforcing the Israelite belief that David was a remorseless killer who would stop at nothing to seize the throne of Israel.

If the assassination of Eshbaal was intended to make David king, at least in the minds of the assassins, then it was imperative to also kill the surviving sons of Saul or Jonathan. This the assassins may have attempted, but their effort failed when a nurse managed to escape with Jonathan's son, Mephibosheth, before they could do him in. She brought the child to Machir, son of Ammiel. Saul appears to have had some additional sons, perhaps by concubines, and they sought refuge with an ally of Saul named Barzillai, whose son had married one of Saul's daughters.

The loss of Abner and Eshbaal greatly demoralized Israel and David continued to demand Israel's surrender. Backed by a Philistine army in addition to his own, David prepared to strike the final blow against Israelite independence. Israel, already significantly weakened and unable to mount any further resistance against such a large force, gave in and yielded the crown of Israel to David.

The Resistance Continues

The surrender of Israel took place at Mahanaim. David marched there with three columns of soldiers, one of which consisted of Philistines. An Ammonite contingent from Nahash joined David's troops when they arrived at Mahanaim. En route to meet with the Israelites, a Benjaminite named Shimei, from the House of Saul, cursed David for his bloody overthrow of the House of Saul, but Shimei commanded a substantial Benjaminite army and David didn't want to disturb the pending surrender negotiations. So, he let Shimei depart.

When David arrived at Mahanaim, he was met by the titular heads of the defeated Israelites, Machir, who cared for Jonathan's son, and Barzillai, whose son had married one of Saul's daughters, and who had cared for five of her children. David insisted that Jonathan's son and all of the children by Saul's daughter be turned over to him.

In addition, David wanted Barzillai to return with him, but Barzillai, who was quite elderly, declined and sent one of his sons in his stead.

This gave David physical control over the various branches of Saul's family, and he kept them under house arrest in Jerusalem. Within about three years, the children of Saul's daughter were executed, allegedly as a sacrifice to end a famine, an event we will discuss shortly.

On the journey back, hostilities between the two camps, Judah and Israel, remained high and another Benjaminite, Sheba, called for renewed fighting. A possible guerilla resistance imperiled David's hold on the throne. As Sheba raised a battle cry, Mephibosheth, the son of Saul, not to be confused with the son of Jonathan, declared, "Today shall the House of Israel restore me the kingdom of my father" (2 Sam. 16:3). But the revolt failed when Joab captured Sheba and had him beheaded by the townspeople who had provided shelter to the rebel.

The bible recounts all of these events about the surrender of Israel but reshapes the stories and rearranges the pieces to hide the fact that David had to force himself on Israel in order to become king and that he took hostages from Saul's family to insure that there would be no resistance.

The biblical editors record the taking of Jonathan's son as an act of kindness in fulfillment of a promise. The march to Mahanaim appears not as a capture of Israel but as a retreat from Absalom's seizure of Jerusalem; the negotiations for surrender appear as a welcoming of David by the remaining Saulide leaders when he arrives at Mahanaim; the seizure of Mephibosheth appears as an act of kindness early in David's reign as the fulfillment of a promise to Jonathan; the seizure of Saul's other children and grandchildren appears as part of a separate and unrelated event involving a famine; and Sheba's revolt is transferred in time from the post-surrender negotiations to the post-Absalom peacemaking.

DAVID'S EARLY YEARS AS KING

One of David's first acts as king over Israel and Judah was to seize Jerusalem as his capitol, with an order to kill the blind and lame Jebusites residing within. Despite the depiction of David's typically cruel mindset, there are a number of questions about how Jerusalem came under his sway. One likely possibility is that David initially shared Jerusalem with the Jebusites and later purchased portions of it from the Jebusite king. Evidence shows that early in David's reign (or perhaps late as the bible has it), a Jebusite king maintained a granary on the outskirts of Jerusalem and very probably continued to rule over the Jebusites within. David may have physically seized complete control over Jerusalem at a later date, after sharing it with the Jebusites in his early years.

Also very early in David's reign, the king ordered a census be conducted throughout the kingdom. No event in David's history seems to have been as devastating a blow to his reputation as this command. The author of Chronicles attributes the act to the influence of Satan, while the author of Samuel assumes that God must have put the idea in David's mind in order to punish Israel for some unmentioned evil. Even the homicidal Joab appears stricken with horror at the glee David takes in performing this deed. The biblical editors tried to place this event in David's last days to diminish its import, but the examination of the evidence shows that it occurred early on.

The reality, of course, was that the census enabled David to know how much treasure he could seize in the name of the throne. Joab set out to conduct the count but did not obtain any numbers for the Benjaminites and the Levites (the priests). This shows both a continued Benjaminite resistance to David's reign and a strong religious opposition to his concentration of power.

The religious opposition seems to have been in the priestly city of Gibeon, close to Saul's home base. During Samuel's split from Saul, Gibeon probably became the religious center of Israel. The census story indicates that David feared to go to Gibeon because the sword of the Lord was there, a good indication of the hostility between the Gibeonite priests and David.

The census appears to have been conducted at the time of a famine that lasted three years. We can't say when in the course of the three years the census occurred, or when during those three years David became king over Israel, but after the third year of famine, David declared that the famine was a punishment from God because Saul had done wrong to Gibeon, the nature of the wrongful act not being described. The bible depicts Gibeon as asking for seven of Saul's children to be executed as a sacrifice to God in order to end the famine. Conveniently, David had those seven children under his control and promptly had them hung.

The role of Gibeon in this affair is troublesome. Gibeon appears to be a Saulide stronghold and evidence presented in chapter 14 suggests that, despite claims that David brought the Ark to Jerusalem, the Ark of the Covenant remained in Gibeon throughout David's reign and into the beginning of Solomon's. I suspect that David may have negotiated a quid pro quo with Gibeon, to wit, in return for being allowed to keep the Ark in Gibeon, the Gibeonites would preside over the sacrifice of Saul's children. Such a conclusion remains highly speculative but consistent with David's modus operandi.

During the course of the famine, but because of the census, the prophet Gad offered David a way of making penance for his sin against Israel. The choice involved three days of pestilence or three months on the run from his enemies. Faced with a choice between hardship for himself and hardship for his subjects, he chose hardship for his subjects. While he was prepared to leave the fate of his people in the hands of God, he was not prepared to leave his own fate in the very same hands, a telling comment on his true commitment to the God of Israel.

Although Samuel and his Shilohite priesthood provided the religious and moral pretext for David's ascension to the throne of Israel, and Abiathar, who appeared to be Samuel's successor, fought by David's side during the entire outlaw period, David did not give Shiloh sole control over the religious life of Israel when he became king over Israel. Instead, he split the religious authority between Abiathar and Zadok, the latter most likely being the chief priest in Judah while David ruled from Hebron.

The bible provides no explanation for Zadok's sudden appearance on the scene. From out of nowhere David appointed him co-priest with Abiathar. The likelihood is that the biblical editors, in their continuous effort to obscure the fact that David became king of Judah while Saul ruled in Israel, eliminated any earlier references to Zadok while he presided over religious affairs in Judah. Under the co-priest arrangement, Zadok probably administered to the religious affairs of Judah while Abiathar performed the same function with regard to Israel.

The bible records two different lists of government administrators in David's reign, one of which provided for a minister of forced labor. This would have been consistent with David conducting a census in order to determine what kind of taxes the people could afford.

David required forced labor in order to pursue an expensive rebuilding program in Jerusalem, including the construction of his house, the wall around the city, and the expansion of the city boundaries. David also needed labor to supply the provisions for his army, including the Pelethites and Cherethites, the Thirty or the Mighty Men as they were also known, and a large standing army that freed him from reliance on the volunteer muster from the tribes, which could not be counted on to remain loyal.

THE BATHSHEBA AFFAIR

The Bathsheba affair, capped by David's arrangement to have her husband killed in battle in order to cover up his affair with the woman, stands out as the great glaring mistake in David's career, at least among his defenders who overlook all the other moral disasters attached to David's reputation. Its presence in the biblical account raises the question of how such a story came to be included in Samuel, especially when the Chronicler omitted it altogether.

As noted in chapter 10, the story serves a theological purpose. It was intended to show that even a king as "good" as David can succumb to evil if he fails to consult with God before his actions. Here the claim is that David failed to consult with Nathan about something or other, although what that something was is not very clear. It could be the failure to confess his sexual desire to Nathan before dallying with Bathsheba, or it could be that he should have consulted about what steps to take after she became pregnant, or it could have been he should have consulted with Nathan about whether he should have remained behind in Jerusalem instead of leading his troops into battle.

In any event, Nathan, the man of God, charged David with murder and the king confessed his sin. Nathan subsequently declared that God forgave David, but added that David would suffer punishment and humiliation at the hands of his family. Most people who follow this story overlook David's killing of Uriah and focus instead on how sexual desire can sometimes cause you to do foolish things. They see David's actions as just a one-time mistake about sex rather than as evidence of a murderous life style.

ABSALOM

The Absalom story is the longest episode within the history of David, suggesting that there existed an independent earlier epic about Absalom that was well known at the time Samuel was written and couldn't be overlooked. How much or how many of the incidents are factually based we can't say, but it does stand for the idea that David's reign had been characterized by earlier writings as wanting in justice, and that his failures led to his temporary ouster from Jerusalem.

What strikes one as particularly unusual about this accusation is that it seems to flow not from the traditional anti-David northern opposition but rather from the southern Judahite viewpoint, from David's home base. The story shows little connection with northern themes and the revolt against David seems centered directly in Judah, with little or no involvement from the north.

The alienation of David's base is made quite specific in the biblical account. Not only did Absalom drive David out of Jerusalem with the help of the Judahite army, Judah failed to rush out and greet him on his triumphant defeat of Absalom's forces. As an effort to win back Judah's confidence, David offered to appoint Amasa, head of the Judahite army, as the replacement for Joab, commander-in-chief for David's army. This promise turned the tide and Judah returned to the fold. But once David returned to Jerusalem and regained control, Joab slaughtered Amasa and resumed his command of David's army.

The murder of both Absalom and Amasa by David's chief lieutenant appears to have left a sour legacy among elements of political factions in Judah and those lingering resentments no doubt added substance to the Judahite charges that David lacked a concern for justice.

While attempting to spin and defend against northern accusations of Davidic wrongdoing can be aided by allegations of prejudice or bias in the making of the charges, countering an indictment out of one's own political base is much more difficult. Cleverly, the biblical editors decided to go with the flow, tying Absalom's revolt to the punishment of David for his wrongdoing in the Bathsheba affair. This focused attention away from the charges of judicial wrongdoing under David, suggesting that Absalom served merely as God's instrument in punishing David's earlier sin in the Bathsheba affair. This approach directed the reader's attention away from Absalom's accusation of a lack of justice and towards the earlier lesson about the need of kings to consult with God.

As a side note, it seems worth mentioning that wherever the Shilohite priests show up, charges of corruption seem to follow close behind in their footsteps. Eli administered over corrupt priests, Samuel administered over corrupt judges, and, David, with Abiathar as co-priest, had a corrupt court. And they may have been responsible for the assassination of Jeroboam's son and successor.

The Size of David's Kingdom

One of the interesting questions that must remain unresolved is the scope of David's kingdom, and that of Solomon's after him. But the evidence suggests that we must remain skeptical of David's claims of extensive conquest.

When the Philistines defeated Saul they captured most of the central core of Israel, driving through a large swatch of territory that separated the far northern portion of Israel from David's kingdom in Judah. David came to power in Israel as a Philistine vassal and as late as Absalom's revolt, the Philistines of Gath appear to have remained friendly with David and independent of his rule. We have no clear, unambiguous account of David recapturing the central core of Israel from Philistine hands.

We do have one notice of a battle with the Philistines over a narrow strip along the Benjaminite borders, which theoretically enable a transportation of the Ark from Kiriath-Jearim to Jerusalem. And we do have an account of a battle in which David's army defeated some Philistines from Gath, which took place towards the final days of David's reign (although the chronology of events in David's history can rarely be trusted). But we have no clear battle reports that David liberated central Israel from the Philistines or that he conquered the Philistines.

The biblical evidence suggests that in David's time the Philistines controlled most of the western coast along the Mediterranean Sea and continued in possession of the central portion of Israel. This would have made the far northern portion of Israel vulnerable to attack and isolated from David's defenses. It's not unlikely that the far northern territories came under Philistine or Syrian influence if not complete domination.

Also in the north, the king of Geshur, a Syrian enclave, seems to have remained independent of David but allied with him through marriage to the Syrian king's daughter, Absalom's mother.

To the south, David almost certainly dominated Judah and the sparsely populated Simeon.

As to the Transjordan, David probably retained control over that portion of Israel situated there, Reuben, Gad, and half of Manasseh. In addition, it's not difficult to except that he obtained functional control over

Moab, and maybe Edom. He may also have defeated Ammon as alleged in the bible, or he may have inherited it through family connections.

How far north into Syrian territories he eventually exercised authority is hard to say. There are descriptions in the bible of Syrian defeats at the hand of David, and they may be true. Independent evidence is nonexistent, and even in the biblical accounts we can't be sure that David's influence was anything more than transitory.

To a large extent, the picture of David controlling a vast empire seems to be a fictional projection backwards from an earlier time. The idea that he was a great king generated a belief that he must have ruled over the entire region. Not long after the collapse of the United Monarchy, King Omri of Israel may have presided over much of the territory believed to have been ruled over by David. Judahite scribes may have assumed that if Omri could preside over such a large kingdom perhaps David did too.

Solomon added no territory through military conquest, but he may have strengthened his control and expanded the kingdom's reach through his numerous marriages. Again, we are in the realm of speculation, as we have no hard evidence for the extent of Solomon's kingdom.

Perhaps the most telling evidence against the existence of David's huge empire is the lack of any mention of such a kingdom in the annals of any of the other nations that were allegedly conquered by or neighbors with Israel. The most likely scenario is that David ruled over a modest territory centered on Judah, Simeon, and Benjamin plus the Transjordan portion of Israel, with perhaps nominal control over Israel's far northern territories. He may have extended his boundaries into the south Transjordan states of Edom, Ammon, and Moab. All the while he may have remained as a vassal to his earlier Philistine overlords.

His Religious Contributions

Much is made of David as a religious reformer and thinker who developed many of the basic principles of Jewish worship. Chronicles gives him a much larger role in this regard than does Samuel.

In Chronicles, David devotes much of his final years to planning the details of the great Temple, assembling the materials to be used, organizing the priesthood according to clans and defining their functions, including the use of music, and setting forth many of the procedures.

Samuel presents a very different picture. There, the narrative depicts him as wanting to erect a house for God to dwell in, but Nathan tells him that he has too much blood on his hands to build such a religious facility. It's hard to imagine that if David really cared about building a house for God that religious leaders would stop him if they shared the same goal.

David's failure to build a house for God in Jerusalem stems more from financial realities and religious opposition than it does for any impurity on his own part. It's not difficult to see a deep internal schism between the Zadokites and the Shilohites over the control of religious facilities as well as an external schism between the priests in Jerusalem and the priests throughout the countryside. And the negative feedback from the census episode no doubt contributed to his hesitation to raise the funds necessary.

On the other hand, on a pragmatic level, one can see David suggesting artistic flourishes and protocols for religious ceremonies, such as the use of musical instruments and the preparation of religious hymns and songs, especially if he was the musically talented young lad depicted in Samuel.

The bible also credits David with bringing the Ark to Jerusalem and centralizing worship in that city but, as argued in chapter 14, there is a substantial question as to whether David ever brought the Ark to Jerusalem. And, for all the fuss against Saul for not consulting the Ark, there is little evidence that David did either. In fact, after David allegedly brought the Ark to Jerusalem there is hardly any reference to it at all. Just about the only times it is even mentioned are on the occasions when David talks about building a house for it and when the priests carry it out of Jerusalem during Absalom's rebellion.

There are religious figures prominent in David's court, but little religious theology. They appear to have been selected more for political purposes than for religious thinking, to balance factions rather than to promote ideas. To this end, he appointed co-priests, one from Judah and one from Israel, each presumably to administer to their own separate religious constituencies.

To the extent that he centralized worship in Jerusalem, this, too, had a political motivation, forcing the tribes to show him allegiance so that they could perform their religious obligations. The importance of centralized worship became apparent in the time of Jeroboam, when he led Israel away from Judah and feared what would happen once the people had to go to David's city for required festivals. Jeroboam solved the problem by changing the dates of the ceremonies and setting up separate temples.

What religious teachings we do find in the story of David seem to be a projection backwards from the time of Josiah in the late seventh century BCE. It was at this time that Samuel may have been written and Josiah aggressively organized many theological reforms, including the centralization of worship in Jerusalem and the destruction of idols and icons that detracted from the monotheistic teachings of his time. What little theology we get in the story of David comes more from the Deuteronomistic themes of Josiah than it does from any teachings of David.

The Aftermath

David's reign carried the seeds of its own destruction. Built on a desire for personal power, he attempted to impose a centralized dictatorship over a people fanatically devoted to a decentralized individualistic lifestyle. Systems of forced labor and high taxes ran counter to the wants and needs of the Israelite community. They wanted justice and peace. David gave them neither. His lack of justice triggered a rebellion and his expansionist goals subjected Israel to constant threats of war.

Having seized by force what had earlier been built on democratic principles, we shouldn't be surprised by the fact that his successor, too, seized the throne forcibly from its rightful successor. Solomon, who appears to have been a vainglorious dilettante dedicated to self-aggrandizement, exhausted what little patience was left for an intolerant ruler.

He far exceeded David's grasp in the area of forced labor, property confiscation, and public monuments to his greatness. Having given Israel its
greatest religious symbol, the great Temple, he polluted the religious life of
Israel with a total lack of concern for religious principles, setting up pagan
idols, icons, alters, and temples wherever it was politically convenient and
without regard to how this undermined Israel's religious concerns.

It did not take long for public resistance to mount. During his reign
Jeroboam sought to overthrow him but failed, fleeing to Egypt to avoid
Solomon's death sentence. But when Solomon died, Jeroboam returned
and led Israel out of confederation with Judah. He liberated Israel from
its tyranny, restored a sense of royal dignity and public democracy, and for
his troubles the Judahite scribes and Shilohite priests slandered him as
the worst of Israel's kings, the anti-David.

David's reputation is an accident of history. He was a brutal and cruel
tyrant, who routinely slaughtered the innocent in his grab for power. He
was unjust and unpopular in his time, widely feared and deeply hated. He
betrayed Saul and committed treason against Israel by consorting with
and fighting for its enemies. He even volunteered to aid the Philistines in
their efforts to destroy the kingdom of Israel.

By contrast, Saul was a good and decent man, who provided justice,
brought peace, and had the love of his people. Unfortunately for history,
the Assyrians destroyed the northern kingdom of Israel in 722 BCE, and
the praise songs for Saul were heard no more. Judah survived and had the
final word. Its lies and distortions and cover-ups were what were passed
on for truth. History was not well served by its efforts.

Appendix A
BIBLICAL QUOTES USED
AS CHAPTER INTRODUCTIONS

1 *Good David and Bad David*

But the word of the LORD came to me [i.e., David], saying, Thou hast shed blood abundantly, and hast made great wars: thou shalt not build an house unto my name, because thou hast shed much blood upon the earth in my sight. (1 Chr 22:8.)

2 *Make Us a King*

In those days there was no king in Israel: every man did that which was right in his own eyes. (Judg 21:25.)

3 *Who Killed Goliath?*

Elhanan son of Jaare-oregim, the Bethlehemite, killed Goliath the Gittite, the shaft of whose spear was like a weaver's beam. (2 Sam 21:19. Revised Standard Version.)

4 *A Failed Coup*

Then Saul said unto his servants that stood about him, Hear now, ye Benjamites; will the son of Jesse give every one of you fields and vineyards, and make you all captains of thousands, and captains of hundreds; That all of you have conspired against me, and there is none that showeth me that my son hath made a league with the son of Jesse, and there is none of you that is sorry for me, or showeth unto me that my son hath stirred up my servant against me, to lie in wait, as at this day? (1 Sam 22:7-8.)

5 *The Outlaw King*
And Achish believed David, saying, He hath made his people Israel utterly to abhor him; therefore he shall be my servant for ever. (1 Sam 27:12.)

6 *The Suspicious Death of King Saul*
The LORD hath returned upon thee [i.e., David] all the blood of the House of Saul, in whose stead thou hast reigned; and the LORD hath delivered the kingdom into the hand of Absalom thy son: and, behold, thou art taken in thy mischief, because thou art a bloody man. (2 Sam 16:8.)

7 *Civil War*
Now there was long war between the House of Saul and the House of David: but David waxed stronger and stronger, and the House of Saul waxed weaker and weaker. (2 Sam 3:1.)

8 *Kill the Lame and the Blind: The Taking of Jerusalem*
And David said on that day, Whosoever getteth up to the gutter, and smiteth the Jebusites, and the lame and the blind, that are hated of David's soul, he shall be chief and captain. (2 Sam 5:8.)

9 *Consolidation*
Now Joab was over all the host of Israel: and Benaiah the son of Jehoiada was over the Cherethites and over the Pelethites: And Adoram was over the tribute [i.e., forced labor]: and Jehoshaphat the son of Ahilud was recorder: And Sheva was scribe: and Zadok and Abiathar were the priests: And Ira also the Jairite was a chief ruler about David. (2 Sam 20:23-26.)

10 *The Murder of Uriah*
Wherefore hast thou despised the commandment of the LORD, to do evil in his sight? thou hast killed Uriah the Hittite with the sword, and hast taken his wife to be thy wife, and hast slain him with the sword of the children of Ammon. Now therefore the sword shall never depart from thine house; because thou hast despised me, and hast taken the wife of Uriah the Hittite to be thy wife. (2 Sam 12:9-10.)

11 Absalom's Rebellion: No Justice, No Peace!

And Absalom said unto him, See, thy matters are good and right; but there is no man deputed of the king to hear thee. Absalom said moreover, Oh that I were made judge in the land, that every man which hath any suit or cause might come unto me, and I would do him justice! And it was so, that when any man came nigh to him to do him obeisance, he put forth his hand, and took him, and kissed him. And on this manner did Absalom to all Israel that came to the king for judgment: so Absalom stole the hearts of the men of Israel. (2 Sam 15:3-6.)

12 Sheba's Rebellion: No Part in David!

We have no part in David, neither have we inheritance in the son of Jesse: every man to his tents, O Israel. So every man of Israel went up from after David, and followed Sheba the son of Bichri: but the men of Judah clave unto their king, from Jordan even to Jerusalem. (2 Sam 20:1-2.)

13 The Devil Made Him Do It!

And Satan stood up against Israel, and provoked David to number Israel. (1 Chr 21:1.)

14 Bringing the Ark to Jerusalem

And David was afraid of the Lord that day, and said, How shall the Ark of the Lord come to me? So David would not remove the Ark of the Lord unto him into the city of David: but David carried it aside into the house of Obededom the Gittite. (2 Sam 6:9-10.)

15 A Successful Coup

And he said, Thou [i.e., Bathsheba] knowest that the kingdom was mine [i.e., Adonijah's], and that all Israel set their faces on me, that I should reign. (1 Ki 2:15.)

16 Collapse

And now whereas my father [i.e., Solomon] did lade you [i.e., Israel] with a heavy yoke, I will add to your yoke: my father hath chastised you with whips, but I will chastise you with scorpions. (1 Ki 12:11.)

Appendix B

THE CENSUS SIN:
A COMPARISON BETWEEN
1 CHR 21-22:1 AND 2 SAM 24

1 Chronicles 21	2 Samuel 24
1 And Satan stood up against Israel, and provoked David to number Israel.	1 And again the anger of the LORD was kindled against Israel, and he moved David against them to say, Go, number Israel and Judah.
2 And David said to Joab and to the rulers of the people, Go, number Israel from Beersheba even to Dan; and bring the number of them to me, that I may know it.	2 For the king said to Joab the captain of the host, which was with him, Go now through all the tribes of Israel, from Dan even to Beersheba, and number ye the people, that I may know the number of the people.
3 And Joab answered, The LORD make his people an hundred times so many more as they be: but, my lord the king, are they not all my lord's servants? why then doth my lord require this thing? why will he be a cause of trespass to Israel?	3 And Joab said unto the king, Now the LORD thy God add unto the people, how many soever they be, an hundredfold, and that the eyes of my lord the king may see it: but why doth my lord the king delight in this thing?

4 Nevertheless the king's word prevailed against Joab. Wherefore Joab departed, and went throughout all Israel, and came to Jerusalem.

4 Notwithstanding the king's word prevailed against Joab, and against the captains of the host. And Joab and the captains of the host went out from the presence of the king, to number the people of Israel.

5 And Joab gave the sum of the number of the people unto David. And all they of Israel were a thousand thousand and an hundred thousand men that drew sword: and Judah was four hundred threescore and ten thousand men that drew sword.

5–9 And they passed over Jordan, and pitched in Aroer, on the right side of the city that lieth in the midst of the river of Gad, and toward Jazer: Then they came to Gilead, and to the land of Tahtim-hodshi; and they came to Danjaan, and about to Zidon, And came to the strong hold of Tyre, and to all the cities of the Hivites, and of the Canaanites: and they went out to the south of Judah, even to Beersheba. So when they had gone through all the land, they came to Jerusalem at the end of nine months and twenty days. And Joab gave up the sum of the number of the people unto the king: and there were in Israel eight hundred thousand valiant men that drew the sword; and the men of Judah were five hundred thousand men.

6 But Levi and Benjamin counted he not among them: for the king's word was abominable to Joab.

No corresponding verse.

7–8 And God was displeased with this thing; therefore he smote Israel. And David said unto God, I have sinned greatly, because I have done this thing: but now, I beseech thee, do away the iniquity of thy servant; for I have done very foolishly.

9–11 And the LORD spake unto Gad, David's seer, saying, Go and tell David, saying, Thus saith the LORD, I offer thee three things: choose thee one of them, that I may do it unto thee. So Gad came to David, and said unto him, Thus saith the LORD, Choose thee

12 Either three years' famine; or three months to be destroyed before thy foes, while that the sword of thine enemies overtaketh thee; or else three days the sword of the LORD, even the pestilence, in the land, and the angel of the LORD destroying throughout all the coasts of Israel. Now therefore advise thyself what word I shall bring again to him that sent me.

10 And David's heart smote him after that he had numbered the people. And David said unto the LORD, I have sinned greatly in that I have done: and now, I beseech thee, O LORD, take away the iniquity of thy servant; for I have done very foolishly.

11–13a For when David was up in the morning, the word of the LORD came unto the prophet Gad, David's seer, saying, Go and say unto David, Thus saith the LORD, I offer thee three things; choose thee one of them, that I may do it unto thee. So Gad came to David, and told him, and said unto him,

13b Shall seven years of famine come unto thee in thy land? or wilt thou flee three months before thine enemies, while they pursue thee? or that there be three days' pestilence in thy land? now advise, and see what answer I shall return to him that sent me.

[Note: KJV says seven years, NRSV says three years.]

13 And David said unto Gad, I am in a great strait: let me fall now into the hand of the LORD; for very great are his mercies: but let me not fall into the hand of man.

14 So the LORD sent pestilence upon Israel: and there fell of Israel seventy thousand men.

15 And God sent an angel unto Jerusalem to destroy it: and as he was destroying, the LORD beheld, and he repented him of the evil, and said to the angel that destroyed, It is enough, stay now thine hand. And the angel of the LORD stood by the threshing-floor of Ornan the Jebusite.

16–17 And David lifted up his eyes, and saw the angel of the LORD stand between the earth and the heaven, having a drawn sword in his hand stretched out over Jerusalem. Then David and the elders of Israel, who were clothed in sackcloth, fell upon their faces. And David said unto God, Is it not I that commanded the people to be numbered? even I it is that have sinned and done evil

14 And David said unto Gad, I am in a great strait: let us fall now into the hand of the LORD; for his mercies are great: and let me not fall into the hand of man.

15 So the LORD sent a pestilence upon Israel from the morning even to the time appointed: and there died of the people from Dan even to Beersheba seventy thousand men.

16 And when the angel stretched out his hand upon Jerusalem to destroy it, the LORD repented him of the evil, and said to the angel that destroyed the people, It is enough: stay now thine hand. And the angel of the LORD was by the threshingplace of Araunah the Jebusite.

17 And David spake unto the LORD when he saw the angel that smote the people, and said, Lo, I have sinned, and I have done wickedly: but these sheep, what have they done? let thine hand, I pray thee, be against me, and against my father's house.

indeed; but as for these sheep, what have they done? let thine hand, I pray thee, O LORD my God, be on me, and on my father's house; but not on thy people, that they should be plagued.

18–19 Then the angel of the LORD commanded Gad to say to David, that David should go up, and set up an altar unto the LORD in the threshingfloor of Ornan the Jebusite. And David went up at the saying of Gad, which he spake in the name of the LORD.

18–19 And Gad came that day to David, and said unto him, Go up, rear an altar unto the LORD in the threshingfloor of Araunah the Jebusite. And David, according to the saying of Gad, went up as the LORD commanded.

20 And Ornan turned back, and saw the angel; and his four sons with him hid themselves. Now Ornan was threshing wheat.

No corresponding verse.

21–23 And as David came to Ornan, Ornan looked and saw David, and went out of the threshingfloor, and bowed himself to David with his face to the ground. Then David said to Ornan, Grant me the place of this threshingfloor, that I may build an altar therein unto the LORD: thou shalt grant it me for the full price: that the plague may be stayed from the people. And Ornan said unto David, Take it to thee, and let my lord the king do

20–22 And Araunah looked, and saw the king and his servants coming on toward him: and Araunah went out, and bowed himself before the king on his face upon the ground. And Araunah said, Wherefore is my lord the king come to his servant? And David said, To buy the threshingfloor of thee, to build an altar unto the LORD, that the plague may be stayed from the people. And Araunah said unto David, Let my lord the king take and offer that which is good in his eyes: lo, I give thee the oxen also for burnt offerings, and the threshing instruments for wood, and the wheat for the meat offering; I give it all.

No corresponding verse.

24–25 And king David said to Ornan, Nay; but I will verily buy it for the full price: for I will not take that which is thine for the LORD, nor offer burnt offerings without cost. So David gave to Ornan for the place six hundred shekels of gold by weight.

26–27 And David built there an altar unto the LORD, and offered burnt offerings and peace offerings, and called upon the LORD; and he answered him from heaven by fire upon the altar of burnt offering. And the LORD commanded the angel; and he put up his sword again into the sheath thereof.

28–30 At that time when David saw that the LORD had answered him in the threshingfloor of Or-

up what seemeth good unto him: behold, here be oxen for burnt sacrifice, and threshing instruments and other instruments of the oxen for wood.

23 All these things did Araunah, as a king, give unto the king. And Araunah said unto the king, The LORD thy God accept thee.

24 And the king said unto Araunah, Nay; but I will surely buy it of thee at a price: neither will I offer burnt offerings unto the LORD my God of that which doth cost me nothing. So David bought the threshingfloor and the oxen for fifty shekels of silver.

25 And David built there an altar unto the LORD, and offered burnt offerings and peace offerings. So the LORD was entreated for the land, and the plague was stayed from Israel.

No corresponding verse.

nan the Jebusite, then he sacrificed there. For the tabernacle of the LORD, which Moses made in the wilderness, and the altar of the burnt offering, were at that season in the high place at Gibeon. But David could not go before it to inquire of God: for he was afraid because of the sword of the angel of the LORD.

1 Chronicles 22   No corresponding verse.

1 Then David said, This is the house of the LORD God, and this is the altar of the burnt offering for Israel. (1 Chronicles 22:1.)

Appendix C
GLOSSARY OF NAMES AND PLACES

Abiathar A Shilohite priest who survived Saul's attack on the Nob sanctuary. He joined David's outlaw army, and when David became king Abiathar became co-chief priest with Zadok.

Abigail The wife of Nabal and possibly the daughter of Nahash, the Ammonite king. She gave supplies to David's outlaw army, and when her husband died she married David. She was the mother of Chileab (also called Daniel), David's second son. There is another Abigail who is described as David's sister. This Abigail appears to be the mother of Amasa. Some evidence suggests that both Abigails are one and the same person.

Abishag A young virgin brought to the elderly David to keep his sickly body warm. She may have become David's wife. She became the subject of a dispute between Solomon and Adonijah, rivals for the right to succeed David on the throne.

Abishai Brother of Joab and Asahel. Their mother was Zeruiah, sister of Abigail (but which Abigail is uncertain). These brothers were among David's closest allies, best soldiers, and chief military leaders.

Abner Saul's uncle and chief military leader. When Saul died Abner placed Saul's son, Eshbaal, on the Israelite throne and held off David's army for about two years. When Joab assassinated Abner, Israelite opposition to David's succession collapsed.

Absalom David's third son and brother of Tamar. After Amnon, David's eldest son, raped Tamar, Absalom killed him. Subsequently, he led a rebellion against his father and temporarily drove David out of Jerusalem. He died during the battle between his forces and David's when his hair got caught in a tree branch and Joab had him put to death. Absalom was the grandson of the king of Geshur.

Achish   King of the Philistine city of Gath, who befriended David during his outlaw days and appointed David to be his personal bodyguard. He invited David to join him in an assault on Israel and David agreed. But some Philistine lords distrusted his loyalty and convinced Achish to leave David behind.

Adonijah   David's fourth son and heir-apparent to the throne after the death of Absalom. He lost out when Solomon staged a military coup and became David's successor. Solomon initially spared Adonijah's life, but had him put to death when Adonijah asked permission to marry Abishag, interpreting his request as a claim on the throne.

Adriel   A son of Barzillai, who married Merab, Saul's oldest daughter. They had five sons. King David had these five children executed in order to propitiate God and terminate a famine. Adriel may have been one of the titular leaders of Israel after Eshbaal's death. His marriage to Saul's daughter may have given him or one of his sons a claim to the throne of Israel.

Agag   A king of the Amalekites. When Samuel ordered the death of all Amalekites and Saul spared Agag's life, Samuel denounced Saul and told him that God had rejected him as king.

Ahijah   A Shilohite prophet who urged Jeroboam to rebel against Solomon.

Ahimelech   Priest of Nob, Ahimelech was apparently a descendant of the Shilohite House of Eli. He gave food and a weapon to David when he fled from Saul's house and Saul, in response, ordered the execution of all the priests of Nob. Only Abiathar escaped death.

Ahinoam   The name of two women in the story of David. One was Saul's wife, whom Saul denounced as an ally of David. The other was David's first wife who joined with him prior to his marrying Abigail. The two Ahinoams may be one and the same person.

Ahithophel   A highly respected wise man who sided with Absalom during the revolt against David. When Absalom rejected his strategic advice, Ahithophel committed suicide.

Amalekites A nomadic tribe that fought against Israel during the Exodus from Egypt. Several hundred years later, Samuel ordered Saul to destroy all the Amalekites as punishment for their earlier actions. *See* Agag.

Amasa The son of Abigail and a relative of David. As head of the army of Judah he supported Absalom's revolt against David. After Absalom's death, David, in order to win back Judah's support, appointed him in place of Joab as chief military officer of the kingdom. Joab killed him shortly after the appointment and resumed his position as chief military officer.

Ammon The Ammonites, in southern Jordan, were traditional enemies of Israel.

Amnon David's eldest son. He lusted after his half-sister Tamar and raped her. Tamar's brother Absalom subsequently killed Amnon in revenge.

Araunah A Jebusite king who owned a granary on the outskirts of Jerusalem. David bought the granary site from him so that he could offer a sacrifice to God and stop a pestilence from destroying his kingdom. Later, Solomon built his great Temple at that location.

Ark of the Covenant Israel's holiest relic. It housed the Ten Commandments and served as a throne for God. The Israelites believed that God was present on the Ark and they carried it into battle and made inquiries of it. The bible has two different descriptions of the Ark. In Exodus it is an ornate gold-encased box with golden cherubim mounted atop. In Deuteronomy it is a simple box made of shittim wood. Saul was accused of paying too little attention to the Ark.

Asahel Brother of Joab and Abishai, and one of Israel's greatest warriors. Abner allegedly killed him before David became king and Joab killed Abner, allegedly in revenge for the death of Asahel. But elsewhere in the bible, after Abner's death, Asahel appears as a member of King David's administrative team.

Ashtoreth A Canaanite goddess. She was one of the many foreign deities for whom Solomon set up places of worships.

Baanah A soldier in the Israelite army who, with his brother Rechab, participated in the murder of King Eshbaal. When they brought the dead king's head to David, David had them put to death.

Barzillai Father of Adriel. He greeted David on the king's flight from Absalom and gave him provisions. He appears to have been the grandfather of five sons born to Adriel and Merab, a daughter of Saul. King David had these five grandsons executed in order to propitiate God and terminate a famine.

Bathsheba The wife of Uriah the Hittite, one of David's most loyal and pious soldiers. David had an affair with her, got her pregnant, and then had Joab arrange for Uriah to be killed in order to cover up the affair. After Uriah was killed, David married her. The child she was pregnant with died at birth. Later she gave birth to Solomon.

Beer-Sheba The southernmost boundary of the kingdom of the united Israel.

Belial, sons of A term occasionally used to denounce evil people.

Benaiah A military hero who once killed an Egyptian giant. David appointed him over his mercenary forces, the Pelethites and Cherethites. He supported Solomon in the coup against Adonijah, killed Joab on Solomon's orders, and become Solomon's chief military officer.

Benjamin The smallest of the tribal groups, Benjamin was centrally located between Judah and Ephraim. Saul was a Benjaminite. The city of Jerusalem was located on the Benjamin side of the border with Judah.

Chemosh The chief deity of Moab and one of the foreign deities for whom Solomon built a place of worship.

Cherethites A band of foreign mercenaries in service to King David. They may have been Mycenaean Greeks from Crete. Together with the Pelethites, another foreign mercenary group, they became an institutional force within the administrations of David and Solomon.

Chileab David's second son, about whom nothing is known except that he was born in Hebron to Abigail. On occasion, he is also called Daniel.

Dagon A chief deity among the Philistines.

Dan The northernmost boundary of united Israel.

David The son of Jesse, from Bethlehem in Judah. When Samuel the priest broke off relations with King Saul, he transferred his support to David. A charismatic figure, he became quite popular in Saul's court, both as a warrior and as a personality with musical and poetic talents. He was betrothed to Saul's daughter, Michal, and became fast friends with Saul's son and heir, Jonathan. When Saul feared that David sought to replace him as king, both of Saul's children helped David escape from Saul's grasp. When Saul and Jonathan died in battle, David, as King of Judah, waged a civil war against Eshbaal, king of Israel and Saul's successor. About two years after the struggle began, Joab killed Abner, the Israelite general, and others killed Eshbaal. The weakened Israel accepted David as their king. David ruled for about seven and a half years as king of Judah and another thirty-three years as king over Judah and Israel combined. During his last year or so, he may have been co-regent with Solomon.

Doeg the Edomite A servant of King Saul who witnessed Ahimelech, the priest of Nob, give food and a weapon to David on his flight from Saul. He reported the incident to Saul and the king ordered the priests of Nob executed. When the Israelite military leaders refused to carry out the assignment, Doeg volunteered to do the job and carried out Saul's directive.

Edom A Jordanian nation that traditionally fought with Israel.

Eli Head of the Shiloh priesthood that governed Israel in the pre-monarchical period. He took Samuel under his guidance and trained him for the priesthood. Eli's administration was marked by corruption and he died at the age of ninety-eight when he learned his sons had been killed in battle and the Philistines captured the Ark of the Covenant.

Endor, Witch of The woman visited by Saul before the battle in which he was killed. He had her summon up the spirit of Samuel for consultation.

Ephraim One of two tribes allegedly descended from Joseph. Its southern boundary lay along the northern border of Benjamin. When Israel split from Judah following Solomon's death, Ephraim became the northern capitol.

Eshbaal The original name of Ishbosheth, the son of Saul who ruled Israel after Saul's death. Later biblical editors changed the "baal" element of his name, which signified one of the chief Canaanite deities, to "bosheth," meaning "shame." He also appears in biblical texts under the names Ishbosheth, Ishvi and Ishui. Eshbaal ruled for about two years before being assassinated by two of his soldiers. Upon his death, David became king over Israel.

Gad A prophet who gave David advice. He may have been the author of or the subject of a lost book known as the Book of Gad the Seer, cited as a source work in 1 Chr 29:29.

Gath One of the five chief cities of the Philistines. The giant Goliath came from Gath, and Achish, the king of Gath, had a close relationship with David.

Geshur A territory in the Syrian region. David married the daughter of the king of Geshur, and that daughter gave birth to Absalom and Tamar.

Gibeah Saul's home base. Biblical editors may have occasionally confused it with nearby Gibeon, a large priestly city.

Gibeon A priestly city that housed the Tabernacle during portions of David's reign and Solomon's reign. The people of Gibeon allegedly told David that Saul did them a great wrong and that as a punishment on Israel God ordered a famine. To end the famine, Gibeon allegedly requested the execution of seven of Saul's sons. Biblical editors may have occasionally confused Gibeon with nearby Gibeah, Saul's home base.

Gilboa A mountain where Saul and his sons were slain during a battle with the Philistines.

Goliath A Philistine giant from the city of Gath, allegedly slain by either David, according to one part of the Book of Samuel, or Elhanan, according to another portion of Samuel.

Hannah The mother of Samuel.

Hanun, son of Nahash Hanun became king of the Ammonites after Nahash died. King David sent a delegation to congratulate him, but Hanun treated them as spies and sent them home under humiliating conditions. This triggered a war between David and the Ammonites, which David won.

Hebron One of the chief cities of Judah. When the wealthy Nabal died and David married Abigail, Nabal's widow, he became an influential leader in Hebron. When David became king of Judah, Hebron served as his capitol for seven and a half years.

Hiram, king of Tyre A wealthy Phoenician monarch who supplied David and Solomon with building materials, especially the famous cedars of Lebanon, and artisans. When Solomon became king he formed a naval alliance with Hiram.

Hophni One of the corrupt sons of Eli, who died in battle with the Philistines.

Hushai A loyal member of King David's administration who pretended to support Absalom's revolt in order to undermine the military strategy used against David.

Ishbosheth *See* Eshbaal.

Israel During the United Monarchy, Israel signified ten tribal units and Judah signified the remaining two (Simeon probably being the other one). When Solomon's kingdom split in two, the northern and Transjordan portions became Israel, and the remainder became Judah.

Ittai A Philistine military commander who came to David's aid during Absalom's revolt and helped David regain his throne.

Jabesh-Gilead A non-Israelite territory closely allied with Saul. When Saul saved Jabesh-Gilead from an Ammonite attack, the people of Israel made Saul king. When Saul died and the Philistines displayed his body on the walls of the Philistine cities, a raiding party from Jabesh-Gilead rescued the remains and gave them a proper burial.

Jebusites Apparently the pre-Israelite inhabitants of the city of Jerusalem, which may have been known as Jebus before David took possession of it.

Jedidiah An alternative name for Solomon, conferred on him at birth by Nathan.

Jeroboam A northern leader who rebelled against Solomon, fled to Egypt for safety, and returned after Solomon's death to lead Israel out of confederation with Judah. He became the first king of the new Israel. Allied at first with the Shilohite priests, he lost their support when he failed to give them control over Israelite religion.

Jesse Father of David and a wealthy Judahite from Bethlehem.

Joab A loyal supporter of David, as were his brothers Abishai and Asahel. Under David he was the head of the military. In the course of his career he murdered Abner, Amasa, and Absalom. He was not afraid to talk back to David and on several occasions chastised him for failing to carry out his kingly duties. When David died, Joab supported Adonijah over Solomon, and when Solomon consolidated power, he put Joab to death.

Jonathan Son of and heir-apparent to Saul. A skilled fighter, he and David became fast friends. Despite Jonathan's position, he frequently helped David escape from Saul. Jonathan died in battle against the Philistines, in the same conflict that took his father's life.

Judah The home territory of David. It served as David's power base and he became king of Judah while Saul still ruled over Israel. After the split between Israel and Judah, the latter became the name for the southern kingdom. Judah survived long after Israel disappeared, and the term "Jew" refers to those who later lived in the kingdom of Judah. Those later residents included many people from other tribes in addition to Judah.

Kirjath-Jearim Part of a confederation with Gibeon, it served as the home of the Ark of the Covenant after its recapture from the Philistines. David allegedly brought the Ark from that city to Jerusalem.

Kish Father of Saul.

Machir Looked after Mephibosheth, the son of Jonathan, after Jonathan's death. He supposedly greeted David in Mahanaim when David fled from Absalom. He may have been one of the titular leaders of Israel after the death of Eshbaal.

Mahanaim After Saul's death, and the defeat of Israel by the Philistines in the central portion of Israel, Abner led the retreating Israelites to Mahanaim, on the other side of the Jordan, and installed Eshbaal as king over Israel. According to the biblical account, when David fled from Absalom, he, too, went to Mahanaim for refuge.

Manasseh The largest tribal territory in Israel, with portions on both sides of the Jordan.

Mephibosheth The name of both a son of Saul and a son of Jonathan. (The original name would have been Mephibaal.) The biblical editors may have confused the two as one person. David ordered Mephibosheth, the son of Jonathan, to remain with him in Jerusalem, supposedly as the fulfillment of a promise to Jonathan. When Mephibosheth was a child, he was accidentally dropped and became lame.

Merab Saul's oldest daughter, previously pledged to marry David she subsequently married Adriel. She and Adriel had five sons, all of whom David had executed in order to propitiate God and end a famine.

Michal Saul's daughter, who loved David and who was betrothed to him. She helped David escape from Saul's grasp. The marriage was never consummated and she married another. But during the civil war between David and Eshbaal, David demanded that she be returned to him and Abner brought her to Jerusalem. When David became king over Israel, she had nothing but loathing for him.

Moab One of Israel's traditional enemies. David's ancestor Ruth had Moabite ties and when David fled from Saul he brought his family to Moab for safety.

Molech Chief deity of the Ammonites and one of the foreign deities for whom Solomon built a place of worship.

Nabal A wealthy rancher from Hebron who refused David's request for aid. David sent a military expedition against him, but Nabal's wife Abigail intervened by praising David and offering provisions. Shortly after Nabal learned of what his wife did, he keeled over and died. Abigail then married David.

Nahash King of the Ammonites and a bitter enemy of Saul and the Israelites. He was also a good friend of David. He may be the Nahash who is described as the father of Abigail and Zeruiah, which suggests a familial relationship between David, Joab, and the Ammonite king.

Nathan An influential man of God who served as an advisor to David. He planned the coup that put Solomon on the throne. He may have been the author of or subject of a lost book known as the Book of Nathan the Prophet, cited as a source in 1 Chr 29:29.

Nob A sanctuary of some sort that seems to have housed a branch of Shilohite priests. However, some evidence suggests that Nob was originally a Philistine sanctuary. When Ahimelech, a priest at Nob, gave aid to David on his flight from Saul, the king ordered all the priests at Nob put to death.

Obededom Served as a caretaker for the Ark of the Covenant after David's failed attempt to bring it to Jerusalem.

Omri One of the later kings of Israel whose name appears in the archaeological record. House of Omri became synonymous with Israel, even after his dynasty ended.

Pelethites A band of foreign mercenaries in service to King David. Their name may be a variation on Philistine. Together with the Cherethites, another foreign mercenary group, they became an institutional force within the administrations of David and Solomon.

Philistines The main enemy of Israel, located mostly along the Mediterranean coast of southern Canaan.

Phinehas One of the corrupt sons of Eli, who died in battle with the Philistines.

Rechab A soldier in the Israelite army who, with his brother Baanah, participated in the murder of King Eshbaal. When they brought the dead king's head to David, David had them put to death.

Rehoboam Solomon's son and successor. When he refused to lighten the burden of Israelites, Jeroboam led Israel out of confederation with Judah.

Rizpah Concubine of Saul and the mother of two children executed by David. Abner's interest in Rizpah caused Eshbaal to distrust his general.

Samuel Successor to Eli as leader of the Shiloh priesthood. He also presided over a corrupt administration, giving rise to a demand for a king to replace him. Samuel resisted these efforts but lost out in the power struggle, and the Israelites made Saul the first king over Israel. When Saul wouldn't follow Samuel's instructions Samuel sought to overthrow Saul and joined forces with David.

Saul The first king over Israel. He took over many of the functions of Samuel and replaced theocratic domination with democratic principles. When he listened to the voice of the people over the dictates of Samuel, an irreparable schism arose between the two. Saul perceived that David's popularity as a warrior would give him a base to challenge Saul for the throne. The bible attributes Saul's fears of David's ambition to paranoia, but other biblical evidence shows that Saul's worries were solidly rooted in fact. Saul made several efforts to capture David, but when David allied himself with the Philistines, Saul abandoned his pursuit. Saul fell in battle during a Philistine assault on Israel, but some evidence suggests that David had Saul assassinated.

Sheba A Benjaminite who led a major military revolt against David after David became king over Israel. Joab trapped Sheba inside the city of Abel of Beth-Maacah, and demanded that the citizens behead him in return for the lifting of the siege. The citizens acquiesced to Joab's demand and the revolt collapsed.

Sheba, Queen of A foreign ambassador who came to visit Solomon in order to open up trade relationships. The location of Sheba is not known but most scholars place it either in Arabia or Ethiopia.

Shiloh The home base of the priesthood that ruled over Israel in the premonarchical period. The city seems to have been destroyed in the time of Eli, and the priesthood resettled elsewhere.

Shimei, son of Gera When David fled from Absalom, Shimei, a Benjaminite, cursed David as a bloody murderer who wrongfully displaced the House of Saul. After Absalom's revolt collapsed, Shimei greeted David with an army of one thousand Benjaminites and asked forgiveness, which David granted. Shimei may have supported Solomon over Adonijah in the struggle to succeed David.

Shishak The biblical name of an Egyptian pharaoh who gave shelter to Jeroboam when he fled from Solomon and who raided Jerusalem in the time of Rehoboam, seizing the treasures of Solomon's temple as a payoff for not sacking the city. Scholars identify Shishak as Sheshonk I, founder of Egypt's twenty-second dynasty at about 945 B.C.E.

Shobi A son of Nahash, king of the Ammonites. He greeted David on his arrival at Mahanaim.

Solomon David's successor on the throne who seized power in a military coup that ousted Adonijah, the rightful heir. He was the son of Bathsheba. His greatest contribution to Israel was the building of a glorious temple for the worship of God. Although famous as a wise man, he alienated the religious establishment by building places of worship for the many foreign deities worshipped by his numerous wives. The breakup of Israel and Judah after his death was viewed as a punishment for his heresy, but the biblical texts also indicate that the people of Israel considered him an oppressive ruler.

Tabernacle A special tent designed to serve as a house for the Ark of the Covenant.

Talmai, king of Geshur David married his daughter, who gave birth to Absalom and Tamar.

Tamar A sister of Absalom who was raped by Amnon, David's oldest son.

Thirty, the A term used to describe an elite fighting force comprised of Israel's greatest heroes. Also known as the Mighty Men.

Uriah the Hittite An Israelite hero, a member of the Thirty, and husband of Bathsheba. David had an affair with his wife and when she became pregnant David had him brought back from battle under the pretense of getting a status report. He had hoped that Uriah would use the occasion to sleep with his wife, but Uriah thought it wrong to do so while Israel was engaged in battle and remained in David's house rather than go home to Bathsheba. Finally, David had Uriah carry a secret letter to Joab, which directed Joab to place Uriah in the thick of battle and withdraw support. As a result, enemy soldiers killed Uriah. The bible portrays Absalom's revolt as a punishment for what David, did to Uriah.

Uzzah When David tried to bring the Ark to Jerusalem, Uzzah reached out to steady it and keep it from falling. Because he was unauthorized to touch the Ark, God struck him dead.

Zadok One of the two co-chief priests of Israel under David's administration. His background is omitted from the story of David, but it is likely that he may have been chief priest of Judah while David ruled in Hebron. The other co-chief priest was Abiathar, who represented the Shilohites. Zadok allied himself with Solomon and Abiathar with Adonijah. As a result, when Solomon became king, he appointed Zadok as the sole chief priest and demoted Abiathar.

Zeruiah Sister of Abigail, daughter of Nahash, mother of Joab, Abishai, and Asahel. It is not clear which Abigail she is the sister of. Nahash may be the Ammonite king who befriended David. If so, then Joab and his brothers were Ammonites.

Ziba A servant from the House of Saul charged with caring for the property of Mephibosheth, son of Jonathan. When David fled from Absalom, Ziba provided the king with provisions and accused Mephibosheth of supporting the revolution. Subsequently, Mephibosheth, reminding David of his lameness, blamed Ziba for not waiting for him during the flight from Absalom.

Ziklag A city given to David by Achish, king of Gath, as a reward for his faithful service to the Philistines. The city had a reputation as a royal city for the kings of Judah.

Index

PERE∫ET PRE∫∫

If you enjoyed this book by Gary Greenberg be sure to look for this Pereset Press release

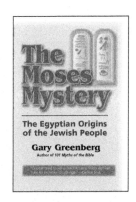

The Egyptian Origins of the Jewish People

Gary Greenberg
Author of *101 Myths of the Bible*

THE MOSES MYSTERY
The Egyptian Origins
of the Jewish People

What do history and archaeology *really* say about the origins of ancient Israel?

Although the bible says that Israel's formative history took place in ancient Egypt, biblical scholars and Egyptologists have steadfastly refused to explore the role of Egyptian history and literature on the origins of Jewish religion. *The Moses Mystery* attempts to set the record straight. Based on extensive research into biblical and Egyptian history, archaeology, literature and mythology Greenberg argues that the first Israelites were Egyptians, followers of the monotheistic teachings of Pharaoh Akhenaten.

Some of the many intriguing revelations in *The Moses Mystery* include:

- Ancient Egyptian records specifically identify Moses as Akhenaten's chief priest and describe the Exodus as the result of a civil war for control over the Egyptian throne

- Abraham, Isaac, and Jacob were characters from Egyptian mythology

- The Twelve Tribes of Israel never existed

An ingenious comparison of Biblical
and Egyptian history.– St. Louis Post-Dispatch

A must read for those interested
in biblical scholarship. – Tennessee Tribune

Insightful and valuable. – KMT magazine

Also by Gary Greenberg
101 Myths of the Bible: How Ancient Scribes Invented Biblical History
The Judas Brief: Who Really Killed Jesus?
Manetho: A Study in Egyptian Chronology

CPSIA information can be obtained at www.ICGtesting.com
Printed in the USA
BVOW06s1822030416

442801BV00014B/115/P